PENGUIN BOOKS

WILD ORCHIDS AND TROTSKY

Mark Edmundson graduated from Bennington College and Yale. His first book, *Towards Reading Freud*, was published by Princeton in 1990. He is at work on another critical study, *The Function of Theory*, forthcoming from Cambridge. A literary journalist, he has published articles and reviews in such places as *TLS*, *London Review of Books*, *The Nation*, *The New Republic*, and *The Washington Post Book World*. He serves as a contributing editor to *Raritan* and *Harper's* and teaches English at the University of Virginia, where he is currently a Commonwealth Center fellow.

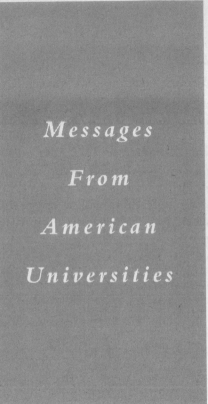

Messages

From

American

Universities

PENGUIN BOOKS

WILD

ORCHIDS

AND

TROTSKY

EDITED BY
MARK EDMUNDSON

PENGUIN BOOKS
Published by the Penguin Group
Penguin Books USA Inc., 375 Hudson Street,
New York, New York 10014, U.S.A.
Penguin Books Ltd, 27 Wrights Lane, London W8 5TZ, England
Penguin Books Australia Ltd, Ringwood, Victoria, Australia
Penguin Books Canada Ltd, 10 Alcorn Avenue,
Toronto, Ontario, Canada M4V 3B2
Penguin Books (N.Z.) Ltd, 182–190 Wairau Road,
Auckland 10, New Zealand

Penguin Books Ltd, Registered Offices: Harmondsworth, Middlesex, England

First published in Penguin Books 1993

1 3 5 7 9 10 8 6 4 2

LIBRARY OF CONGRESS CATALOGING IN PUBLICATION DATA
Wild orchids and Trotsky: messages from American universities/
edited by Mark Edmundson.
p.   cm.
Includes bibliographical references.
ISBN 0 14 01.7078 2
1. Humanities—United States.   2. Humanities—Study and teaching
(Higher)—United States.   I. Edmundson, Mark, 1952–
AZ505.W55   1993
001.3—dc20   92-28407

Printed in the United States of America
Set in Bembo
Designed by Brian Mulligan

ACKNOWLEDGMENTS

This book attempts to give an accurate picture of the current ferment in the humanities at American colleges and universities. A lot is going on now, so accuracy means variety and sometimes complexity. Adding to the challenge is the fact that the academy has been under consistent attack, much of it error-ridden, much of it opportunistic, over the last few years. There have been few chances for those in the humanities to tell their side of the story, to write back. In fact, there has been no little resistance on the part of large-circulation media to representing the academy's side.

Our editor at Viking, Nan Graham, was willing to take the chance of letting professors speak their minds. Rather than retreating from a challenging topic, as too many others have, she took it on directly. Many thanks are due her, from the academy and from readers without. Nan's assistant editor, Gillian Silverman, was of great help in developing this book—she was consistently spirited, well informed, and effective. Thanks too to Courtney Hodell, who did remarkable work seeing the project through its final stages.

Thanks as well to my friends and colleagues who helped in preparing the book: Chip Tucker, Richard Rorty, Jason Bell, Kim Benston, Frank Lentricchia, Betsy Tucker, Gordon Hutner, Gena McKinley, Rob Sheffield, and Richard Poirier. Gerry Marzorati was crucial in getting this project off the ground. Michael Pollan contributed generously to its completion. My wife, Elizabeth Denton, gave shrewd editorial advice—and much more than that.

CONTENTS

INTRODUCTION

THE
ACADEMY
WRITES
BACK

*Mark
Edmundson*

I

IS IT TRUE WHAT THEY'RE SAYING ABOUT LIBERAL ARTS EDUCATION
in America? Have hordes of tenured radicals, the flotsam and
jetsam of the countercultural 1960s, who failed then to take over
the government, reappeared two decades later to take over the
English departments and to threaten Western culture from inside
its former citadels of defense? One hears that the light of humane
learning is dying out, the victim of feminism, deconstruction,
pragmatism, Lacanian psychoanalysis, cultural studies, and all
of the other arcane druidic faiths the professors are practicing.
It's said that the wisdom of genius, the best that is known and
thought, is being systematically maligned as mere ideology, the
wishful dream-life of the master class. In its place students are
learning—if anything—politically correct hymns, intoned in
forced harmony, on race, class, and gender oppression.

Clearly it's time for someone to step out of the shaded groves
of academe, look the general public in the eye, and set the record
straight by saying, for instance, that all the commotion is coming from a few splinter groups of academic malcontents, and
that the business of educating America's young is, in the
main—though with a few embarrassing exceptions—going
along pretty much as always. There have been misunderstand-
ings; here and there a regrettable lapse; "mistakes have been

3

made"; but the educational economy of America is fundamentally sound.

The truth is that things *are* changing. Relatively new ways for talking about literature and the arts are coming rapidly into prominence and are being used in both scholarship and the classroom. It would be foolish to pretend that all of these new vocabularies count as legitimate breakthroughs, or that they are always well deployed. The last twenty years have produced some astoundingly bad academic writing, work both dull and pretentious. But some extraordinarily fine things have been said and written, too. What Lynne Cheney, William Bennett, and many others have viewed with alarm and dismissed with contempt has, quite frequently, been evidence of fruitful changes in the humanities.

The contributors to this volume have been actively engaged with those changes. In the pages to come, they account for their involvement: They describe what they do as writers and teachers, why they do it, and what path brought them to their current position. Most of the pieces, in other words, are compressed intellectual autobiographies. What the essays have in common is an intense interest in the relationship between politics and art, between the claims of social responsibility and those of aesthetics. It is this relationship (and contention) that Richard Rorty evokes in his essay with the images of Trotsky and wild orchids.

Many of the contributors to this volume have been among the most frequently named, and most frequently maligned, by those claiming to expose an intellectual scandal in the humanities. J. Hillis Miller has been excoriated for bringing deconstruction, the demonic European import, to American shores. Richard Rorty, who in actuality carries on the tradition of American pragmatism, has been denounced as a promulgator of relativism, the belief that any one idea or value is just as good as any other. Frank Lentricchia combines an engagement with pragmatism with a commitment to leftist politics and populism, for which he's been dubbed criticism's Dirty Harry.

As feminist critics, Susan Fraiman and Nancy K. Miller

have, so the story goes, been obsessed with one category, gender, at the expense of every other human concern. But the argument of feminist criticism—and once understood in its full implications, it is not easily dismissed—is that a good deal of Western culture has been obsessed precisely with *not* thinking about gender, with ignoring the achievements and the sufferings of women living, by and large, under the law of men. Eve Sedgwick is a feminist critic as well, but she is best known as an advocate for the rights of gay men, an advocacy that, in a homophobic culture, has incurred an all-too-predictable response. Then there are Michael Bérubé and Judith Frank: Perhaps the most frequently attacked, they are members of the so-called PC generation of critics. These are the younger professors who, as Bérubé observes, are reputed to combine the Sex Pistols' political tact with a Puritanical good cheer and sense of rhythm: the generation of Rotten Mather.

Harold Bloom dislikes a good deal of what is going on in contemporary criticism, and he says so emphatically here. (The field of literary studies is in anything but a state of consensus.) Bloom—whose Oedipal theory of poetic influence shocked the orthodox twenty years ago and whose view that the Bible's J author is probably female is enjoying a comparable effect now—has always been a sect of one. It's possible that the most radical professor in the collection is one who quite dislikes literary radicalism. Richard Poirier values an artistic self that performs beyond the confines of political and social consensus and that, on balance, contributes nothing, either as a paragon or a cautionary example, to the creation of solid citizens. William Kerrigan has about the same taste for recent theory as Bloom and Poirier do (though for all three it's a *well-informed* disagreement that's proffered). Kerrigan is a born-again humanist who's sworn off theory in favor of a criticism that keeps alive the Renaissance ideal he finds in Jacob Burckhardt. Edward Said, associated in the popular mind with the Palestinian struggle—and hence, for some, with "terrorism"—is committed, as writer and teacher, to a form of humanism that goes back to Lionel

Trilling and Matthew Arnold. His hope is simply to persuade the West to apply that humanistic standard in its dealings with non-Western cultures.

In general, scholarly convention dictates that professors refrain from private reflection and fit their thoughts to the various analytical vocabularies (the products, presumably, of collective work over time) that their disciplines offer. This volume departs from such convention, and for a few reasons. The first is accessibility: We hope to communicate with a general audience that, thus far, has heard only one side of the story. The academy simply hasn't responded forcefully to the multiple attacks against it, and the attackers, made bolder by the relative silence, seem to be growing more irrational and less well informed. As Michael Bérubé puts it: "Journalists, disgruntled professors, embittered ex-graduate students, and their families and friends now feel entitled to say anything at all about the academy without fear of contradiction by general readers. The field is wide open, and there's no penalty for charlatanism (quite the contrary), since few general readers are informed enough to spot even the grossest form of misrepresentation and fraud."

True. But it's also true that the academy hasn't put enough energy into making its case to the public. We have been slow to remember, I think, that our intellectual freedom and whatever cultural authority we possess are based on the consent of the American people. The gap into which the academy-bashers have inserted their wedge is an information gap, one created in some measure by the arrogance of the professors. "They could never understand," we seem to have been saying to ourselves, while forgetting that "they" are, at least in part, our former students.

The risk in writing accessibly is obvious: When professors are compelled to abandon their terminological weaponry, it may be revealed that—let us put it bluntly—these overschooled, pampered, and privileged types really aren't very bright. The pieces that follow are cast almost exclusively in plain language. By writing back, members of the academy are putting their authority at risk, which in a democracy is where authority should be.

But intellectual autobiography seems a useful mode for other reasons, too. By offering part of their personal history as readers and writers, the contributors here remind one of a fact often obscured: The changes occurring in the humanities have a long history. They're not the result of perversity or whim. What is under way is not a repudiation of the past, but a reconsideration that aims sometimes for dramatic transformation, as in the work of Eve Sedgwick, and sometimes for renewal, as in that of Richard Poirier. Personal history, here, can reflect intellectual history.

Then, too, the personal dimension of these essays may counter attempts by the academy-bashers to render their foes as caricatures, creatures markedly less human than themselves or their readers. Academia isn't always and everywhere Plato's Symposium, but it's not inevitably a Jonsonian comedy of humours either. Challenging the caricatures with personal voices and self-portraits may enrich and complicate a debate that has been reduced to didactic simplicity.

These essays demonstrate (against the claims of many of the academy-bashers) how much variety now exists in the liberal arts. Here one will encounter New Historicism, pragmatism, feminism, gay studies, deconstruction and cultural studies, as well as recent variations upon traditional humanism. And the variety here hardly compares to the differences flourishing in literary study overall. Literature departments are, I believe, where the mental fight is fiercest—and perhaps where the most is at stake. But the contentions in literary studies are multiplied time and again throughout the humanities: in history, philosophy, and religion.

Variety. There's a lot going on. This would seem an elementary point, except that most of the academy's critics have labored to depict literary studies as an appalling monolith—all of the parts stitched together to create one grotesque amalgam: Frankenstein (or, when feminists are involved, the Bride of) lurching through the once safe corridors in search of young minds.

Roger Kimball's modus operandi in *Tenured Radicals* is to dissolve that variety and to mock indiscriminately every development he surveys. All is dismissed with an even sweep of the imperial arm: "pretentious nonsense"; "patent drivel"; "rebarbative nonsense"; "blather." He makes no effort to understand why others might not think as he does. In *Tenured Radicals*, one finds none of the tendency, which is always part of humanism at its best, to enter into dialogue with adversaries. Kimball's chief weapon is ridicule, and his guiding assumption is that anything that can be made to look absurd must be so. He forgets that every new way of thinking, from Socrates to Freud, has been readily mocked at its inception, by those who prefer to avoid the intellectual and moral burdens presented by troubling new ideas. Kimball summarizes his dispiriting intellectual procedures and his ethical position in a quotation from Nietzsche: "We do not refute a disease. We resist it."

Like Kimball, Dinesh D'Souza is out to simplify a difficult subject. The author of *Illiberal Education*, as well as an admiring biography of the Reverend Jerry Falwell, D'Souza claims that two critics, René Wellek and Austin Warren (both deeply learned humanists), are the men behind the curtain of Oz (Great and Powerful). His sense that they set off the theory explosion in America is the first in a long-running sequence of errors on the subject.

D'Souza's objective here is to show that pernicious literary theories—theories that promulgate "relativism"—have led to the hiring of unqualified faculty at Duke and to the depression of that university's academic standards. Relativism is the view that any one idea is as good as any other, and apart from a precocious college freshman or two, no one in the entire world holds it. What D'Souza incorrectly calls relativism is the idea, which is in fact sustained by many literary critics, myself included, that no standards of evaluation or judgment are eternal and exist on high. All that means is that when we argue about values, we do not appeal to god, or to some substitute for god;

we are compelled to refer to other standards and other ideals. These tend to be communal, and secular rather than religious. As Richard Rorty puts it, "There is nothing to be said about either truth or rationality apart from descriptions of the familiar procedures of justification which a given society—*ours*—uses in one or another area of inquiry." D'Souza seems to feel that if you don't have transcendent values, you don't have any values at all. When he tries to prove that theoretical "relativism" has led to hiring unqualified faculty members at Duke, or to giving arbitrary grades to students there, he cannot come up with a single example that bears him out.

The best academy-bashing book I've read is David Lehman's *Signs of the Times*. What interest and distinction it possesses derive from the fact that Lehman is more honest than his colleagues. Curiously enough, Lehman feels that deconstruction —of which his understanding is spotty—is all right when it's put to work by a novelist like Calvino or a poet like Ashbery. (Lehman has edited a collection of admiring essays on the latter.) It's when deconstructive values enter literary critical practice that Lehman draws back. But his chief complaint isn't that deconstruction is mistaken, but that it challenges certain views he holds dear, views in particular about the autonomy of the individual.

What's worst about deconstruction, the book frequently hints (and here Lehman's relative honesty comes into play), is that it might be on the right track. In fact, Lehman is sufficiently attracted to the mode to give a rather witty quasi-deconstructive reading of the word *deconstruction* itself—this he calls (close readers, prick up your ears) a layman's approach. Deconstruction (which I'll try to characterize accurately before this introduction closes) is wrong, Lehman asserts, because if it were right matters would simply be too depressing. This doesn't count as much of an argument, but it's a good bit more attractive than ridicule and error, the respective techniques of Kimball and D'Souza.

Anyone who reads through *Wild Orchids and Trotsky* will emerge with a more complex and a more accurate picture of the debate. If they've been fed on Kimball, D'Souza, and Lehman (or George Will, or Jonathan Yardley, or a dozen others), they will be giving up some of the satisfactions of control. William S. Burroughs has said that Americans are control junkies; they'd jump down their own throats and digest their dinners for themselves if they could. A premise of this book is that Burroughs had it wrong, at least for a number of Americans. There are, I think, plenty of people out there who don't want the story of academic ferment predigested for them but want to make up their own minds. If this volume does its job, readers will leave it with a richer, more intricate sense of the issues. Some readers may become even more hostile to what's going on in the liberal arts (none of the contributors are pulling their punches), but at least it will be an informed hostility. No more skewering of criticism on the point of a clever phrase ("Derrida's deconstruction—masturbation without pleasure"; "the mafioso theorist: he'll make you an offer you can't understand"). We aim to confirm criticism's subtlety, its perils and promise.

Yet some things, one must admit, are simply not worth having an intricate view of. Is criticism really worth thinking about? Are any of its dialects worth picking up? (And why are they so grindingly ugly at times?) Once you acquire these languages, what good do they do you? The next two sections of this introduction will offer my own answers to these questions. Let me say, to start with, that I am inclined to look for a productive angle of vision, not "the whole truth and nothing but." Every contributor would tell the story in a different way—a fact central to the story that, overall, this volume has to tell.

2

"There is not a creed which is not shaken, not an accredited dogma which is not shown to be questionable, not a received tradition which does not threaten to dissolve." The voice of Jacques Derrida? Michel Foucault? Gayatri Spivak? No, that is

Matthew Arnold, patron saint of the new traditionalists, protector of the humanistic tradition. Arnold is calling attention to the central condition now addressed by literary study: a crisis of authority. Creeds, dogmas, and traditions are being discredited left and right. What remains when faith in established institutions, and particularly in religion, is all but lost to at least some significant part of the population? Arnold did not retreat from the question. "The future of poetry is immense," he writes in the same passage, "because in poetry, where it is worthy of our high destinies, our race, as time goes on, will find an ever surer and surer stay."

Arnold's humanism is born of a conviction that when faith wanes, poetry—or, to speak more broadly, as Arnold himself will, culture—must take its place. Thus his desire to contribute to the creation of a sustaining culture by selecting and exposing his contemporaries to "the best that is known and thought." Note how heavy is the burden being placed on culture. Even in Arnold's time one would have to doubt—as Arnold himself surely did on occasion—whether texts of a secular sort were equal to the civilizing task. Much of literary criticism, from Arnold's time to the present, has absorbed itself with asking whether great writing does indeed have the resources to act as what Arnold's great heir Northrop Frye called "secular scripture."

No wonder then that literary study has become the source of anxious contestation. No wonder that critics, no longer happy with mere appreciation, ask the most difficult questions of their books. Is reading Shakespeare—a poet with no apparent ethical position, who seems delighted, as Keats said, as much by Iago as by the virtuous Imogen—genuinely conducive to moral improvement? Can Wordsworth, uncritically assimilated, lead one to overestimate the benevolence of Nature and, accordingly, of one's own human nature? Do he and Rousseau contribute to liberal presumptions about individual perfectability? Is Emerson's insistence on worshipping personal power an ingredient in a national ideology that celebrates blind imperial force? Does Milton contribute to oppression in the present by reaffirming stereotypes about female narcissism? Such questions become inevitable, it seems to me, as soon as you are willing to take Arnold's assumptions about the future of poetry seriously.

Though Arnold's wording of the famous line does vary, he asks on more than one occasion that we discover the best that is known and thought: *is*, not *was*. Criticism, according to Arnold, must involve an ongoing review, a judgment on the part of the present as to what is valuable in the past. T. S. Eliot, Arnold's most influential heir and another champion of literary humanism, insists on something very much like this in "Tradition and the Individual Talent" when he observes that the "existing monuments" of culture form an order among themselves "which is modified by the introduction of the new (the really new) work of art among them." That order can also be modified, most contemporary critics would insist, by the passage of time and by the exercise of critical intelligence, whether that intelligence be deployed by poet or scholar.

One might disagree with Arnold's high assessment of poetry's role—for what it's worth, I do. But what attracts many (if not most) critics to literary study is the possibility that Arnold is right and that theirs is potentially a central cultural activity. Those who champion Arnold against today's radicalism argue that he never probed great literature for its mystified views of knowledge, of gender, of class. He was by and large a celebratory critic. He pointed to touchstones—great moments in the great works that might shed light on our struggles, might buoy us in the midst of adversity. Arnold was not a censor, this line of response continues; he did not strive to be politically correct. Why is so much criticism now so heavily "politicized"? And, too, Arnold wrote well. One could understand him the first time through.

These two issues, of politics and of critical style, are central to the current controversies. Investigating them will clarify some issues in our story about the uses and abuses of contemporary literary studies.

First, politics. Let me take a moment and provide that cant-ing phrase "politically correct" with a bit of historical context. Where did PC criticism come from? Is it the legacy of Abbie Hoffman and the "modernism in the streets" prolific in the demonic sixties? Or does it have, perhaps, a somewhat earlier genesis?

The first, and still the most influential, politically correct critic in our culture is a short, ugly, balding man, reputedly a sexual pervert. He mesmerizes young people with his eloquence and turns them against their elders. (He is in fact executed for precisely this crime.) This PC critic says that he loves literature, but he also points out that poetic beauty lulls the moral senses to sleep. Poetry overcomes reason, incites passion, and diverts one from the true and the good. For this reason the PC critic Socrates decides, painfully, that poets have no real place in a just state. When he constructs his version of Utopia, he banishes them outside its walls.

Socrates initiated the dialogue between poetry and philosophy that has been at the center of Western culture for twenty-five hundred years. The feminist who offers a critique of Milton's gender politics focusing on his equation of femininity with narcissism, if she's arguing adroitly, is proceeding in his spirit. She will assert, perhaps, that Milton's disposition continues to inhere in various cultural forms (from Freudian psychoanalysis, which equates women and Narcissus, to the latest MTV video) and to the detriment of women (and men) right now. Milton's standing in culture, according to this view, helps to legitimize current oppressions.

In the language of Socrates, this critic is finding Milton incompatible with her version of the good and may eventually move to banish him from her department's community of anointed texts—those, that is, that turn up on the syllabus for the required survey course in English literature. What she's more likely to do, though, is to teach Milton against what she perceives to be his own resistant grain. She needs him to make her points just as much as Socrates needed Homer.

Someone who proceeds in this fashion now is likely to be charged by the new guardians of public morality with corrupting the young. But what she's really doing is continuing the age-old debate between poetry and philosophy. (The best characterization of literary criticism that I have been able to come up with is that it's what takes place between poetry and philosophy.) What makes matters a bit confusing is that this critic is likely to hold an appointment not in the philosophy department, but in English. Still, she's lining up on the side of those philosophers who, in the final analysis, will opt for ethical standards over and against aesthetic prowess. One point here is central. All of the modes of reading that presume to "demystify" literature ought to be understood as ways—more or less sophisticated, more or less persuasive—of reiterating Socrates's charges against the poets: which is, to put it unceremoniously, that they're a pack of liars. The irony of the general perception that deconstruction, feminism, and the like are rabidly amoral —the death knell of Western culture—is that these are highly ethical initiatives. To some of us, sometimes, they are rather claustrophobically so.

Is "demystifying" criticism destined to win out? No more than philosophy is destined to win its battle with poetry. Only the best of the negative critique really hurts, and those disposed against it have an obligation to learn the new philosophical languages and to attempt, with whatever intellectual and spiritual resources they might have, to defend poetry against them. All affirmative criticism—and there is still a lot of it being written—strives to answer Socrates and his descendants: Operating in the mode of Sir Philip Sydney and Percy Bysshe Shelley, affirmative critics write and rewrite the defense of poetry.

But the great originals here are Aristotle and Longinus. Longinus understood how sublime poetry dramatizes humanity's power to reach beyond itself in gestures of what Nietzsche would call self-overcoming. Longinus is little concerned with ethics. Aristotle, for his part, was probably answering Socrates when he argued in *The Poetics* that though tragedy does stir up dangerous, potentially revolutionary emotions, it does so to exorcise them. *Catharsis* is the much-remembered word for the process. Tragedy, in this account, helps to keep the community safe. It preserves the polis—which is to say that Aristotle's rebuttal, like Socrates's critique, is political. Whatever current critics of the academy may say, the humanities have been politicized from their beginnings. If Aristotle's rebuttal is, for some of us, too conservative, it nonetheless gets the dialogue between poetry and philosophy going.

What Aristotle did not do is denounce Socrates as a promulgator of opaque jargon (look back into Plato and you'll see that there are passages a good deal less than transparent) who was corrupting the young. Instead he set about the task of refuting his opponents with a serious and subtle analysis in praise of a great work, *Oedipus Rex*. He attempted to persuade his audience that a play—whatever Socrates might think—could be of enduring ethical value.

It's this sort of hard critical work that Kimball, Lehman, D'Souza, and other academy-bashers have largely refrained from doing. They've failed to learn the new critical languages so that they can refute them knowingly. They haven't provided better readings of Shakespeare, Milton, Wordsworth, and Emerson than their opponents. Instead, they've taken the short-cut method, offering blanket denunciations and shrill keenings about a crisis in literary studies.

Of course the libraries house many great humanistic readings of the major poets, and those studies are often almost all that the conservative critics claim them to be. To read A. C. Bradley or Harold Gooddard on Shakespeare is an instructive and moving experience (at least for me), but their work does not speak fully to the present cultural and political situation. Art may *sometimes* be eternal, but criticism almost never is. The task of the humanistic critic now is to return to the great works and to show how they bear on contemporary experience. The best that *is* known and thought: That is criticism's quest.

And if literature is to provide a focus for life, if it is to criticize and refine life in response to a perceived crisis of authority, then the stakes are very high. But one more major development intervenes between Arnold and the present. And it is this development, I think, that makes contemporary criticism so baffling to nonpractitioners and accounts for the eccentricities of content and style in much current work. To put it crudely, one might say that on the practice of criticism initiated by Socrates, and on the crisis of authority described by Arnold, there intervenes the thought of Sigmund Freud, the man whom W. H. Auden, in his great elegy, called "a whole climate of opinion / under whom we conduct our different lives." Thus my second topic in this account of contemporary criticism, that of critical style.

3

Beginning around the second decade of the twentieth century, Freud began to see a change in the kinds of patients coming to him. Most were suffering not from overinsistent drives (the most common diagnosis during the early period of psychoanalysis), but from the excessive severity of the *Uber-Ich*. Their superegos had not matured, and the inner agency of authority remained harshly delimiting, providing the sort of strictures a child might need but not, presumably, a mature adult.

Why had this happened? Freud suggested that it was due to the absence of creditable cultural authority. There was nothing to provide a rational replacement for religion and to develop the atavistic superego into a more tolerant form. Thus far Freud doesn't sound much different from the Arnold I've been describing, the Arnold who took it that the quest for a substitute for waning religious authority was the major cultural responsibility of the day.

But Freud adds something else to the diagnosis, an addition that, as I see it, goes a long way to founding contemporary theory. To him the superego is not only sick but unconscious. That is to say, *contra* Arnold, it may not be susceptible to disinterested appeals, may not be able to embrace or even to recognize the best that is known and thought when it is manifest. In fact, Freud's superego grows more remorseless and more irrationally insistent as time goes on, accruing energy whenever it impels the ego to renounce a given pleasure.

Perhaps most disturbing about the vision of authority taken ill that Freud lays out so brilliantly in *Civilization and Its Discontents* is the reciprocal relationship he sees between what is going on inside individuals and developments in the world at large. With every passing generation, civilization tightens its grip on people, forcing them to renounce more and more instinctual satisfactions. The price for the security civilization brings—impotence, depression, despair—is a very high one, and even Freud, who loved culture as much as anyone, is compelled to wonder if the exchange is worthwhile.

Now, the superego, even when it is ill, speaks with the voice of reason. In fact, it can even infiltrate the reasoning powers. Freud believes that at its worst the superego and reason can become infected by the death drive. Think for a moment of the implications. If what Freud says is so, then the Enlightenment faith that free reason (the reason available to Socrates and Arnold alike) can conquer superstition and renovate life is cast into doubt. Reason, once the savior, is now, potentially, the destroyer.

A number of events in recent history serve to corroborate Freud's dire vision. One in particular is worth bringing yet again into focus. It is not only its unprecedented barbarism that makes the Holocaust a point of still unresolved and unresolvable crisis in the history of the West. It is that the barbarism was underwritten, elaborated, refined, made more barbarous still, by resources that one can only associate with intellection. The killing factories, designed for maximum efficiency; the scrupulous care with which medieval versions of hell were constructed above the ground; the exquisite planning that appropriated and put to use the horrible by-products (hair, gold fillings, skin)—all of these attest, for some, to reason's capacity to betray Enlightenment hopes. Such horrors compelled Max Horkheimer and T. W. Adorno, intellectuals of the Frankfurt School, to make a statement that, if finally extreme, cannot be dismissed out of hand: They argue in *Dialectic of Enlightenment* that the Final

Solution was the logical outcome of—and not a deviation from—the Age of Reason.

Granted, Freud did not live to see the Final Solution in its full force; it is doubtful that under any conditions he would have turned and renounced the Enlightenment. His belief that the disinterested mind could commune with the Reality Principle went to the core of his work. Freud was devoted to providing a form of reason, embodied in his therapeutic voice and in the voice of his writings, to contend with the cruel voice he located in the social and the private superego. His sense was that a kind of reason that truly recognized and respected the irrational could successfully war against it. But even that form of reason frequently needed to be augmented by what Freud called the transference, an effect whereby the subject seeking therapeutic relief came to regard the therapist as something of a father. In his practice and in his writing, Freud often strove for paternal status. In doing so, he risked becoming an authority on whom readers and patients would be as dependent as they were on the unreasonable superego he hoped to displace.

One might describe a good deal of contemporary theory as a form of writing that follows upon Arnold's perception of a crisis of authority but is informed by doubts, akin to Freud's, about the role of reason in resolving that crisis. Which is not to say that all theorists accept Freud's premises out and out— no more than they accept Arnold's. Many, if not most, ambitious theorists set out, first of all, to rewrite Freud's account of the crisis of reason. Jacques Derrida speaks of the triumph of the metaphysics of presence; Michel Foucault of the reign of Power/Knowledge; Paul de Man of the drive for truth; Harold Bloom of the inhibiting power of the precursors on the poet striving for autonomy; feminists speak of patriarchy; Marxists of class domination and its by-product, ideology. There are dramatic disparities among these accounts, but all evoke a form of reason that has gone awry and exists beyond the range of habitual consciousness.

Then the question: How does one challenge reason that has turned irrational? Is it necessary to counter deranged authority with an equally compelling counterauthority, fire with fire? Must one use a voice just as commanding as the voice one wishes to reform or displace? Naturally, one risks becoming a mere mirror image of the kind of authority one most detests. (I take this to have happened to Michel Foucault, and not to him alone.) And what about the conventions of logic? Suppose those conventions are part of the problem. Jacques Derrida, in fact, has come to believe that the principles that make thinking possible in the West are intrinsically violent. And yet one cannot signify without deploying those principles, that logic. From this perplexity arises many of the vagaries of theoretical style. Suspicious of conventional argument and presentation but committed to it as both a necessary vehicle for communication and an object of critique, Derrida and others play a double game, attempting to dart in and out of metaphysical nets.

From such a perception about language and reason stems much of the difficulty of contemporary theoretical criticism. For some critics the desire to write in an unaccustomed language—a language labeled "jargon," by the enemies of current academic form—arises from opposition to the coercive authority that is understood as investing established verbal practices. Obviously, writing under such assumptions is sometimes disastrous. One of the implications of the high theory style can be that the theorist is in sync with a higher reality.

This stance has drawn the ire of a constituency that ought, on the face of it, to be in alliance with the professors: liberal intellectual journalists. Journalists have achieved a great deal over the last few decades in keeping the country honest, and they've achieved it in plain language. They aren't terribly receptive to theory's fancy dancing. One of the hopes of this volume is to open up another kind of line of communication between the professors and the press, two groups that may have a lot to learn from one another.

Until now they have been using each other chiefly to score points; each has been trying to enhance its cultural authority by making itself look good at the other's expense. Cultural journalists have been inclined to point their fingers at the English

department and say, "Look how unworldly, jargon-ridden, pretentious, bumbling." (The implied corollary is, of course, "See
how clear-minded, practical, down-to-earth, honest, and urbane is our guild.") To which the professors respond, "They're
superficial, ignorant corporate hirelings." Which in turn is saying something about the professoriat that does not need spelling
out. These kinds of tensions can have their values, provoking
each side to think critically about itself. But when the conflict
reaches the level of obsessive vituperation, as it did during the
scandal surrounding the exposure of Paul de Man's wartime
journalism (all of which was published in collaborationist pe-
riodicals, some of which is disgustingly anti-Semitic), it provides a fertile ground for opportunists like Roger Kimball,
David Lehman, and Dinesh D'Souza.

Rather than fighting each other, I'd suggest we go in for
some mutual edification. (Perhaps I'm compelled to say this,
since, as a contributing editor to *Harper's* and a writer for a
number of other nonacademic publications, I am about three
parts academic to one part journalist.) But the professors *could*
use a dose of worldliness, and the journalists could use, if not
having their ears washed out with strong doses of Derrida, at
least the time, occasionally, to join up with an academic community for a year or so and teach, sit, read, and think. Neither
group, under the salutary influence of the other, would be likely
to leave its habits, especially its linguistic habits, unchanged.
How much accommodation to the ways of the world lies in
journalistic plain-speak? How much is the theorist hiding out
within the intricacies of a displaced religion? It would be of
value for both groups—and for their various constituencies—
to know.

4

So far I've considered the genesis and the range of theory, and
struggles for cultural power, on a fairly large scale. But what
happens when the professor of literature steps into the class-

room? What happens when people like those writing in this volume actually settle down to the discussion of poems, novels, short stories? The best answer lies in the essays at hand, but it will be worthwhile to introduce some of the contributors' concerns by way of practical criticism. I say criticism, not theory, and it will do now to make slightly firmer a distinction between a pair of terms I have been using loosely. Criticism, one might say, involves the questioning, description, evaluation, celebration, derogation of cultural works; theory intensifies that activity, providing a stylistic and conceptual challenge to extant forms of cultural authority. The borders between criticism and theory are infinitely permeable, but the distinction is not without its practical uses.

As a way of demonstrating some of the concerns that now animate literary criticism, I want to consider Robert Browning's marvelous poem "My Last Duchess" (reproduced at the close of the introduction). Probably the most influential reading of that poem is by Robert Langbaum, my colleague at the University of Virginia. Like most readers, Langbaum regards Browning's monologuist, the duke, as a despicable character. Yet there is something engaging, almost mesmerizing, in his account of his charming former wife. Unveiling a portrait of her to a visiting envoy, the duke calls attention to "that spot of joy" on the duchess's cheek, captured perfectly, he says, by the painter, Fra Pandolf. But to the duke's taste, that spot was too easily called forth: "She had/A heart—how shall I say?— too soon made glad."

At one time, many things could call forth the duchess's lovely erotic blush: a sunset, a bough of cherries, her white mule, and, too, her husband's "favour at her breast." Insulted by being lumped with such commonplace affections, the duke takes corrective steps: "I gave commands;/Then all smiles stopped together." All but one, that is. For now, possessing the work of art, the duke possesses his wife's "spot of joy" exclusively.

Surely the duke's behavior is outrageous. And yet one is drawn to him. "What interests us more than the duke's wickedness," says Langbaum, is "his immense attractiveness." Like the envoy, we find ourselves drawn to the duke's "conviction of matchless superiority, his intelligence and bland amorality, his poise, his taste for art, his manners." The result is that moral judgment is, if only temporarily, suspended in favor of sympathy. What compels this response is the power of verbal artistry. And yet it is by this amoral suspension of judgment that we are, in a paradoxical way, morally edified. By identifying with the duke, we enlarge the borders of our experience. We know more, and the knowledge is not merely intellectual, but combines feeling and thought. By reading "My Last Duchess" in the spirit that Langbaum commends, I come closer to being able to say, with the Roman playwright Terence, that nothing human is foreign to me.

Langbaum's reading, which dates from 1957, still finds favor among contemporary humanists and, as you would expect, it is a reading from which a deconstructive critic would likely depart. As a deconstructor might see it, the duke is an archmetaphysician. He is driven toward a form of knowledge that completely subordinates—even overwhelms—the thing known. In this case, that "thing" is a living being, the duchess. The duke prefers to that relatively autonomous living being a picture, something over which he can exercise complete control—"since none puts by/The curtain . . . but I."

Similarly, though less dramatically, the metaphysician is devoted to picture theories of knowledge. He writes and thinks in a way that presumes that the world may be understood outside of time and chance, in a static, pictorial way. He creates models for understanding that suppress distinctions, like those that might exist among the spots of joy that come to the duchess's cheek on different occasions, for diverse reasons, in favor of one true and representative spot—like the one the duke reveals, as he chooses, when he chooses, in the process of drawing back the curtain. The spot, the trace, the play of signs and their mutual interpretability are all subordinated to the one spot, the one sign, the "truth." Since, from the deconstructor's point of view, the motive for this subordination is a drive for power over the multiple world of creatures and things, it is possible that, in its most extreme, obsessive form, the fruit of that drive is the kind of violence that the duke exemplifies. Have we in the West, during what Heidegger calls "the age of the world picture," treated nature and others somewhat as the duke has treated his last duchess, as something to be dominated unto death? We murder to dissect, said Wordsworth.

So, is Browning a sort of poststructuralist prophet, a deconstructor before the letter? Maybe not. For observe the way he ends the poem—a master stroke, many critics have thought. "Notice Neptune," he says to the envoy as they head downstairs,

> Taming a sea-horse, thought a rarity,
> Which Claus of Innsbruck cast in bronze for me!

Yes, exactly, one is inclined to observe, a perfect ironic image for the dramatic action of the poem overall: The duke is himself Neptune, the sea horse is resistant nature in general, the duchess, perhaps, in particular; the bronze itself is an illustration of how willing some kinds of art and artists can be to align themselves with metaphysics and serve power ("cast in bronze for *me!*"), celebrating its predatory excesses.

But wait a minute. By reading the conclusion this way, aren't we thinking somewhat in the manner of the duke? Aren't we fixing his identity and the meaning of the poem in something like the way he fixes the identity of the duchess? Are we using this poem as he uses the painting? Yes, we leave those lines saying; it's clear what Browning wants to get across.

But do we truly understand the poem? Do we in fact know even what became of the duchess? Almost every reader thinks that the duke has had her killed, but the poem itself never says so. "All smiles stopped together"—but murder, who knows? If we do not know this elementary fact about the poem, how can we walk away with the feeling of assurance that the last lines apparently dispense? Is there something in Browning that is in complicity with the duke's way of knowing? Is the poet compelled, by his own disposition, or by the pressures of conventional Western thinking, to provide a form of comforting closure that removes the reader from complicity (that bronze depicts the duke, not me) but that leaves him in the state of smug assurance that the duke so desires? Is the poem "My Last Duchess" a more civil, a more sublimated, version of Fra Pandolf's artwork?

The kind of reading I have sketched out here might, in a more elegant form, be the content of a class taught by a deconstructive critic like J. Hillis Miller. But the poem would be of interest to others as well. What happens, for instance, when you read Browning's lyric with gender in mind, as Susan Fraiman and Nancy K. Miller would be inclined to do? Surely it matters here that the "object" of control is a woman. Are we seeing, in Browning's poem, a representation of the ways in which men have characteristically "known" women through the endless writing of medical treatises, psychological studies, ethnographic commentaries, poems, and novels that have attempted to work out confining definitions of femininity, to depict it accurately? Is there a sense in which the duke is trying to dominate female sexuality? (Remember, it's the duchess's promiscuous blush that provokes the duke's jealous response.)

One wonders too if the duke's particular way of knowing, his commissioning of an image that consolidates his power, might have analogues in other regions of Western culture. Edward Said in his remarkable study of Orientalism, as well as Judith Frank, might be interested in enlarging this reading to compare the duke's mode of comprehending the feminine with the ways in which Western culture has understood—and in understanding attempted to dominate—other non-Western cultures. For their parts, Houston Baker and Michael Bérubé would be interested in how these ways of knowing have been applied to an internal other, African-American culture.

Eve Sedgwick, I take it, would be intrigued by questions of knowledge in this poem, but also by the way it dramatizes certain sexual dynamics. Notice how the duke attempts to create a bond between himself and the envoy by calling attention to the desire that, he implies, the sight of the painting provokes in them both. The image of the woman thus becomes a relay point for an exchange of desire between the two men. Sedgwick might be inclined to call this unequal bonding a version of the homosocial, a mode she takes to be pervasive in the West. What, then, are the full dynamics of power and sexuality between the duke and the envoy? How does the duke use the occasion of the unveiling to learn something, or even to force something to light, about the envoy's sexuality?

Questions of epistemology and questions of ethics would be secondary, I think, in the ways that Harold Bloom and Richard Poirier, two critics who descend from Emerson, read the poem. Bloom is inclined to see Browning as a Romantic quester confined by the achievements of Romantics past. Browning's fascination with evil characters like the duke, and inveterate second-raters like the painter Andrea del Sarto, might proceed, in this view, from his desire to anatomize the parts of himself incapable of embarking on an idealistic quest like that of Percy Bysshe Shelley, a poet he vastly admired and hardly resembles at all. But this inability, this failure to overcome influence, results in grand verse, in eloquent loss. That song of loss is to Bloom the characteristic song of post-Miltonic poetry. Browning's poem would qualify, among other things, as a testimonial to the weariness and infertility of contemporary culture, a condition Bloom is capable of describing with extraordinarily exuberant invention.

Richard Poirier, on the other hand, would be drawn to Browning and his duke as artists of performance. Poirier is an evaluative critic on the highest level: He follows Frost's observation that criticism ought to spend at least some of its time responding to the feats of poetry, which are, ultimately, feats of metaphor making. The duke's pragmatic prowess, his ability to use splendidly eloquent language—both intimidating and charming—to get what he wants (another duchess) would activate Poirier's prowess as a respondent. In the complete compatibility between wickedness and verbal power Poirier could find affirmation for his view that literature at its best works on behalf of no particular social or moral program.

In a similar way, William Kerrigan might view the duke as the dark underside of the Renaissance ideal, the self-delighting solipsist who dwells in the courtier's breast. That solipsist is likely to understand the duchess, as he would comprehend any woman of importance to him, as Nature possessed with twin potentialities, virgin and whore. She is forever being married, found faithless, then murdered, only to be embraced again in an eternal recurrence.

Richard Rorty would be less interested, I would guess, in reading Browning than in reflecting on the kinds of readings that are possible. Rorty is always attuned to the tensions between originality and conformity in a given work. He is a connoisseur of fresh creations, of what he calls new vocabularies. He'd value the reading of "My Last Duchess" that gave us something new, some fresh verbal access to experience, under the assumption that language must always be renovated to keep pace with changing events.

Though they could be better articulated by the critics themselves, the concerns I have been enumerating are representative of those informing humanistic study now. Some of these approaches strike me as more fruitful than others; some seem flush with promise, others less useful. But I find it hard to believe that any of these kinds of enquiry sound the death knell of Western culture, or entail the lowering of academic standards or the onset of interpretive anarchy. Nor are they easily written off as pretentious nonsense, patent drivel, blather, and the rest.

Admittedly something has changed: Critics now are willing, in their quest to find the best that is known and thought, to resist, even to denounce, works that humanism once prized. We now face the unaccustomed, and disturbing, presence of literary scholars whose relation to poetry and fiction can be critical to the point of repudiation. That is, we now have many literary critics who are ready to address literature with the skepticism that was once the exclusive property of the philosophers. Some of this skepticism is smug in tone and untenable in its claims to comprehensive application. But the best contemporary criticism allows us to look anew on the literature of the past and compels ambitious poets and novelists of the present to create works that assimilate, exceed, or scorn the strictures the professors are issuing. Contemporary criticism, when it is working effectively, continues the age-old contention between poets and philosophers, an endless process of mental fight without which neither poetry nor philosophy can achieve its proper vital strength.

My Last Duchess

That's my last Duchess painted on the wall,
Looking as if she were alive. I call
That piece a wonder, now: Frà Pandolf's hands
Worked busily a day, and there she stands.
Will 't please you sit and look at her? I said
'Frà Pandolf' by design, for never read
Strangers like you that pictured countenance,
The depth and passion of its earnest glance,
But to myself they turned (since none puts by
The curtain I have drawn for you, but I)
And seemed as they would ask me, if they durst,
How such a glance came there; so, not the first
Are you to turn and ask thus. Sir, 't was not
Her husband's presence only, called that spot
Of joy into the Duchess' cheek: perhaps
Frà Pandolf chanced to say 'Her mantle laps
'Over my lady's wrist too much,' or 'Paint
'Must never hope to reproduce the faint
'Half-flush that dies along her throat:' such stuff
Was courtesy, she thought, and cause enough
For calling up that spot of joy. She had
A heart—how shall I say?—too soon made glad,
Too easily impressed; she liked whate'er
She looked on, and her looks went everywhere.
Sir, 't was all one! My favour at her breast,
The dropping of the daylight in the West,
The bough of cherries some officious fool

Broke in the orchard for her, the white mule
She rode with round the terrace—all and each
Would draw from her alike the approving speech,
Or blush, at least. She thanked men,—good! but thanked
Somehow—I know not how—as if she ranked
My gift of a nine-hundred-years-old name
With anybody's gift. Who'd stoop to blame
This sort of trifling? Even had you skill
In speech—(which I have not)—to make your will
Quite clear to such an one, and say, 'Just this
'Or that in you disgusts me; here you miss,
'Or there exceed the mark'—and if she let
Herself be lessoned so, nor plainly set
Her wits to yours, forsooth, and made excuse,
—E'en then would be some stooping; and I choose
Never to stoop. Oh sir, she smiled, no doubt,
Whene'er I passed her; but who passed without
Much the same smile? This grew; I gave commands;
Then all smiles stopped together. There she stands
As if alive. Will 't please you rise? We'll meet
The company below, then. I repeat,
The Count your master's known munificence
Is ample warrant that no just pretence
Of mine for dowry will be disallowed;
Though his fair daughter's self, as I avowed
At starting, is my object. Nay, we'll go
Together down, sir. Notice Neptune, though,
Taming a sea-horse, thought a rarity,
Which Claus of Innsbruck cast in bronze for me!

TROTSKY
AND
THE WILD
ORCHIDS

Richard
Rorty

Richard Rorty is America's most controversial philosopher. His books, which include Philosophy and the Mirror of Nature, Contingency, Irony and Solidarity, *and* Consequences of Pragmatism, *defend the possibility of durable ethical and political allegiances that do not ground themselves in transcendental truths. Rorty teaches now at the University of Virginia and has taught at Princeton and Wellesley College. He holds degrees from Yale and the University of Chicago.*

IF THERE IS ANYTHING TO THE IDEA that the best intellectual position is one equidistant from the right and from the left, I am doing very nicely. I am often cited by conservative culture warriors as one of the relativistic, irrationalist, deconstructing, sneering, smirking intellectuals whose writings are weakening the moral fiber of the young. Neal Kozody, writing in the monthly bulletin of the Committee for the Free World, an organization known for its vigilance against symptoms of moral weakness, denounces my "cynical and nihilistic view" and says "it is not enough for him [Rorty] that American students should be merely mindless; he would have them positively mobilized for mindlessness." Richard Neuhaus, a theologian who doubts that atheists can be good American citizens, says that the "ironist vocabulary" I advocate "can neither provide a public language for the citizens of a democracy, nor contend intellectually against the enemies of democracy, nor transmit the reasons for democracy to the next generation." My criticisms of Allan Bloom's *Closing of the American Mind* led Harvey Mansfield—recently appointed by President Bush to the National Council for the Humanities—to say that I have "given up on America" and that I "manage to diminish even Dewey." (Mansfield recently described Dewey as a "medium-sized malefactor.")

Yet Sheldon Wolin, speaking from the left, sees a lot of

31

similarity between me and Allan Bloom: Both of us, he says, are intellectual snobs who care only about the leisured, cultured elite to which we belong. Neither of us has anything to say to blacks, or to other groups who have been shunted aside by American society. Wolin's view is echoed by Terry Eagleton, Britain's leading Marxist thinker. Eagleton says that "in [Rorty's] ideal society the intellectuals will be 'ironists,' practicing a suitably cavalier, laid-back attitude to their own belief, while the masses, for whom such self-ironizing might prove too subversive a weapon, will continue to salute the flag and take life seriously." *Der Spiegel* said that I "attempt to make the yuppie regression look good." Jonathan Culler, one of Derrida's leading American disciples, says that my version of pragmatism "seems altogether appropriate to the age of Reagan." Richard Bernstein says that my views are "little more than an ideological *apologia* for an old-fashioned version of cold war liberalism dressed up in fashionable 'post-modern' discourse." The left's favorite word for me is "complacent," just as the right's is "irresponsible."

The left's hostility is partially explained by the fact that most people who admire Nietzsche, Heidegger, and Derrida as much as I do—most of the people who either classify themselves as "postmodernist" or (like me) find themselves thus classified willy-nilly—participate in what Jonathan Yardley has called the "America Sucks Sweepstakes." Participants in this event compete to find better, bitterer ways of describing the United States. They see our country as embodying everything that is wrong with the rich post-Enlightenment West; they see us as living in what Foucault called a "disciplinary society," one dominated by an odious ethos of "liberal individualism" that produces racism, sexism, consumerism, and Republican presidents. By contrast, I see America pretty much as Whitman and Dewey did, as opening a prospect on illimitable democratic vistas. I think that our country—despite its past and present atrocities and vices, and despite its continuing willingness to elect fools and knaves to high office—is an example of the best kind of society so far invented. To think that is, in leftist eyes, about as politically incorrect as you can get.

The right's hostility is largely explained by the fact that rightist thinkers don't think that it is enough just to *prefer* democratic societies. One also has to believe that they are Objectively Good, that the institutions of such societies are grounded in Rational First Principles. Especially if one teaches philosophy, as I do, one is expected to tell the young that their society is not just one of the better ones so far contrived, but one that embodies Truth and Reason. Refusal to say this sort of thing counts as "the treason of the clerks"—as an abdication of professional and moral responsibility. My own philosophical views —views I share with Nietzsche and Dewey—forbid me to say this kind of thing. I do not have much use for notions like "objective value" and "objective truth." I think that the so-called "postmodernists" are right in most of their criticisms of traditional philosophical talk about "Reason." So my philosophical views offend the right as much as my political preferences offend the left.

I am sometimes told, by exasperated people on both sides, that my views are so weird as to be merely frivolous. They suspect that I will say anything to get a gasp, that I am just amusing myself by contradicting everybody else. This hurts. So I have tried, in what follows, to say something about how I got into my present position—how I got into philosophy, and then found myself unable to use philosophy for the purpose I had originally had in mind. Perhaps this bit of autobiography will make clear that, even if my views about the relation of philosophy to politics are odd, they were not adopted for frivolous reasons.

When I was twelve, the most salient books on my parents' shelves were two red-bound volumes: *The Case of Leon Trotsky* and *Not Guilty*. These made up the report of the Dewey Commission of Inquiry into the Moscow Trials. I never read them with the wide-eyed fascination I brought to books like Krafft-Ebing's *Psychopathia Sexualis*, but I thought of them in the way other children thought of their family's Bible: They were books that radiated redemptive truth and moral splendor. If I were a really *good* boy, I would say to myself, I should have read not only the Dewey Commission reports but also Trotsky's *History of the Russian Revolution*, a book I started many times but never managed to finish. For in the 1940s the Russian Revolution and its betrayal by Stalin were, for me, what the Incarnation and its betrayal by the Catholics had been to precocious little Lutherans four hundred years before.

My father had almost, but not quite, accompanied John Dewey to Mexico as P.R. man for the Commission of Inquiry that Dewey chaired. Having broken with the American Communist Party in 1932, my parents had been classified by the *Daily Worker* as "Trotskyites," and they more or less accepted the description. When Trotsky was assassinated in 1940, one of his secretaries, John Frank, hoped that the GPU would not think to look for him in the remote little village on the Delaware River where we were living. Using a pseudonym, Frank was our guest in Flatbrookville for some months. I was warned not to disclose his real identity, though it is doubtful that my schoolmates at Walpack Elementary would have been interested in my indiscretions.

I grew up knowing that all decent people were, if not Trotskyites, at least socialists. I also knew that Stalin had ordered not only Trotsky's assassination but also Kirov's, Ehrlich's, Alter's, and Carlo Tresca's. (Tresca, gunned down on the streets of New York, had been a family friend.) I knew that poor people would always be oppressed until capitalism was overcome. Working as an unpaid office boy during my twelfth winter, I carried drafts of press releases from the Worker's Defense League office off Gramercy Park (where my parents worked) around the corner to the home of Norman Thomas (the Socialist Party's candidate for president) and also to A. Phillip Randolph's office at the Brotherhood of Pullman Car Porters on 125th Street. On the subway, I would read the papers I was carrying.

They told me a lot about what factory owners did to union organizers, plantation owners to sharecroppers, and the white locomotive engineers' union to the colored firemen (whose jobs white men wanted, now that diesel engines were replacing coal-fired steam engines). So at twelve I knew that the point of being human was to spend one's life fighting social injustice.

But I also had private, weird, snobbish, incommunicable interests. In earlier years these had been in Tibet. I had sent the newly enthroned Dalai Lama a present, accompanied by warm congratulations to a fellow eight-year-old who had made good. A few years later, when my parents began dividing their time between the Chelsea Hotel and the mountains of northwest New Jersey, these interests switched to orchids. Some forty species of wild orchids occur in those mountains, and I eventually found seventeen of them. Wild orchids are uncommon, and rather hard to spot. I prided myself enormously on being the only person around who knew where they grew, their Latin names, and their blooming times. When in New York, I would go to the 42nd Street Public Library to reread a nineteenth-century volume on the botany of the orchids of the eastern U.S.

I was not quite sure why those orchids were so important, but I was convinced that they were. I was sure that our noble, pure, chaste North American wild orchids were morally superior to the showy, hybridized, tropical orchids displayed in florists' shops. I was also convinced that there was a deep significance in the fact that the orchids are the latest and most complex plants to be developed in the course of evolution. Looking back, I suspect that there was a lot of sublimated sexuality involved (orchids being a notoriously sexy sort of flower), and that my desire to learn all there was to know about orchids was linked to my desire to understand all the hard words in Krafft-Ebing.

I was uneasily aware, however, that there was something a bit dubious about this esotericism—this interest in socially useless flowers. I had read (in the vast amount of spare time given to a clever, snotty, nerdy only child) bits of *Marius the Epicurean* and also bits of Marxist criticisms of Pater's aestheticism. I was afraid that Trotsky (whose *Literature and Revolution* I had nibbled at) would not have approved of my interest in orchids.

At fifteen I escaped from the bullies who regularly beat me up on the playground of my high school (bullies who, I assumed, would somehow wither away once capitalism had been overcome) by going off to the so-called "Hutchins College" of the University of Chicago. (This was the institution immortalized by A. J. Liebling as "the biggest collection of juvenile neurotics since the Childrens' Crusade.") Insofar as I had any project in mind, it was to reconcile Trotsky and the orchids. I wanted to find some intellectual or aesthetic framework that would let me—in a thrilling phrase I came across in Yeats—"hold reality and justice in a single vision." By "reality" I meant, more or less, the Wordsworthian moments in which, in the woods around Flatbookville (and especially in the presence of certain coralroot orchids, and of the smaller yellow ladyslipper), I had felt touched by something numinous, something of ineffable importance, something *really* real. By "justice" I meant what Norman Thomas and Trotsky both stood for, the liberation of the weak from the strong. I wanted a way to be both an intellectual and spiritual snob and a friend of humanity—a nerdy recluse and a fighter for justice. I was very confused, but reasonably sure that at Chicago I would find out how grown-ups managed to work the trick I had in mind.

When I got to Chicago (in 1946), I found that Hutchins, together with his friends Mortimer Adler and Richard McKeon (the villain of Pirsig's *Zen and the Art of Motorcycle Maintenance*), had enveloped the University of Chicago in a neo-Aristotelian mystique. The most frequent target of their sneers was John Dewey's pragmatism. That pragmatism was the philosophy of my parents' friend Sidney Hook, as well as the unofficial philosophy of most of the other New York intellectuals who had given up on dialectical materialism.

But according to Hutchins and Adler, pragmatism was vulgar, "relativistic," and self-refuting. As they pointed out over and over again, Dewey had no absolutes. To say, as Dewey did, that "growth itself is the only moral end" left one without a criterion for growth, and thus with no way to refute Hitler's suggestion that Germany had "grown" under his rule. To say that truth is what works is to reduce the quest for truth to the quest for power. Only an appeal to something eternal, absolute, and good—like the God of St. Thomas or the nature of human beings, as described by Aristotle—would permit one to answer the Nazis, to justify one's choice of social democracy over fascism.

This quest for stable absolutes was common to the neo-Thomists and to Leo Strauss, the teacher who attracted the best of the Chicago students (including my classmate Allan Bloom). The Chicago faculty was dotted with awesomely learned refugees from Hitler, of whom Strauss was the most revered. All of them seemed to agree that something deeper and weightier than Dewey was needed if one was to explain why it would be better to be dead than to be a Nazi. This sounded pretty good to my fifteen-year-old ears. For moral and philosophical absolutes sounded a bit like my beloved orchids—numinous, hard to find, known only to a chosen few. Further, since Dewey was a hero to all the people among whom I had grown up, scorning Dewey was a convenient form of adolescent revolt. The only question was whether this scorn should take a religious or a philosophical form, and of how it might be combined with striving for social justice.

Like many of my classmates at Chicago, I knew lots of T. S. Eliot by heart. I was attracted by Eliot's suggestions that only committed Christians (and perhaps only Anglo-Catholics) could overcome their unhealthy preoccupation with their private obsessions, and so serve their fellow humans with proper humility. But a prideful inability to believe what I was saying when I recited the General Confession gradually led me to give up my awkward attempts to get religion. So I fell back on absolutist philosophy.

I read through Plato during my fifteenth summer, and convinced myself that Socrates was right—virtue *was* knowledge. That claim was music to my ears, for I had doubts about my own moral character and a suspicion that my only gifts were intellectual ones. Besides, Socrates *had* to be right, for only then could one hold reality and justice in a single vision. Only if he were right could one hope to be both as good as the best Christians (such as Alyosha in *The Brothers Karamazov*, whom I could not—and still cannot—decide whether to envy or despise) and as learned and clever as Strauss and his students. So I decided to major in philosophy. I figured that if I became a philosopher I might get to the top of Plato's "divided line"—the place "beyond hypotheses" where the full sunshine of Truth irradiates the purified soul of the wise and good: an Elysian field dotted with immaterial orchids. It seemed obvious to me that getting to such a place was what everybody with any brains really wanted. It also seemed clear that Platonism had all the advantages of religion, without requiring the humility that Christianity demanded, and of which I was apparently incapable.

For all these reasons, I wanted very much to be some kind of Platonist, and from fifteen to twenty I did my best. But it didn't pan out. I could never figure out whether the Platonic philosopher was aiming at the ability to offer irrefutable argument—argument that rendered him able to convince anyone he encountered of what he believed (the sort of thing Ivan Karamazov was good at)—or instead was aiming at a sort of incommunicable, private bliss (the sort of thing his brother Alyosha seemed to possess). The first goal is to achieve total argumentative power over others—e.g., the ability to convince bullies that they should not beat one up, or the ability to convince rich capitalists that they must cede their power to a cooperative, egalitarian commonwealth. The second goal is to enter a state in which all doubts are stilled, but in which you no longer wish to argue. Both goals seemed desirable, but I could not see how to fit them together.

At the same time I was worrying about this tension within Platonism—and within any form of what Dewey had called "the quest for certainty"—I was also worrying about the familiar problem of whether it is possible to get a noncircular justification of any debatable stand on any important issue. The more philosophers I read, the clearer it seemed that each of them could carry their views back to first principles that were incompatible with the first principles of their opponents, and that none of them ever got to that fabled place "beyond hypotheses." There seemed to be nothing like a neutral standpoint from which these alternative first principles could be evaluated. But if there were no such standpoint, then the whole idea of "rational certainty," and the whole Socratic–Platonic idea of replacing passion by reason, seemed not to make much sense.

Eventually I got over the worry about circular argumentation by deciding that the test of philosophical truth was overall coherence, rather than deducibility from universally granted truths. But this didn't help much. For coherence is a matter of avoiding contradictions, and St. Thomas's advice—"When you meet a contradiction, make a distinction"—makes this pretty easy to do. As far as I could see, philosophical talent was largely a matter of proliferating as many distinctions as were needed to wriggle out of dialectical corners. More generally, it was a matter, when trapped in such a corner, of redescribing the nearby intellectual terrain in a way that made the terms used by one's opponent seem irrelevant, or question-begging, or jejune. I turned out to have a flair for such redescription. But I became less and less certain that developing this skill was going to make me either wise or virtuous.

Since that initial disillusion (which climaxed about the time I left Chicago to get a Ph.D. in philosophy at Yale), I have spent forty years looking for a coherent and convincing way of formulating my worries about what, if anything, philosophy is good for. My starting point was the discovery of Hegel's *Phenomenology of Spirit*, a book that I read as saying: Granted that philosophy is just a matter of out-redescribing the last philosopher, the cunning of reason can make use even of this sort of competition. It can use it to weave the conceptual fabric of a freer, better, more just society. If philosophy can be, at best, only what Hegel called "its time held in thought," still, that might be enough. For by thus holding one's time, one might do what Marx wanted done—change the world. So even if there was no such thing as "understanding the world" in the Platonic sense—an understanding from a position outside of time and history—perhaps there was still a social use for my talents, and for the study of philosophy.

For quite a while after I read Hegel, I thought that the two greatest achievements of the species to which I belonged were *The Phenomenology of Spirit* and *Remembrance of Things Past* (the book that took the place of the wild orchids once I left Flatbrookville). Proust's ability to weave intellectual and social snobbery together with the hawthorns around Combray, his grandmother's selfless love, Odette's orchidaceous embraces of Swann and Jupien's of Charlus, and with everything else he encountered—to give each of these their due without feeling the need to bundle them together with the help of a religious faith or a philosophical theory—seemed to me as astonishing as Hegel's ability to throw himself successively into empiricism, Greek tragedy, Stoicism, Christianity, and Newtonian physics, and to emerge from each ready and eager for something completely different. It was the commitment to temporality that Hegel and Proust shared—the specifically anti-Platonic element in their work—that seemed so wonderful. They both seemed able to weave everything they encountered into a narrative without asking that that narrative have a moral, and without asking how that narrative would appear under the aspect of eternity.

About twenty years or so after I decided that the young Hegel's willingness to stop trying for eternity, and just be the child of his time, was the appropriate response to disillusionment with Plato, I found myself being led back to Dewey. Dewey now seemed to me a philosopher who had learned all that Hegel had to teach about how to eschew certainty and eternity, while immunizing himself against pantheism by taking Darwin seriously. This rediscovery of Dewey coincided with my first encounter with Derrida (which I owe to Jonathan Arac, a colleague at Princeton). Derrida led me back to Heidegger, and I was struck by the resemblances between Dewey's, Wittgenstein's, and Heidegger's criticisms of Cartesianism. Suddenly things began to come together. I thought I saw a way to blend a criticism of the Cartesian tradition with the quasi-Hegelian historicism of Michel Foucault, Ian Hacking, and Alasdair MacIntyre. I thought that I could fit all these into a quasi-Heideggerian story about the tensions within Platonism.

The result of this small epiphany was a book called *Philosophy and the Mirror of Nature*. Though disliked by most of my fellow philosophy professors, this book had enough success among nonphilosophers to give me a self-confidence I had previously lacked. But *Philosophy and the Mirror of Nature* did not do much for my adolescent ambitions. The topics it treated—the mind-body problem, controversies in the philosophy of language about truth and meaning, Kuhnian philosophy of science—were pretty remote from both Trotsky and the orchids. I had gotten back on good terms with Dewey; I had articulated my historicist anti-Platonism; I had finally figured out what I thought about the direction and value of current movements in analytic philosophy. I had sorted out most of the philosophers whom I had read. But I had not spoken to any of the questions that got me started reading philosophers in the first place. I was no closer to the single vision that, thirty years back, I had gone to college to get.

As I tried to figure out what had gone wrong, I gradually decided that the whole idea of holding reality and justice in a single vision had been a mistake—that a pursuit of such a vision had been precisely what led Plato astray. More specifically, I decided that only religion—only a nonargumentative faith in a surrogate parent who, unlike any real parent, embodied love, power, and justice in equal measure—could do the trick Plato wanted done. Since I couldn't imagine becoming religious, and indeed had gotten more and more raucously secularist, I decided that the hope of achieving a single vision by becoming a philosopher had been a self-deceptive atheist's way out. So I decided to try to write a book about what intellectual life would be like if one could manage to give up the Platonic attempt to hold reality and justice in a single vision.

That book—*Contingency, Irony and Solidarity*—argues that there is no need to weave together one's personal equivalent of Trotsky and one's personal equivalent of my wild orchids. Rather, one should try to abjure the temptation to tie in one's responsibilities to other people with one's relation to whatever idiosyncratic things or persons one loves with all one's heart and soul and mind (or, if you like, the things or persons one is obsessed with). These two will, in some lucky people, coincide—as they do in Christians, for whom the love of God and the love of other human beings are inseparable, or Trotskyites, who are moved by nothing but the thought of justice. But they need not coincide, and one should not try too hard to weave them together. So, for example, Jean-Paul Sartre seemed to me right when he denounced Kant's self-deceptive quest for certainty, but wrong when he denounced Proust as a useless bourgeois wimp, a man whose life and writings were equally irrelevant to the only thing that really matters, the struggle to overthrow capitalism.

Proust's life and work were, in fact, irrelevant to that struggle. But that is a silly reason to despise Proust. It is as wrongheaded as Savonarola's contempt for the works of art he called "vanities." Single-mindedness of this Sartrean or Savonarolan sort is the quest for purity of heart—the attempt to will one thing—gone rancid. It is the attempt to see yourself as an incarnation of something larger than yourself (the Movement, Reason, the Good, the Holy) rather than accepting your finitude. The latter means, among other things, accepting that what matters most to you may well be something that may never matter much to most people. Your equivalent of my orchids may seem merely weird, merely idiosyncratic, to practically everybody else. But that is no reason to be ashamed of, or downgrade, or try to slough off, your Wordsworthian moments, your lover, your family, your pet, your favorite lines of verse, or your quaint religious faith. There is nothing sacred about universality that makes the shared automatically better than the unshared. What you can get everybody to agree to (the universal) merits no automatic privilege over what you cannot (the idiosyncratic).

This means that the fact that you have obligations to other people (not to bully them, to join them in overthrowing tyrants, to feed them when they are hungry) does not entail that what you share with other people is more important than anything else. What you share with them when you are aware of such moral obligations is not, I argued in *Contingency*, "rationality" or "human nature" or "the fatherhood of God" or "a knowledge of the Moral Law," or anything other than ability to sympathize with the pain of others. There is no particular reason to expect that your sensitivity to that pain, and your idiosyncratic loves, are going to fit within one big overall account of how everything hangs together. There is, in short, not much reason to hope for the sort of single vision that I went to college hoping to get.

So much for how I came to the views I currently hold. As I said earlier, most people find these views repellent. My *Contingency* book got a couple of good reviews, but these were vastly outnumbered by reviews saying that the book was frivolous, confused, and irresponsible. The gist of the criticisms I get from both left and right is pretty much the same as the gist of the criticisms aimed at Dewey by the Thomists, the Straussians, and the Marxists, back in the thirties and forties. Dewey thought, as I now do, that there was nothing bigger, more permanent and more reliable, behind our sense of moral obligation to those in pain than a certain contingent historical phenomenon—the gradual spread of the sense that the pain of others matters, regardless of whether they are of the same family, tribe, religion, nation, or intelligence as oneself. This idea, Dewey thought, cannot be shown to be true by science, or religion, or philosophy—at least if "shown to be true" means "capable of being made evident to anyone, regardless of background." It can be made evident only to people whom it is not too late to acculturate into our own particular, late-blooming, historically contingent form of life.

This Deweyan claim entails a picture of human beings as children of their time and place, without any significant metaphysical or biological limits on their plasticity. It means that a sense of moral obligation is a matter of conditioning rather than of insight. It also means that the notion of insight (in any area, physics as well as ethics) as a glimpse of what is *there* apart from any human needs and desires cannot be made coherent. As William James put it, "the trail of the human serpent is over all." More specifically, our conscience and our aesthetic taste are, equally, products of the cultural environment in which we grew up. We decent, liberal, humanitarian types (representatives of the moral community to which both my reviewers and I belong) are just luckier, not more insightful, than the bullies with whom we struggle.

This view is often referred to dismissively as "cultural relativism." But is it not relativistic, if that means saying that every moral view is as good as every other. *Our* moral view is, I firmly believe, much better than any competing view, even though there are many people whom you will never be able to convert to it. It is one thing to say, falsely, that there is nothing to choose between us and the Nazis. It is another thing to say, correctly, that there is no neutral, common ground to which a philosophical Nazi and I can repair to argue out our differences. That Nazi and I will always strike each other as begging all the crucial questions, arguing in circles.

Socrates and Plato suggested that if we tried hard enough we should find beliefs that *everybody* found intuitively plausible, and that among these would be moral beliefs whose implications, when clearly realized, would make us virtuous as well as knowledgeable. To thinkers like Allan Bloom (on the Straussian side) and Terry Eagleton (on the Marxist side), there just *must* be such beliefs—unwobbling pivots that determine the answer to the question "Which moral or political alternative is *objectively* valid?" For Deweyan pragmatists like me, history and anthropology are enough to show that there are no unwobbling pivots, and that seeking objectivity is just a matter of getting as much intersubjective agreement as you can.

Nothing much has changed in philosophical debates about whether there is more to objectivity than intersubjectivity since the time I went to college—or, for that matter, since the time Hegel went to seminary. Nowadays we philosophers talk about "moral language" instead of "moral experience," and about "contextualist theories of reference" rather than "the relation between subject and object." But this is just froth on the surface. My reasons for turning away from the anti-Deweyan views I imbibed at Chicago are pretty much the same reasons Dewey had for turning away from evangelical Christianity and from the neo-Hegelian pantheism he embraced in his twenties. They are also pretty much the reasons that led Hegel to turn away from Kant, and to decide that both God and the Moral Law had to be temporalized and historicized to be believable. I do not think that I have more insight into the debates about our need for "absolutes" than I had when I was twenty, despite all the books I have read and arguments I have had in the intervening forty years. All they did was to let me spell out my disillusionment with Plato—my conviction that philosophy was no help in dealing with Nazis and other bullies—in more detail, and to a variety of audiences.

At the moment there are two cultural wars being waged in the United States. The first is the one described in detail by my colleague James Davison Hunter in his comprehensive and informative *Culture Wars: The Struggle to Define America*. This war is important. It will decide whether our country continues along the trajectory defined by the Bill of Rights, the Reconstruction Amendments, the building of the land-grant colleges, female suffrage, the New Deal, *Brown v. Board of Education*, the building of the community colleges, Martin Luther King's civil rights movement, the feminist movement, and the gay rights movement. Following this trajectory would mean that America will continue to set an example of increasing tolerance and equality.

But it may be that this trajectory could be maintained only while Americans' average real income continued to rise. So 1973 may have been the beginning of the end: the end both of rising economic expectations and of the political consensus that emerged from the New Deal. The future of American politics may be just a series of increasingly blatant and increasingly successful variations on the Willie Horton spots. Sinclair Lewis's *It Can't Happen Here* may become an increasingly plausible scenario. Unlike Hunter, I feel no need to be judicious and balanced in my attitude toward the two sides in this first sort of culture war—the sides he calls "progressivist" and "orthodox." I see the "orthodox" (the people who think that hounding gays out of the military promotes traditional family values) as the same honest, decent, blinkered, disastrous people who voted for Hitler in 1933. I see the "progressivists" as defining the only America I care about.

The second cultural war is being waged in magazines like *Critical Inquiry* and *Salmagundi*, magazines with high subscription rates and low circulations. It is between those who see modern liberal society as fatally flawed (the people handily lumped together as "postmodernists") and those (including typical left-wing Democrat professors like myself) who see ours as a society in which technology and democratic institutions can, with luck, collaborate to increase equality and reduce suffering. This war is not very important. Despite the conservative columnists who pretend to view with alarm a vast conspiracy (encompassing both the postmodernists and the pragmatists) to politicize the humanities and corrupt the youth, this war is just a tiny little dispute within what Hunter calls the "progressivist" ranks.

People on the "postmodernist" side tend to share Noam Chomsky's view of the United States as a nation run by a corrupt elite that aims at enriching itself by impoverishing the Third World. From that perspective, ours is not so much a country in danger of slipping into fascism as it is a country that has always been quasi-fascist. These people typically think that nothing will change unless we get rid of "humanism," "liberal individualism," and "technologism." People like me see nothing wrong with any of these -isms, nor with the political and moral heritage of the Enlightenment—with the least common denominator of Mill and Marx, Trotsky and Whitman, William James and Vaclav Havel. Typically, we Deweyans are sentimentally patriotic about America—willing to grant that it could slide into fascism at any time, but proud of its past and guardedly hopeful about its future.

Most people on my side of this second, tiny, upmarket, cultural war have given up on socialism in light of the history of nationalized enterprises and central planning in Central and Eastern Europe. We are willing to grant that welfare-state capitalism is the best we can hope for. Most of us who were brought up Trotskyite now feel forced to admit that Lenin and Trotsky did more harm than good, and that Kerensky (the hapless social democrat whom Lenin shoved aside) has gotten a bum rap for the past seventy years. But we see ourselves as still faithful to everything that was good in the socialist movement. Those on the other side, however, still insist that nothing will change unless there is some sort of total revolution. Postmodernists who consider themselves post-Marxists still want to preserve the sort of purity of heart that Lenin feared he might lose if he listened to too much Beethoven.

I am distrusted by both the orthodox side in the important war and the postmodern side in the unimportant one because I think that the orthodox are philosophically wrong as well as politically dangerous, and that the postmoderns are philosophically right though politically silly. Unlike both the orthodox and the postmoderns, I do not think that you can tell much about the worth of a philosopher's views on topics such as truth, objectivity, and the possibility of a single vision by discovering his politics, or his irrelevance to politics. So I do not think it counts in favor of Dewey's pragmatic view of truth that he was a fervent social democrat, nor against Heidegger's criticism of Platonic notions of objectivity that he was a Nazi, nor against Derrida's view of linguistic meaning that his most influential American ally, Paul de Man, wrote a couple of anti-Semitic articles when he was young. The idea that you can evaluate a writer's philosophical views by reference to his political utility seems to me a version of the bad Platonic-Straussian idea that we cannot have justice until philosophers become kings or kings philosophers.

Both the orthodox and the postmoderns still want a tight connection between people's politics and their views on large theoretical (theological, metaphysical, epistemological, meta-philosophical) matters. Some postmodernists who initially took my enthusiasm for Derrida to mean that I must be on their political side decided, after discovering that my politics were pretty much those of Hubert Humphrey, that I must have sold out. The orthodox tend to think that people who, like the postmodernists and me, believe neither in God nor in some suitable substitute, must feel that everything is permitted, that everybody can do what they like. So they tell us that we are either inconsistent or self-deceptive in putting forward our moral or political views.

I take this near-unanimity among my critics to show that most people—even a lot of purportedly liberated postmodernists—still hanker for something like what I wanted when I was fifteen: a way of holding reality and justice in a single vision. More specifically, they want to unite their sense of moral and political responsibility with a grasp of the ultimate determinants of our fate. They want to see love, power, and justice as coming together deep down in the nature of things, or in the human soul, or in the structure of language, or *somewhere*. They want some sort of guarantee that their intellectual acuity or their aesthetic sensitivity, and those special ecstatic moments that such acuity or sensitivity sometimes affords, are of some relevance to their moral convictions. They still think that virtue and knowledge are somehow linked—that being right about philosophical matters is important for right action.

I do not want to argue that there is *no* linkage—that philosophy is socially useless. Had there been no Plato, the Christians would have had a harder time selling the idea that all God really wanted from us was fraternal love. Had there been no

Kant, the nineteenth century would have had a harder time reconciling Christian ethics with Darwin's story about the descent of man. Had there been no Darwin, it would have been harder for Whitman and Dewey to detach the Americans from their belief that they were God's chosen people, to get them to start standing on their own feet. Had there been no Dewey and no Sidney Hook, American intellectual leftists of the 1930s would have been as buffaloed by the Marxists as were their counterparts in France and in Latin America. Ideas do, indeed, have consequences.

But the fact that ideas have consequences does not mean that we philosophers, we specialists in ideas, are in a key position. We are not here to provide principles or foundations or deep theoretical diagnoses, or a synoptic vision. When I am asked (as, alas, I often am) what I take contemporary philosophy's "mission" or "task" to be, I get tongue-tied. The best I can do is to stammer that we philosophy professors are people who have a certain familiarity with a certain intellectual tradition, as chemists have a certain familiarity with what happens when you mix various substances together. We can offer some advice about what will happen when you try to combine or to separate certain ideas, on the basis of our knowledge of the results of past experiments. By doing so, we may be able to help you hold your time in thought. But we are not the people to come to if you want confirmation that the things you love with all your heart are central to the structure of the universe, or that your sense of moral responsibility is "rational and objective" rather than "just" a result of how you were brought up.

There are still, as the nineteenth-century American pragmatist C. S. Peirce put it, "philosophical slop-shops on every corner" that will provide such confirmation. But there is a price. To pay the price, you have to turn your back on intellectual history and on what Milan Kundera calls "the fascinating imaginative realm where no one owns the truth and everyone has the right to be understood . . . the wisdom of the novel." You risk losing the sense of finitude, and the tolerance, that result from realizing how very many synoptic visions there have been, and how little argument can do to help you choose between them. Despite my relatively early disillusionment with Platonism, I am very glad that I spent all those years reading philosophy books. For I learned something that still seems very important: to distrust the intellectual snobbery that originally led me to read them. If I had not read all those books, I might never have been able to stop looking for what Derrida calls "a full presence beyond the reach of play," for a luminous synoptic vision.

By now I am pretty sure that looking for such a presence and such a vision is a bad idea. The main trouble is that you might succeed, and your success might let you imagine that you have something more to rely on than the tolerance and decency of your fellow human beings. The democratic community of Dewey's dreams is a community in which nobody imagines that. It is a community in which everybody thinks that it is human solidarity, rather than knowledge of something not merely human, that really matters. The actually existing approximations to such a fully democratic, fully secular community now seem to me the greatest achievements of our species. In comparison, even Hegel's and Proust's books are optional, orchidaceous extras.

MY
KINSMAN,
T.S. ELIOT

*Frank
Lentricchia*

Frank Lentricchia is a leading American critic whose work combines elements of Marx and Gramsci with the native strain found in Emerson and William James. His writing has been central in focusing university intellectuals on the political content of their teaching and scholarship, and on the strategic responses of imaginative writers to the pressures that emanate from social and political arrangements. Lentricchia's most influential books are After the New Criticism, Criticism and Social Change, and Ariel and the Police. He did his graduate work at Duke University and has taught at the University of California at Irvine and at Rice. He is currently Katherine Everett Gilbert Professor of English at Duke.

I seemed to be the same person, and I was
the same person, I was still myself, I was
more myself than I had ever been, and yet
I was nothing.
                              —Thomas Merton

I wish that I could say that it wrote itself,
but New York wrote it.
                    —caption, *New Yorker* cartoon

A WEEK AFTER MOVING TO NEW YORK, where for the fall semester
of '91 I'm to direct a Duke University program for seniors
interested in literature and the other arts, a letter arrives from
Mark Edmundson of the University of Virginia. He asks me if
I'd like to write something for a volume that Viking will be
publishing on the "current state of literary studies," a presentation of my side in response to numerous harsh attacks on the
academy, where I reside in partial beatitude. No, I wouldn't.
Then, page two, and a first-order temptation: Edmundson tells
me that it would be desirable if I could write a "brief intellectual
autobiography that would somewhere contain a statement of
my present allegiances. The piece could be quite personal, a
chance for some self-reflection." I can't resist, I've been thinking
of doing this kind of thing, I say yes, not too eagerly, I hope.
But I don't tell Edmundson that I don't, anymore, know what
my allegiances in literary criticism are, or what my "position"
is, as they say, or that I'll try self-reflection with the desire not
to have a self to reflect upon. I don't tell him that I'd like to
mix up the personal and the intellectual to the point where it
would be impossible to separate them, not as an exercise in
high-wire theory (this I know how to do), but as an act of
homage to the real state of my affairs.

———

Some of my students are going to have trouble adjusting to New York. My wife, no question. But not me. People I've met from other parts of the country think I'm from the city itself (actually I'm from upstate New York—Utica). Queens, I was once told by a woman who grew up in Queens. The misidentification thrills me, and a couple of times I don't bother to correct the mistake. I think I learned to sound the way I sound because as a teenager in the 1950s I lived in *On the Waterfront*. I learned to sound the way a real man sounds, tough (I'm not, of course, referring to Italian American manhood, another level altogether), but not tough where you-know-where. The Brando character in *Waterfront* is a cliché I like to draw tightly around me.

I've been coming here regularly since the '50s for weekends; now I am becoming a member of my heart's second home, the first one being Hillsborough, North Carolina, a village of 3,000. On my second day, I tell someone who thinks I'm making a radical change that it isn't so. Because, I say, Manhattan and Hillsborough are the same. I shall pay for saying this, pay double for writing it—two islands of tranquility necessary for writing, the former more peaceful even than the latter. Manhattan is where walking the streets I lose the "I" easily, in two seconds, and sentences and phrases come into me, shape themselves as forms of sensation, good stuff, keepers, like Wordsworth peripatetic, composed, in the Lake District composing, me on Seventh Avenue South, through the gates.

I'm not supposed to be doing this, I'm supposed to be writing the last chapter of my never-ending book on modernism, I'm supposed to be writing on T. S. Eliot. The day after I say yes to Mark Edmundson, I write in my little red notebook, "My Kinsman, T. S. Eliot." I wonder how I could explain that to my parents (answer: I'll never bring it up), born to Southern Italian immigrants, who moved into my mother's father's house when I was in single digits, where we lived until I was twenty-one. Three generations in a two-family house on Mary Street.

How would I explain that to my grandparents, all four of whom lived into my early thirties? Eliot, my kinsman, from St. Louis, a premier WASP who went to Harvard, then to England for good, where he took on a different sound, like a complete Englishman. Absurd.

I admit that I can see a fragile connection. We both wanted to sound like somebody else. But I never wanted to sound like Eliot. In my neighborhood? And we were both drawn to acting. Theater as the medium of our kinship. What did we sound like originally? Is that a relevant question? I don't want to get into it. Maybe the connection isn't so fragile. Maybe we'd prefer not to remember, because maybe we'd prefer not to know what we know.

My allegiance is not to a literary theory but to the sum total of my liberating literary experiences, and, I have told you, have I not, what I want liberating from? Most of these experiences are text-triggered, but not all. Most of the triggering texts are what a literary culture less guilty than ours used to call "great," "major," and "classic," but not all. I take my liberation where I find it. When I say "but not all" I give the impression that I like the performing and visual arts, which I do, but that's not what I was thinking about. I was thinking about experiences whose sources virtually none would call "art" or "esthetic," which most would call "life." The "art" and "life" distinction, so venerable and so important, makes "life" harder for me. I can't exactly say to hell with the distinction because I half believe in it. The fun is all in disrespecting it by finding art in life, or, if you can't, by making it up in concert with the givens, the gifts, which need to have their say—a desire we ought to respect. The ethics of interpretation: Be decent to your materials.

Is it becoming obvious to you that I'm a somewhat uneasy Italian American esthete who finds Walter Pater, unofficial mentor of Oscar Wilde, almost sufficient? "Of this wisdom, the poetic passion, the desire of beauty, the love of art for art's sake has most; for art comes to you professing frankly to give nothing but the highest quality to your moments as they pass, and simply for those moments' sake." When I experience art, I feel good because I feel the specificity of the moment, the act, the image, the scene, but before and after I don't feel too good, so I seek out more experiences of art's particularity because art is the only place I know where to find deliverance of the specific from the habits of abstraction. Pater means "art" in the traditional sense, a good enough sense. But if I limit myself to what he intends, I don't feel good that often. That's why I look for the beautiful everywhere, why I coax and stroke it when I find it stirring in front of me. And I do mean "in front of me," in a restaurant in Little Italy, 146 Mulberry Street (honor to the site), at Angelo's (everything's in a name). Art as stubborn specificity, as untheorizable peculiarity. Art for life's sake.

I had walked down to Angelo's from Bleecker and Carmine where I attended *la messa Italiana* at Our Lady of Pompeii, sparsely populated by retired immigrants who take me back to Utica's eastside, the world of my grandparents, St. Anthony's on St. Anthony Street, one of Utica's three Italian churches. There it is: the same elaborate imitation Renaissance interior, with a roof after Michelangelo's Sistine Chapel, the Italian women, old, in black, severely devoted, the affectless manner of the priest droning formulas, and the same old me, disconnected, cold. I was looking for something good I thought I had met in a monastery in South Carolina, six months before, Mepkin Abbey, then met again, four Sundays in a row, at Holy Family, a Catholic church in Hillsborough that looks as if it should have been a subject for a photograph by Walker Evans, like the one captioned "Wooden Church, South Carolina, 1936." In Evans's photo: weather-beaten raw wood, dried to a crisp, flaking and warping under mean sunlight, a child's stick drawing of a house with a tiny bell tower perched on the peak above the front face, saying this is a church. Holy Family doesn't look like the church in the Evans photo but it has a tendency, and someday when the funds fail completely that's what it will look like, and then it will have fulfilled its architectural and religious promise. In its shocking plainness it will become es-

sence of church, the esthetic and spiritual negation of Our Lady
of Pompeii and St. Anthony's. The American Protestant half
of my soul is getting the best of the Italian Catholic half. (What
is a church supposed to look like, anyway?) At Our Lady of
Pompeii I am myself. I cannot give in and had no expectation
that at Angelo's I'd meet again what I thought I had found at
Mepkin Abbey.

> "What happens is a continual surrender of himself as
> he is at the moment to something which is more
> valuable."
> —T. S. Eliot, "Tradition and the Individual Talent"

SCENE: A little after noon, Mulberry Street, almost deserted,
Angelo's, a long and narrow space, expensively decorated, not
in the family style. They seat me toward the front, back to wall,
clear view of door and street and assassins, should they decide
that this is the place, this is the moment, it's you, Frank. At a
front corner table, on a clean diagonal with mine, a couple has
gotten here before me. Here when the place opened, maybe
before (yes, before) because they have already killed half a bottle
of wine and a large antipasto is about to go, too. Angelo's opens
at 12:00. I got there at 12:10. I wonder how these Chinese people
got into an Italian restaurant well before opening time, in Little
Italy, where the Italians have been leaving in droves, many in
resentment, I hear, of an exploding Chinatown pouring over
the border.

The man and the woman are probably in their early thirties,
probably not married, speaking their native tongue. A waiter
approaches their table and the Chinese man shifts effortlessly
into Italian dialect to the waiter who like all the waiters is Italian
born. The Chinese man tells the waiter that he's from Calabria,
born and raised, *sono di Calabria*, and the waiter says back
quickly, as if picking up his cue, that one of his co-workers
(whom he now calls over) is also *di Calabria*. The Chinese Ca-

labrian and the standard Calabrian shake hands, glad to meet each other. The three men exchange pleasantries with a certain gravity of tone. The waiters depart and the Chinese man who said *sono di Calabria* turns to the woman he's with and they resume speaking in what I thought was their native tongue, intimately, with no quick over-the-shoulder glances at the waiter, no telling grins. I assume they're not talking about Calabria, but who knows.

Either this is all, on both sides, the best deadpan act known to man, or what has been said between the parties is literally true. I try hard to imagine what it would mean, what possibly, if either of my options for reading this scene were valid, and I cannot imagine it. If this is theater, who is it theater for? I check the waiters, hoping to pick up something ironical in that quarter. Nothing. They're talking about someone's son-in-law, *un cazzone proprio* (a true prick).

In his essay on Dante, Eliot says that "genuine poetry can communicate before it is understood." At Angelo's, in cognitive darkness, I sink into delight in the surfaces of whatever it is that is passing before me.

Scene:

Midway through my main course: a dish of potatoes (small spheres thereof), mushrooms, onions, asparagus, artichoke hearts, zucchini, and many little excellent sausages, lucidly spiced in a light red sauce (*alto Italiano*). A couple now seated immediately to my right, a family of three to my immediate left. The woman of the couple to my right orders the fettucini alfredo and then asks the waiter (who is also my waiter) if the alfredo comes with mushrooms. The waiter explains that it's the other fettucini on the menu, in the red sauce, that has the mushrooms. The woman says that she doesn't want that one, she wants the alfredo and she wants it with mushrooms. She's not pushy; she's nice. I have to sneak a glance over my right shoulder to get a look at her. I sneeze. She says, God bless you. I thank her, talking into my coffee.

Scene:

The family of three to my left. The man has an important

body: six foot two, tremendous shoulders, two hundred and seventy-five pounds, steel in the face, a belly of real force. Middle fifties. The wife, not rotund in the stereotypical manner but not slim, glasses, unconcerned. The daughter, sixteen or seventeen, petite, working on petite, unconcerned, elsewhere.

When they come in the man sits and the wife and the daughter do not hesitate, they go straight for the ladies' room. The waiter, the one who took the alfredo with mushrooms order and who introduced his colleague to the Chinese Calabrian, comes over to the big man, who must be a regular and who must know this waiter well, because the waiter without being asked brings him a nice antipasto and when the waiter asks, in Italian, after *la signora*, the big man answers, in Italian, "Attending to her cunt." That is what the man said. You had to be there for this part, you had to have a little Italian because the poetry is traduced by the translation (I've lost most of mine but retain the valuable words).

The man with the important body says the words wearily but with real respect. "Attending to" is my effort to get to the formal and elevated quality of his *Attenta alla sua*. The man with the important body must believe (this is what I believe) that his wife is in reality *signora* #2, that she is attending to *signora* #1, with whom he has a relationship, but not one that could be characterized by the elegance of *Attenta alla sua*. His relations with the two signoras appear to be tinged with the sadness of one who in the not too distant past suffered a sudden, debilitating self-appraisal and then quickly relinquished to destiny. It is perhaps no longer proper to say of the two signoras that they are "his." In the middle years of his marriage, the big man finds himself cast in a new role, by whom or what he does not know. His wife is unreadable. Nevertheless, he is to play, this he knows, *la signora* #3. He will not complain. He will grow into the role. It will be remarked, eventually, that his performance is definitive.

Of course, the impossibly ugly Anglo-Saxon monosyllable is not what he said, and cannot compare to the trochaic rhythm of the two-syllabled Italian slang term, whose spelling I am unsure of. I have never seen it written; I cannot find it in my large Italian dictionary and do not bother to look into the one for tourists. I could call Margaret Brose at the University of California, Santa Cruz, a specialist in the literature and language, but I don't know Margaret that well, haven't spoken to her in years, and do not wish to prepare the elaborate transition that would permit me to pose the overwhelming question.

I believe the second syllable of the word I could spell, because that sound ends my name: c-c-h-i-a. I believe that the first syllable must be spelled m-i-n. Thus: *mincchia*. On the other hand, I am unsure of those "c's." Does "mincchia," like "Lentricchia," have two "c's"? If two "c's," then you must linger on the "c" in order to indicate doubleness. Which leads us to the tricky semantic issue. The word in Italian, while making the same reference as the English word, performs another communicative task which I have overheard undertaken by Italian women of my grandmother's generation and status (of the South, of the turn of the century, of poverty, amongst themselves). You would not, in English, having just been told a startling piece of news, or having just witnessed an astounding event, exclaim "Cunt!" You would not do this. But in Italian you might, some would say you must, say *Mincchia!* In such situations you are expressing your awe, registering the presence of sublimity, you are saying it with two "c's." The man with the important body could manage but one "c." The *mincchia* of defeat.

(My wife, *la vera signora*, has just walked in, I'm not making this up. I tell her, without preface, that I'm writing about cunt. She replies, without preface, "What else is there?" Is it clear why some men long for important bodies? The man on my left had an important, some might even say a major body, and I pray to Our Lady of Pompeii that it gives him some consolation.)

The wife and the daughter return from their respective involvements. The waiter spreads wide his arms, but not too wide, and says, *La signora bella! La signora bella* nods subtly, and the waiter says to the big man, indicating the girl, And this is your niece? The big man says, My daughter. The waiter says, I would not have believed that you had a daughter so young. (On "so young" the daughter tilts, almost imperceptibly.) The big man nods in satisfaction; he feels a little bigger, he must, because right away he complains about the bread, he wants it exchanged. I know bread. In rapid succession I had eaten four pieces, there was nothing wrong with the bread. The waiter says, Of course we shall bring you a new basket (and now the waiter moves in swiftly for the kill—he's known all along how to rank the three signoras) and he says, But of course it will be the same. The new bread arrives and the big man says, This is better (*quest'è meglio*). The waiter grins wide. Another waiter comes up from behind him, close, very close, gives him a big hug around the belly, with one arm, and says that he, the hugged one, cannot resist the bread of this place. The petite one, without asking, picks an olive off her father's plate. *La signora bella* appears oblivious, but who knows.

Am I reporting, or making this up? Is this criticism or something else? What shall I call it? The reading of a text or the making of a text? Do I need to know how much poetry, theater, and story is objectively there, at Angelo's? How much of it lies in this beholder's eye, who spends his nights and days with Western literary masters? Is someone waiting for me to give the sexist and homophobic dimensions of my Angelo's text? Waiting for me to say that the theater of Angelo's is marginal to the traditional interests of mainstream Western culture? The kinship of classic and ethnic cultures in the medium of myself. But what does it mean, exactly, to say "myself" when I say "myself"? If a self is a medium, is it a self?

> "From the point of view of literature, the drama is only one among several poetic forms. . . . Nevertheless, the drama is perhaps the most permanent, is capable of greater variation and of expressing more varied types of society, than any other."
> —T. S. Eliot, "The Possibility of a Poetic Drama"

———

"The really fine rhetoric of Shakespeare occurs in situations where a character in the play sees *himself* in a dramatic light. . . . Is not Cyrano exactly in this situation of contemplating himself as a romantic, a dramatic figure? This dramatic sense on the part of the characters themselves is rare in modern drama. . . . But in actual life, in many of those situations in actual life which we enjoy consciously and keenly, we are at times aware of ourselves in this way. . . . A very small part of acting is that which takes place on the stage! . . . [This dramatic sense] is a sense which is almost a sense of humor (for when anyone is conscious of himself as acting, something like a sense of humor is present)."

—T. S. Eliot, " 'Rhetoric' and Poetic Drama"

SCENE: We sit on the floor, crowded together, at the feet of Miss Beach, who does the narration and the characters in different voices. Miss Beach can read. We can't read. It's not our fault, this is first-term kindergarten. Miss Beach asks if there is a story that we would like her to tell us. Before anyone can say anything I shout out, "Jack and the Beanstalk!" Miss Beach looks at me. She looks at me like she's thinking, What's wrong with this kid? She doesn't say: Francis, I told that story yesterday. She doesn't say a word; she stares. That's how I remember my first literary experience. I remember it not directly but by remembering the bad part whose badness was bad because of how different it was from the day before, when it must have been terrific, at the feet of Miss Beach, living in literature, which I don't remember, when I must have surrendered whatever self I had to something more valuable, something alive in Miss Beach's voice.

At the moment when Miss Beach stared but could not speak, the boy wanted to jump back into yesterday's tale but could not do so unless Miss Beach relented and let herself be the way back. She did not relent. So there he was, at the edge of the storyteller's magic circle, unable to get in, who put himself outside by a request for repetition. Let's do it again, it was so good. Of course, he knew nothing of the sort. He knew nothing. He merely felt shame and, later, when he remembers, when he writes about it, some lingering frustration. He's pissed off at Miss Beach, after all these years (forty-seven, to be exact). Italian men have long memories. Be careful, Miss Beach, wherever you are.

T. S. Eliot was born with a double hernia. His mother wouldn't let him engage in the roughhouse of playground sports. He had to be trussed, down there—think about it. I, on the other hand, when I entered the eighth grade, buried Francis for good (spelled with an "i," don't get smart). I took on Frank. I was not born with a double hernia, there was nothing wrong with me down there.

Eliot, I read, thinks that when one is an adolescent (he often says "one") one reads certain writers—he mentions Shelley—and then he says one grows out of these writers, one matures. I could say that Eliot was insulated by his upper-class experience. I could say that Eliot was effete, that he insults my class and ethnic experience. I could say that in my neighborhood we never heard the word poetry, I never knew anyone who owned a book of poems, I never saw a book of poems, who the hell was Shelley anyway, a girl? For not knowing these things we could be called insulated, but what's the point, it's not like we had a choice. And it's not like Eliot the teenager had a choice either. (But when he wrote what he wrote about what adolescents read he was an advanced adult, and for this he is responsible.) He had to read Shelley, we had to smash things on Halloween night, in our own neighborhood. We didn't know the word "faggot," but we knew what a sissy was, we had that word. Lucky for Eliot that he didn't hang out with us.

My best friend in grade school was a black kid named Nelson Brown, angular, tough, nasty elbows. We called him Nellie. I think I felt close to Nellie because, like me, he had a girl's name only, unlike me, he didn't seem to mind, because if he did he would have been called something else, whatever Nellie wanted, who was going to argue with him? Nellie and Franny. Inseparable.

I have a cousin, a female, of course, who got me a library card when I was seven years old. You had to be seven to qualify. I was a baseball player of neighborhood note. I knew boxing, my father took me to the fights, ringside, a vantage point from which it is clear what boxing is. And there they were on the shelves of the East Utica Branch, Utica Public Library: DiMaggio, Gehrig, Ruth, Joe Louis, I got to take them home with me, to my room, close the door.

In order to get home from the library, arms full of books (I would always take out the maximum, too many to carry), I could walk through the playground where my friends were. That was the shortest way back, a straight line between two points. Instead, I walked around the playground, putting a two-block zone between myself and my friends, whose vile hearts and minds I knew. Me unseen, arms full of books. I think I must have had a double hernia. I think I must have been trussed, down there. Nellie would have walked right through. Nellie had real balls.

Those books were like potato chips. I even tried to read them at the dinner table. My father prohibited it, of course, but he wasn't displeased. Most of my favorite writers now are poets. The ones who aren't love words and rhythms the way the best poets love words, rhythms, and the sounds of different voices. My favorite writers are estheticians of the peculiar, virtuosos (I like that word, it's close to "virtue") like DiMaggio, Joe Louis, the Yankee Clipper, the Brown Bomber. I'm not depressed about being called the "Dirty Harry of contemporary literary theory." Now I get to walk through the playground, carrying the poems of Shelley.

And now I don't have to depend on Miss Beach in order to get inside the magic circle. I am Miss Beach. I have gone to Angelo's twice: once in the flesh, once in writing, where it is even better, where I myself can do the narration and all the voices, enhancing myself with all the bodies in the restaurant I choose to remember, filling out Franny's skinny self, getting bigger all the time. Writing as the medium of kinship.

". . . to be educated above the level of those whose social habits and tastes one has inherited may cause a division within a man which interferes with happiness."
—T. S. Eliot, *Notes towards the Definition of Culture*

SCENE: The high school classroom of Senatro D. LaBella. Senior English with the department chairman, a legend.

We have to read *Macbeth*. We can't read *Macbeth*. So what? In college we'll major in shop, in college they don't force you to read Shakespeare unless you major in English, which is out of the question. We heard that LaBella could read him, the rumor was strong. We heard that he could actually make you like it; this is what was said.

Bald, huge tortoise-shell glasses, short (which we don't notice), he enters. His baldness stuns us, we want to be bald. A face of the highest seriousness, a visage, looking hugely down upon us, bigger than it is, thanks to that great glistening dome, like one of those cardinals Raphael painted.

The man moves swiftly, if only for a few steps, erect, everything pulled together, severely graceful. His body is an edge, space is resistant stuff which he slices through as if his freedom, whose basis we would never guess, were in the balance.

We wait for the smile; we need the smile. It comes suddenly and rarely, but it comes. He had done everything, or was about to do everything—this is what the smile said—and he would do it, or had done it, with maximum sleekness.

In the halls, on the move like a cruising animal, he banters ironically with students, without distance. The athletes like him. This man was raised in Utica, our neighborhood on Bleecker Street. He had returned to live on Bleecker Street, he drives an Olds 88 six blocks long and he speaks English as we have never heard it spoken. On Bleecker Street. No imposed tone, it's the clarity, with respect for every letter and sound of every word, and when he talks words become things, each with its unique identity. To speak the language as he speaks it has to be an erotic experience and just hearing him teaches us that language is a thing that can be loved, that such love (it dare not speak its name in today's academy) will be requited with the favors that quench all desire. He never says that to us directly, it was unsayable in our neighborhood, but this is what he teaches. The way he talks we find funny and awesome. We love him because he is a part of us and we love him because he isn't a part of us.

He enters, not with the class text under his arm but with a book containing all of Shakespeare, two columns, mean print, a fat, frightening thing that he holds without fear. Today we're scared because today we're supposed to discuss *Macbeth*. But we don't discuss *Macbeth*, he knows better. Instead, he reads out loud every line of the play over a period of three weeks. He does all the parts. The thing is clear, we understand the thing, we're shocked, and we feel a little noble.

The classroom of Senatro D. LaBella is set at Proctor High School, east side of Utica, approximately 1,500 students, approximately two of which are not Italian American Catholics whose grandparents came over (for reasons anyone in the neighborhood would understand, I count the Lebanese and the Poles with the Italian American Catholics). We don't know Verdi or Dante (neither do the Lebanese and the Poles), we never heard of them. Most of our parents didn't get to go to high school. We didn't think of ourselves as underprivileged.

Shakespeare is a secret. LaBella tells us the secret. The secret is good but the man who tells it is better than Shakespeare because he makes it possible for us to learn new secrets on our own. He is a teacher, Senatro the Beautiful.

Most of the guys I knew at Proctor High believed he could get it every night, but that he wasn't because he had other things on his mind. (I don't know what the girls thought.) The man was complex. When he taught us, we couldn't separate Shakespeare from LaBella. Shakespeare didn't exist for us except in LaBella, inside him, flowing forth on that voice. It has never occurred to me that such knowledge, of Shakespeare living in the flesh and voice of my teacher, would divide me against myself and my background, that it would, in Eliot's words, "interfere with happiness." I know what Eliot is implying. No one should be able to stomach the idea.

This is what I like to imagine: it is early spring of 1958, I am sitting in LaBella's classroom during his one-man Shakespeare festival. Sitting across from me is T. S. Eliot, recently appointed Inspector of Schools for the United States. Eliot has serious theories and concerns about the relations of education and culture. He wants cultures to be organic wholes, he wants all the activities of culture to serve and express the whole, and he wants us to be, and to feel, connected to something larger than ourselves, something more valuable than our puny individual persons. Eliot believes that this state of affairs doesn't obtain, anywhere. He wants it to obtain. He refuses to admit that he's a utopian, and he thinks that the United States in particular has gone to hell.

He watches LaBella, and he watches the students watch LaBella. I watch him. I can tell he's pleased, I can tell he wants to stay in this classroom all day. He won't, but he wants to. He thinks he needs to be someplace else.

This is also what I like to imagine: the self of the almost eighteen-year-old Frank, magically augmented by the self he would become at fifty-one, carrying a sheaf of quotations neatly copied out from Eliot's essay on Marie Lloyd, the music hall artist whose death moved Eliot to cultural mourning. When the

class is adjourned the two Franks follow Eliot out, accost him, hand him the notes. If Eliot is flustered he doesn't show it. He reads: ". . . it is not always easy to distinguish superiority from great popularity, when the two go together."
And then he reads my marginal note:
"Why would you want to, if they go together?"
And then he reads:
"And popularity in her case . . . is evidence of the extent to which she represented and expressed that part of the English nation which has perhaps the greatest vitality and interest. . . . Marie Lloyd's audiences were invariably sympathetic, and it was through this sympathy that she controlled them."
And then my note:
"His students as audience. LaBella as Marie."
And then he reads:
". . . no other comedian succeeded so well in giving expression to the life of that audience, in raising it to a kind of art. It was, I think, this capacity for expressing the soul of the people that made Marie Lloyd unique, and that made her audience . . . not so much hilarious as happy."
My note:
"I'll try to arrange coffee with you and LaBella. He has a lot on his mind, but he might consent. No promises. I could get you an apartment, cheap, in east Utica, the whole second floor of a two-family house."
He reads:
"In the music-hall comedian they find the expression and dignity of their own lives. . . ."
Me:
"No comment."
And he reads:
"The working man who went to the music-hall and saw Marie Lloyd and joined in the chorus was himself performing part of the act; he was engaged in that collaboration of the audience with the artist which is necessary in all art and most obviously in dramatic art."

Me:

"We fed him, we were part of his performance of *Macbeth*."

Eliot takes a parting shot at young Frank: "But, clearly," he says, "Shakespeare is no expression of your culture." (The emphasis is almost inaudible, but it's there, on "your.") The young Frank fears the tall smart man, but he manages this: "We know guys like Macbeth, we definitely heard of his wife." Eliot is merciless: "You attest to the power of the type to cross cultures, not to the specificity of your own." (Subtle emphasis on "own.") Young Frank doesn't follow that one. Nevertheless, he strikes back: "I heard you were from St. Louis, so how come you talk like that?" Eliot has never been asked this in his life and, stunned by the vulgar thrust, blurts it out, in a tone that might almost be described as passionate: "Because it makes me feel better, because I feel at home in it."

Eliot feels outside but he covers up very well. He leaves, returning to his home in London, the place he describes in *The Waste Land* as "Unreal City," city of the living dead.

In a few weeks I shall introduce my students in the New York program to *The Waste Land*. Can I be their Marie Lloyd? Do they want that? Do I? Will we be able to say, afterwards, We resurrected it, we saw ourselves in Eliot's world, we saw ourselves strangely, but more truly, and we cannot go back to the way we were? To sift their consciousness into the world through the medium of *The Waste Land*. I, the sifter. A good thing, or assault with a deadly weapon?

This time through (how many times have I done this?) I am snagged yet again by a passage which by Eliot's standards is plain, and, out of context, even easy. The passage is shocking for its positive charge, its warm tone, its longing for the actual. It doesn't belong to *The Waste Land* that we have long known. Our guide through the desert of the contemporary, the poem's voice-over, the authoritative voice that opens the poem ("April is the cruellest month") and that reappears frequently in judgment, covert and dour, just as frequently (despite its desire to stay outside) falls inside, becoming itself a subject of waste. This walker in the city suddenly sounds almost happy. This moment, this place, seem almost to suffice. I can't find any other passage in the poem remotely resembling this one. I check the work of the Eliot experts, who have been so helpful in clearing up allusive obscurities. They note that the first line is a quotation from *The Tempest*, but this I knew. Such plainness, such absence of allusive obscurity, does not require their explicating finesse. How does the passage work with the rest of the poem? Why has this passage fascinated me for so long?

> 'This music crept by me upon the waters'
> And along the Strand, up Queen Victoria Street.
> O City city, I can sometimes hear
> Beside a public bar in Lower Thames Street,
> The pleasant whining of a mandoline
> And a clatter and a chatter from within
> Where fishmen lounge at noon: where the walls
> Of Magnus Martyr hold
> Inexplicable splendour of Ionian white and gold.

Another fragment, cut off from what comes before and after by extra spacing. The quotation from *The Tempest:* a line spoken by Ferdinand, part of a complete sentence formed by Eliot's first two lines. One sentence, two voices (*The Waste Land:* one poem, countless voices). Eliot assumes the mask of Ferdinand-in-mourning, who has just lost his father and friends in a storm at sea (so he thinks), and is now being led by strange music (Ariel's song) to this bank, on this island ("Weeping again the king my father's wrack"), the music allaying his passion as well as the storm. In a moment, just a few lines later, Ferdinand will meet Miranda and fall instantly in love, and eventually all will be well.

The music that Eliot's waste-land guide hears as he stands outside a public bar is equally alluring. The sounds of conversation and the other sounds that float out to him from the inside must please him as much as the music of the pleasant mandoline (note the amusing internal rhyme, "clatter" and "chatter"). The mandoline of the new Ariel draws him to the pub. This is his destination, but not his destiny. He does not go in. How come?

And there is a third Ferdinand, this one drawn by the Ariel music that Eliot himself makes in writing this passage as a lyric surge, all the more alluring for being one of the rare lyric surges of the poem. The third Ferdinand: I, the reader. The pub, the fishmen (not fishermen, these are workers from a nearby fish-market), the fishmen who "lounge," the pleasant mandoline (from *mandolino*, an Italian word): the pub as Prospero's island in the waste land of the great modern city. The passage itself, the lyric surge itself, as Prospero's island in *The Waste Land*. The streets are specified. This is the route of a magical journey whose end does not turn out well for Eliot.

From Bleecker and Carmine to Sixth Avenue, south to Broome, east to Mulberry, south onto Mulberry, left hand side of the street: 146. I went in. Angelo's restaurant as Prospero's island. How does it turn out for me?

Eliot looks at the contemporary world through a Shake-spearean lens, and by so doing tells us that he is bereft, like Ferdinand; tells us that he wants it to turn out well, as it did for Ferdinand. In this poem of numerous failures of love, is Eliot telling us that he wants to meet Miranda? Eliot sees the scene, or tries to see the scene, as an episode of romance drama. But at the same time he cherishes the scene for what it is. He gives the names of things, the scene holds its own ground. Eliot is decent to his materials. Shakespeare and *il mandolino* in harmony, the two cultures not at war.

From the pub to Magnus Martyr, adjacent places, shifting attention. The pub and Magnus Martyr are companionable expressions of a unified culture. Eliot doesn't go in, he doesn't belong, though he needs to belong. He needs to be able to move effortlessly, naturally, between pub and church, without think-ing. The "inexplicable splendour": this is good, not to have to explain, splendor is not for explaining. He may write in frag-ments but he doesn't want to live that way. He wants to live in a culture organically whole. Maybe the point about the mandoline episode is that it doesn't fit, as an alternative vision is not supposed to fit.

I could weave Angelo's into the seminar, easily, but it might be a mistake. They might say, You went in, ethnic Frank, Eliot didn't. They might say, You have an inside relation to the ethnic pleasures of the Angelo's text. They might say, You are a privileged reader of the Angelo's text. And then we would all sing the multicultural rag. Better to tell them you were a transparency at Angelo's. Tell them you didn't want to be noticed, that you wanted to disappear into all that you beheld. Tell them you weren't a contributing actor at the Theater of Angelo's. Tell them not to use you to beat up on Eliot. Tell them that your wife is not an Italian American, and she has written the two best Italian American short stories you've ever read. No, I am not Marie Lloyd, nor was meant to be.

I could, but I don't live on the second floor of a two-family house in east Utica. I left Utica for good in 1966.

Having sacrificed yourself to something more valuable, in the text of Angelo's, or in the formal text of a poem, you are tempted to move above, in an effort to explain why you tell the stories you tell about men with important bodies, Miss Beach, Senatro the Beautiful, or some of the *Cantos* of Ezra Pound, which you are reading with your students in the Duke in New York program, hoping to teach them that the *Cantos* are about reading as a medium of kinship. Having yielded, having taken a vacation from who you are, having in a way forgotten yourself in order to find a more satisfying self, you begin to reflect on your "position" and "allegiances." You want to announce principles of literary criticism. You would propound a theory. You've been having a good time, but now, should you yield to the Devil, you're going to have a very bad time. So bad, should you yield, that you'll tell yourself that you made a serious mistake when almost thirty years ago you decided you wanted to teach literature and write about it.

You want to resist, and you do resist by remembering three

passages in written texts that have given pleasure. You tell yourself that you are not evading the task that Mark Edmundson offered and which you accepted. You tell yourself that what you remember will silence the Devil for good, who wants you to become abstract, because abstraction is the stuff of his kingdom. The Devil of Theory: you know him well.

The first passage, from Ralph Waldo Emerson, has for years attracted and repulsed you: "Standing on the bare ground—my head bathed by the blithe air, and uplifted into infinite space— all mean egotism vanishes. I become a transparent eyeball. I am nothing. I see all. The currents of the Universal Being circulate through me; I am part or parcel of God. The name of the nearest friend sounds then foreign and accidental: to be brothers, to be acquaintances, master or servant is then a trifle and a disturbance." You like the phrase "I become a transparent eyeball. I am nothing," because it reminds you of what happens in Angelo's, and on Seventh Avenue, and when reading Wallace Stevens, and in that monastery, Mepkin Abbey, that you visited almost six months ago. Different places. You like the distinction implied by "mean egotism," because you know that some capacity for selfhood and ego must remain, some capacity for reception, that which receives and registers the pleasure of seeing all. The "I" that "sees all" is still an "I," but a different kind of "I." You don't know what "the Universal Being" means, especially with capital letters, and you don't care. You suspect Emerson is saying that he feels good, and that this is his way of putting it. The last sentence, "The name of the nearest friend sounds then foreign and accidental," you don't like at all and you wonder why Emerson didn't go all the way and say "dearest friend." Maybe not even Emerson in that mood could bring himself to such iciness, so he changed "d" to "n." In the last sentence, Emerson sees nothing at all. But you will always read Emerson because the conflict in the famous "transparent eyeball" passage is staged again and again in his work, and you can think of no conflict more basic, and not just to writers and readers.

The second passage is from Thomas Merton's autobiography, *The Seven Storey Mountain*, which you are now reading, though you promised yourself you would never read it. You are gripped as you are rarely gripped by the pages on his decision to enter Our Lady of Gethsemani, in Kentucky, and especially by the pages that describe the moments of entry. Then you read this passage: "I was free. I had recovered my liberty. I belonged to God, not to myself: and to belong to Him is to be free, free of all the anxieties and worries and sorrows that belong to this earth, and the love of things that are in it. What was the difference between one place and another, one habit and another, if your life belonged to God, and if you placed yourself completely in His hands? The only thing that mattered was the fact of the sacrifice, the essential dedication of one's self, one's will. The rest was only accidental." You like the sentence "I belonged to God, not to myself," you understand that he had sacrificed himself to something more valuable (Merton admired Eliot, too), but the rest of the passage causes you to think that if belonging to God entails *that*, then to hell with God. You appreciate, however, the situation whose recollection must have produced those sentences and sentiments, and you know how much the rest of Merton's life will be a repudiation of those sentences and sentiments, how much he will suffer the pains and pleasures of being in place, how much he will cherish the so-called accidents of distinction in persons, things, and places.

The sentence in Merton about what was the difference between one place and another rings a bell. You search through Don DeLillo's *Ratner's Star* and you find this in about ten seconds: " 'What is this but a place?' he said. 'Nothing more than a place. We're both here in this place, occupying space. Everything is a place. All places share this quality. Is there any real difference between going to a gorgeous mountain resort with beautiful high thin waterfalls so delicate and ribbonlike that they don't even splash when they hit bottom—waterfalls that *plash*, is this so different from sitting in a kitchen with bumpy linoleum and grease on the wall behind the stove across the street from a gravel pit? What are we talking about? Two places, that's all. There's nowhere you can go that isn't a place. So what's such a difference? If you can understand this idea, you'll never be unhappy.' " DeLillo tells us that in Ratner's voice (it is Ratner himself who is speaking) there remains only the trace of Brooklyn's "desperate melodies." The man rushes madly into abstraction, but DeLillo lets us hear the traces, this is a Brooklyn Jew, this famous Nobel Laureate, not just anybody, and we hear the music in "So what's such a difference?" You're glad that DeLillo saves Ratner from himself by giving him those long and funny descriptions of place difference which dominate his theme of place sameness. Unabstract representation of a desire for abstraction that subverts itself in the act of announcing its desire. You like that.

DECADES

*Nancy K.
Miller*

Nancy K. Miller is one of a handful of distinguished scholars who pioneered feminist criticism in America. She earned her Ph.D. in French at Columbia, was director of the Women's Studies Program at Barnard College, and is currently on the faculty at Lehman College and the Graduate Center of the City University of New York, where she is Distinguished Professor of English. Miller is the author of The Heroine's Text: Readings in the French and English Novel, 1722–1782; Subject to Change: Reading Feminist Writing; *and* Getting Personal: Feminist Occasions and Other Autobiographical Acts. *She is currently at work on a book about contemporary memoirs.*

THERE'S SOMETHING ALMOST IRRESISTIBLE ABOUT DECADES, about taking them as an index by which to measure social change or to identify the spirit of an age: the culture and values of a generation. A recent *New Yorker* cartoon underlines the difficulty of finding the right emblem for the nineties. Two men in hard hats are standing in a lumberyard. One says to the other: "Well, Al, the sixties was *peace*. The seventies was *sex*. The eighties was *money*. Maybe the nineties will be lumber." What will the nineties be? If not lumber, what?

1: BEFORE FEMINISM: 1962–1968

In the 1950s, as Rachel Brownstein remembers it in *Becoming a Heroine*, we dreamed of going to Paris:

> Ideally, one would be Simone de Beauvoir, smoking with Sartre at the Deux Magots, making an eccentric domestic arrangement that was secondary to important things and in their service. One would be poised, brilliant, equipped with a past, above the fray, beyond it, foreign not domestic. (And ideally Sartre would look like Albert Camus.)

It's 1962. I've just turned twenty-one in Paris. For my birth-day, my roommate at the Foyer International des Etudiantes has given me a copy of the *Lettres portugaises*, which she has inscribed with a message that invites me to consider how wonderful it is to be like the *religieuse portugaise*—young and passionate—and concludes: "dis 'fuck you' à tous les garçons [she was learning English from the Americans who ate down-stairs at the Foyer's student restaurant] et aime-les." This edition of the letters, in which the typeface imitates handwriting, is illustrated by Modigliani drawings of women looking unhappy, or at least poignantly withdrawn. Modigliani is an artist whose images of elongated women I find entrancing. I am knocked out by these letters. They are written, I believe then, by a real Portuguese nun, Mariana Alfocarado, seduced and abandoned by a real, if anonymous, Frenchman, and obsessing about it. I identify completely, even though I'm of course not Portuguese (not to mention a nun). I have only begun to meet Frenchmen myself, and I can tell already that I'm out of my depth.

I'm also studying for my M.A. with the Middlebury Pro-gram in Paris and taking a yearlong seminar on Laclos. Antoine Adam, an authority on the early history of the French novel, standing in front of the lectern in a huge amphitheater of the Sorbonne, produces a weekly lecture on *Les Liaisons dangereuses*. I'm supposed to write an essay on it; the choice of topic is up to me. The program has assigned me a tutor to oversee the writing. I'll call him M. Souilliez. He lives on a dark street in the Latin Quarter, on a steep incline, somewhere near the Sor-bonne, maybe behind the Pantheon. It's April. A first draft of the *mémoire* is long overdue; I haven't begun the outline (the outline, "le plan," is at the heart of the French educational system). I have spent Christmas in Italy with an American boy-friend on a motorcycle; Easter vacation with my roommate at her home in Tunisia, where I have discovered, among other things, the art of leg waxing with lemon and sugar. I don't know how I'm going to write this essay, let alone an outline for it.

In despair I go to see the tutor one evening in his apartment.

We sit in the living room and talk about *Les Liaisons dangereuses;* we talk, that is to say, about sex. I am inwardly panicked because I cannot come up with an essay topic, so I try to appear worldly and unconcerned, and with studied casualness hold forth on sex and love, and men and women. Suddenly I get an idea: I'll write on the women in the novel, how all of them are betrayed by the images others have of them and that they each have of themselves. I sit at a table opposite M. Souilliez and start to make an outline. I'm inspired, excited. As I write, he gets up and walks around the room. I forget about him—I'm so happy that I at last have an idea! Then, as I sit at the table, I feel a hand on my breast. M. Souilliez, standing behind my chair, has reached down and slipped his hand into my blouse around my left breast. I stop writing.

Though I realize the moment I feel the hand feeling me that I have been chattering away about precisely these kinds of moves in the novel, it hasn't really occurred to me to make the connection between seduction (not to say sex) and M. Souilliez. I am now nonplussed. I try to imagine that in the *Liaisons'* cast of characters I'm the sophisticated Madame de Merteuil, not the ingenue Cécile, even though I feel a lot more like a schoolgirl than a libertine (that's Cécile's problem in a nutshell, of course). I don't want to have to go to bed with M. Souilliez (he's "old" and not, I think, my type), but I also don't want a bad grade. The hand is still moving around inside the blouse. I remove the hand and sigh. "Oh, monsieur," I say, pausing, and hoping for the world-weary tone of the Marquise in my best American jeune fille French, "j'ai déjà tant d'ennuis sans cela."

He goes no further, shrugs (in a Parisian gesture that seems to mean either: it's your loss or you can't blame a guy for trying), and lets me leave. I race down the stairs out into the street and up the Boulevard St-Michel to the Foyer. When I get back to my room, I begin to wonder how much harm I've done myself. I finally write the essay—"Women and Love in *Les Liaisons dangereuses:* The Betrayal of Images"—and wait for the grade. The comments in the margins alternate between "b," *bien*, and "md," *mal dit*. In general, I seem to have more insight than argumentative force. I take too long getting to the point: "What you say is true and interesting, but what's happened to your outline ['le plan']?" I expect the quotations to do the work of commentary (they should play only a supporting role). And my favorite: "Never hesitate to be clear." In the light, I suppose, of these weaknesses, and despite a very nice overall comment (he thinks I'm smart), I get a mediocre grade on the essay (my own fault, I tell myself, for doing it all at the last minute; it really wasn't very good, anyway).

In 1968 when, having returned to New York, I decided to apply to graduate school, I went through my box of "important papers" and discovered the M.A. essay. I looked at the grade on the title page, and it suddenly seemed to me—correctly, as it turned out—that the number grade (French style) was the equivalent not of the "B" on my transcript, but an "A"; the number had been mistranscribed. In 1968, it still didn't dawn on me to be angry about M. Souilliez's hand down my blouse. By then, flirting with a libertine incarnation of my own (I took the sexual revolution seriously), I congratulated myself instead, Merteuil-like, for having played the right card (didn't I get an "A"?). Recently I ran into an old friend I knew when I was first living in Paris. I asked her if she remembered my scene with the tutor. "Oh, yes," she said, "at the time we thought that sort of thing was flattering."

I sometimes think that I have missed everything important to my generation: 1968 in Paris, 1968 at Columbia; the sixties really, although on my honeymoon in Ireland I did hear the Beatles sing on (pirate) Radio Caroline, "I Want to Hold Your Hand."

2. DURING FEMINISM: 1969–1977

I'm in graduate school at Columbia, and feminism is in the streets . . . at least in a mainstream kind of way.

August 26, 1970, is the first annual nationwide "Women's

Strike for Equality." Friends and I join the march down Fifth Avenue to celebrate the fiftieth anniversary of suffrage. Kate Millett publishes *Sexual Politics* and makes the cover of *Time* magazine. At Town Hall, it's Germaine Greer (*The Female Eunuch* came out in the States in 1971) and a panel of women critics and writers vs. Norman Mailer. Mailer can't understand why women would become lesbians. After all, he opines, men can do to women what women do to each other—90 percent—and then some. In disgust, Jill Johnston walks off the stage and embraces her lover—to Mailer's despair: "C'mon, Jill, be a lady"—in sight of the audience.

There is, in general, lots of writing and talk about female orgasm, how many (multiple, preferably) and what kind.

In January 1971, after reading an article by Vivian Gornick in *The New York Times Magazine* about consciousness-raising groups, some friends and I start our own. At our first meeting, we are amazed by our commonalities. In particular, we talk about how we don't want to be like our mothers, who we feel did not know what they wanted. What do we want? The specifics are not clear, but the aim is to take charge of one's own life. It is nothing less than a fantasy of total control: not only having what we want, but having it on our own terms and our timetable. The point of the group as we see it is to help one another bring this about, to not be victims.

What does this mean for graduate school? In graduate school, where the men are the teachers and the women the students, it's harder to say when things begin (certainly not in courses); it's more about things coming together—personally. One day, the man who was to be the second reader on my dissertation, an eighteenth-century specialist, a man in his sixties, takes me aside to issue a dire warning: "Don't try to be another Kate Millett"—*Sexual Politics* was originally a Columbia English department Ph.D. thesis—"she wasn't first-rate to begin with." This man, who had co-edited a popular anthology on the Enlightenment, taught a course on eighteenth-century French literature (from the anthology) in which, to see whether we had done the reading, he would pull questions out of a hat and spring them on some hapless student. This had something to do with why I didn't want him as my adviser. But he did tell great stories. In fact, the account he gave of Julie de L'Espinasse's life, the way a real woman (and a great letter writer) "died of love," sealed my fate: Of course I was going to "be" in the eighteenth century.

In June 1972, fortified by our ongoing weekly discussions in the group, I take the plunge. I'm going to get serious about my work (no more reading, it's time, I'm thirty-one years old—old!), and write the dissertation. (Actually, writing the dissertation seemed a solitary undertaking of such enormous moment that I withdrew from the group in order to "work." Holed up in a tiny room in a ground-floor tenement in the West Village, I wrote cut off from the pleasure of the support that had gotten me there in the first place. I guess that was my idea of being a scholar—though I did turn to soap operas for relief.) I buy an electric typewriter, as well as secondhand filing cabinets on 23d Street and a door that when placed on top of them makes a desk. I also declare my thesis topic (equipment first): "Gender and Genre: An Analysis of Literary Femininity in the French and English 18th-century Novel." In those days in the Columbia French department this is also called a stylistic structural analysis. I am going to analyze nine novels according to the principles of narratology and rhetoric: Propp and Greimas, Riffaterre and Genette, Barthes and Kristeva. I am going to do this, I say, as a feminist.

(Rereading these pages after having watched a three-hour profile on Richard M. Nixon on public television, I try to think about what—beyond marching and sit-ins—it might mean to have been writing a dissertation during the Vietnam War and Watergate. I learn, for instance, that on June 23, 1972, as I was, perhaps, drafting an introduction to "Gender and Genre," Richard Nixon was having a conversation with H. R. Haldeman about diverting the F.B.I. I easily remember spending hours glued to the Watergate proceedings in total fascination and indignation, but I seem to have made no visible *conceptual* connections between the preoccupations of my desk and the political upheaval of those public scenes.)

I had become a feminist and a structuralist together. That's a little condensed: This happened at the same time, but on separate tracks. Feminism, for me, meant the group, *Ms.* magazine, feminist fiction, and a whole set of what today we might more portentously call cultural practices. It meant a revolution in relationships—between women, between women and men —and one's perception of the real—in material and symbolic terms, even if we didn't talk that way. Feminism had to do with our lives. And yet despite pockets of local activity—the annual Barnard "Scholar and Feminist" conference, the occasional undergraduate offering—the academic institution was impervious to the dramatic changes occurring in social relations wrought by '68 and by feminism. Affirmative action began officially in 1972, but its immediate effects were almost invisible; the tiny number of tenured women at Columbia remains virtually unchanged since the early seventies.

In 1972, as I remember things, the phrase "feminist criticism" was not yet an acknowledged working category, at least not on the fifth floor of Philosophy Hall, where formalism reigned supreme. There was literary theory (what the good people did), and there was feminism (Kate Millett, English departments). I liked to think that criticism and feminism worked together. After all, I used to argue, both are modes of critique: the one, of the ideology that regulates the relations between men and women in culture and society; the other, of its own blinding assumptions about literature and art. It's hard to see now, but in the early seventies structuralism, as it was understood in American universities, like feminism, seemed to mean a break with a reactionary past: the men's club model of lit. crit., practiced today by people like Denis Donoghue and Helen Vendler. (In 1972 the name of the Men's Faculty Club, noted for its elegant Ladies' Lounge—the wives had to go somewhere, after all—was changed to the Faculty House.) For us, as beleaguered but ambitious graduate students, this "science of lit-

erature" was exciting; it provided a new language and a dream
of transparency to sustain us in what we saw as a long struggle
against "them." I can still remember the moment when in a
study group I understood Saussure's model of the sign: Never
again would I confuse the word and the thing; literature and
the world; sign and referent; signified and signifier (little knowing that Lacan had already turned this upside down, not to
mention Derrida). This epiphany about the processes of sig-
nification was on a par only with the thrill of discovering binary
oppositions and how they organize symbolic and social uni-
verses. Lévi-Strauss delivered the truth of this fact in person in
the Barnard College gym in 1972 (poststructuralism, with a
whole new set of emphases, had already unsettled structuralism
in France, but colonials necessarily live according to belated
cadences). What I mainly remember from this event was the
conviction (Lévi-Strauss's, then rapidly mine) that binary oppositions were embedded functionally in the brain. For me, it
all went together perfectly with Beauvoir's magisterial analyses
of the polarizing operations that opposed man as Same to
woman as Other (Beauvoir herself, of course, relies heavily on
Lévi-Strauss's paradigms), and even, since everything made
sense in these vast systems, with the lowly housewife's "click"
(the sign that she had deciphered the codes of domestic oppression) that Jane O'Reilly dissected famously in *Ms.* Whatever the
cultural material, structuralist models of analysis rescued you
from the murk of ambiguity (not to say personal confusion)
and privileged authority (the variously tweeded "we's" of a
fifties legacy), and feminism showed you what to make of what
you found. Between the capacious categories of narratology and
the stringent lines of feminist hermeneutics, there was no text
the new "we" couldn't crack. It was a heady moment.

Is it true that there was no problem in articulating feminism
and structuralism together? Yes and no. It's probably that combination of enthusiasms that British reviewers of the book my
thesis finally became—*The Heroine's Text* (1980)—found so
deadly: structuralist jargon and feminist ideology. I kept seeing
the same story everywhere, they complained. Well, yes, that's

the whole point (which American academics—at least the feminist ones—generally got): Heroines either die (it's true that Madame de Merteuil survives, but she's exiled and hideously disfigured) or marry (sometimes both, like Rousseau's Julie). The objections to my language (I called these endings "dysphoric" and "euphoric") and approach (plot summary, as the less kind put it) bothered me less (even if they were insulting and sort of true) than a certain feminist rejection of the project for "ideological" reasons. There were those who felt (1) that all formalism was male, and hence incompatible with feminist analysis, and (2) that the task of feminism was to respond to the issues of "real" women. In that sense I was indeed guilty as charged. Women were strikingly absent from my dissertation. When I chose the expression "literary femininity," I meant it to mark my distance from anything real and to sound theoretically advanced (to ward off the ambient disdain that "working on women" generated): women in fiction, but with an emphasis on narrative; female destiny, with an emphasis on plot. This was my way of showing (again) my difference both from Kate Millett, the incarnation of "strident" feminism, and from the mode of "images of women" that had already begun to emerge in English studies. Any historical considerations were necessarily foreclosed. On the one hand, the historical seemed like an antiquated belief in the referent; on the other, the invocation of the historical as the truth value of literature, the dominant mode of eighteenth-century studies, was the very thing I wanted most to escape from and oppose.

In 1972 my corpus, as we then called it, was made up entirely of respected male authors, major figures (with the exception of the bad boys Sade and Cleland, forgiven because of outrageousness and sex), and famous books. It was the canon, although the term wasn't current at that point. And women authors? The entire time I was a graduate student—during lectures, reading for seminars, for the thesis—I never once asked myself the question of female authorship, despite the fact that I must have read some women writers for course work or exams: Marie de France, Louise Labé, Marie-Madeleine de Lafayette, Germaine

de Staël (the last two known then of course as Mme de . . .).
Besides, by the time I started writing my dissertation, the Author (male) was Dead, intentions a fallacy, and all I cared about
was The Text. If I blamed anything, I blamed texts, not authors,
for the representation of women. And not even texts: Texts
were prisoners of ideology just as men were prisoners of sex.

After my thesis defense, it was reported to me that the sole
woman on the jury (one of Columbia's classic tokens) had
praised me for "sitting on my feelings." I've never been absolutely sure what that meant: that I was tautologically angry
because feminist, but my writing was cool and "scientific"? Or
that through the elaborate veils of my narratological tables she
could tell I really cared. About what? About the logic of "female
plot" that killed off heroines—exquisite cadavers, as I called
them in my first article—at the story's close?

What I really cared about then, I think, had as much to do
with my own fate as with the fictional destiny of women in the
eighteenth-century novel. At stake—if buried—in the ponderous prose of my structuralist feminism was the story of *my* plot:
my own "coming to writing"—"as a woman"—to invoke the
language of a feminist literary criticism that was to flower after
the mid-seventies. Despite the hierarchies and abuses of academic conventions, then, I saw writing a dissertation as something radical but also literary: as becoming the heroine of my
life. Despite the so-called feminization of the profession, my
getting a Ph.D. in the early seventies felt like a violation of
gender expectations. In 1961, having gathered my ideas about
appropriate intellectual and domestic arrangements in the America of the late fifties, it seemed natural for my college boyfriend
to get a doctorate (even if that was hardly his—nor indeed our
generation's—idea of creative accomplishment); I was slated to
get an M.A. and teach high school French, unless, of course—
my mother's fifties fantasy for me—I married very well and
got to be a woman of leisure who spoke French only in Europe.
When, a decade later, I started writing and saw the pages pile
up on my desk—a lot of the time spent at my desk involved
admiring the *height* of the chapters—it seemed miraculous: as

though someone else were responsible for producing the work. The man I lived with at the time, who had mixed emotions about my passion for the enterprise, did a drawing of me sitting with my hands thrown up in the air, as if in astonishment, watching the pages—produced by my cat pounding away at the typewriter—fly upward with a life of their own. But when my typist met me with the final version of the manuscript, I burst into uncontrollable tears on Broadway at 116th Street: I suppose that's part of what I was "sitting on" during the defense.

Part, but not the whole story. I was not, of course, merely a tearful heroine overcome by the events taking place around her. I was also the author of her destiny. I had a very clear sense of having done the work and wanting to own it. And so, in 1973, inspired by the example of Judy Chicago, I renamed myself. I had been using my ex-husband's name—I married briefly and unhappily in the mid-sixties—and the idea of seeing the signifier of my misery embossed on my diploma seemed suddenly and thoroughly unacceptable. At the same time, the idea of returning to my father's (also my "maiden") name seemed regressive. Not bold enough to go all the way and call myself Nancy New York, or to pick a name that pleased me out of the phone book, I took my mother's name, Miller. It was not lost on me that this was still to take a man's—my grandfather's—name, nor that I was taking the name of my worthiest adversary, my mother. Despite these contradictions, it seemed the best solution.

(Not my grandfather's real name either—which, according to some family legends, may have been Middlarsky—but the Ellis Island rendition of an immigrant's desire to be a "Yankee." I kept Kipnis as my legal middle name and made the initial K. part of my new signature. My father, who was a lawyer, took care of the change for me and never said how he felt about it. My dissertation director, however, who took the conventions of the patriarchy very seriously, was, to my great amusement, shocked. The woman typing my thesis, a student at General Studies, who was rapidly changing her life, changed her name too, and I felt quite pleased to have inspired her to do it.)

I will admit to a certain nostalgia for the gestures of those years in feminism that we have now come to take for granted, like being called Ms. I sometimes long for the conviction we had then that changing the language counted for something.

3. FEMINIST LITERARY CRITICISM: 1978–1989

And why don't you write? Write! Writing is for you, you are for you; your body is yours, take it.
            —Hélène Cixous, "The Laugh of the Medusa"

By the fall of 1978, when, after having taught my first course —a graduate seminar—on (French) women authors, I wrote "Emphasis Added" (the second of my essays on women's writing), I had both regressed to and returned from the Portuguese nun. I had fully lived out Simone de Beauvoir's analysis of the *grande amoureuse*—the woman hopelessly and desperately in love—and changed literatures. I wrote the essay, which takes its examples from Lafayette's *La Princesse de Clèves* and Eliot's *Mill on the Floss*, in total solitude, in the aftermath of a story with a Frenchman that had turned out badly (let's just say that I had renunciation thrust upon me). When I discovered—by teaching the letters in a course on women writers—that the Portuguese nun was really a man (a literary hack) in drag, I was more embarrassed at my ignorance, I think, than disappointed. Besides, I didn't need her anymore: I didn't need to be in love to write. That was half of the story; the other half was falling in love with the Princess of Clèves: the heroine and the novel.

When I say that I fell in love, I mean both that this book swept me away and that it took me somewhere. Working on "Emphasis Added" six years after starting to write my dissertation was like a second coming to writing. The dissertation was still sitting on my desk, waiting to be revised, transformed (one hoped) into the tenure book. It seemed to me that I needed to do another kind of writing in order to talk about women writers; but the old task demanded its due and the two projects were at odds with each other. As it turned out, writing the new essay allowed me to complete the old book, to finish off a certain past with the flourish of an epilogue. Those few pages are the only part of that book I can still bear to read.

I wrote the epilogue to *The Heroine's Text* in a single sitting, in rage against an anonymous and extremely hostile (female) reader's report. I wish—or I think I wish—I still had a copy of the report. As I recollect it, the reader complained, among other things, that I didn't seem to realize that the novels I analyzed were written by men. This felt at the time an outrageous objection to make to me, of all people! Still, I had to ponder the remark, and it led me to make the point explicitly at the close of the book: that these novels were written by men for men through the double fiction of the female reader and her heroine. It also led me to think about my complete failure to consider what difference women's fictions would have made to my argument about the limited arrangements of closure that I called the heroine's text. That was a point less easily fixed. It seems to me now that a lot of the energy that fueled my writing after the epilogue came from a desire for reparation: How could I not have taken female authorship into account from the beginning?

The move to women's writing had a double effect on my career and on my sense of myself as a feminist critic. Once I started working on women writers and on feminist criticism as literary theory, I felt myself to be instantly losing status. Not within the feminist community at large, of course, but within the little world of French departments that I was used to. (I'm still not sure whether this is true or just what I worried about.) No doubt this anxiety was also linked to the fact that at the same time (i.e., before coming up for tenure) I began to "leave the century"—what would it mean not to "have" a period? But that is the matter of another reflection about the organization of literary studies.

(At a departmental party recently I was deep in conversation with Rachel Brownstein, a friend and colleague. We were interrupted by a male colleague, who asked what we were talking about. When we foolishly revealed the subject of our absorption—our haircuts; we go to the same haircutter—he was jubilant: "Oh," he said, "I always wondered what women talked about when they were alone." I guess I didn't look at him as witheringly as I had hoped, since he went on to pursue his interruption. Did I, he wanted to know, have a period? Being what is called "peri-menopausal," I had to work very hard not to answer in terms of my newly haywire cycle. I censored my "sometimes" and said no, since he was merely looking, as it turned out, for someone to serve on an orals committee. But it's true that not having a period can be a problem.)

At one point, a feminist critic brought me up against this anxiety of authority as we were returning from a conference in which I had given a paper on women's autobiography: "You've always worked on women, haven't you?" she asked. Male authors, I thought, but she had my number: in the shadows of their characters, *women* all the same. I never would be taken seriously. Not for me all the stories of how, having written the first, "real" tenure book for them, one went on, through feminist consciousness raising, to see the light—and *then* worked on women. This was not, I learned many years later, what she was getting at. Still, if I had always been a feminist in my work on male writers, "working on women" seemed to make me into a different (read "lower") order of feminist: soft instead of hard, marginal instead of central. Nonetheless, that was where I was going; nor was I alone. To have resisted the turn to women's writing would perhaps require greater explanation than my seduction by it. Despite (or perhaps because of) the excitement, even the scandal, of *Sexual Politics*, and the success of Judith Fetterley's *Resisting Reader* in 1978, the trend in feminist literary studies in the late seventies was moving massively toward the study of women's writing.

Again I am struck with the difficulty and strangeness of evoking a time when just *saying* "women's writing" had a radical edge to it. When I began to "work on women" in the late seventies, I had no idea of what that was going to mean for me and more generally for developments in feminist theory. In personal terms it meant a new sense of self-authorization that changed my relation to all of the issues in the profession—especially to "theory"—and changed my identity within it. I think this is because in North American feminist criticism, by an interesting process of slippage, authorial subjectivity (itself implicitly constructed on the model of the heroine) became a homologue for female agency. Through these effects of substitution, it became possible for me, a reader of novels (alternately, a critical heroine), to cast myself (at least in my own eyes) as a feminist theorist. Or so it seemed at the time. By the early eighties, the literary appropriation of feminist theory had been accomplished. This process, which can be tracked, if a little too neatly, by two titles that seem to echo each other—*Madwoman in the Attic* (1979) and *Honey-Mad Women* (1988)—was emblematic of the decade's intellectual style. Although differences of position separate these two powerful works, their authors—Sandra Gilbert and Susan Gubar, on the one hand, and Patricia Yaeger, on the other—all rely importantly on imbricated metaphors of literary identity and female experience to make their case. (It's my sense that the appeal of literary metaphors is on the wane in the nineties, along with the attrition of an earlier confidence in figures of gender altogether.)

The eighties also saw the widespread formalization of Women's Studies Programs, many of which had come into being in the late seventies throughout the United States. In 1981, when I moved across the street from Columbia to Barnard as the director of their fledgling Women's Studies Program, it seemed to me (and this was part of what allowed me to take an administrative job I was otherwise unprepared for) that the rise of feminist scholarship as an institutional force derived at least in part from the sense of self-authorization, and ultimately collective authorization, that "working on women" provided. From my office with the decorator-purple (we hoped subversive) walls, I wrote a book-length collection of memos, characterized by the rhetorical turns of feminist righteousness, in a mode a colleague from Political Science taught me called "bullets"; my memo style, she explained, was too narrative.

By 1985, however, that interlocking sense of personal conviction and political solidarity—speaking "as a feminist" *for all women*—had already begun to erode within the feminist community. This was the moment when white mainstream feminists finally began to pay attention to internal divisions that of course had been there from the beginning. The publication, for instance, in 1981 of *This Bridge Called My Back: Writings by Radical Women of Color* clearly marks the terms of dissent from the discourse of unity. By 1985, the date I assign only somewhat arbitrarily to this crisis, women of color refused a definition of feminism that by the whiteness of its universal subject did not include them, and poststructuralist critics looked suspiciously upon a binary account of gender with referential claims; did we really want to posit a *female* experience as the ground of women's identity? Not to be left out, mainstream academics (male and female), who saw themselves as upholders of literary standards, trounced feminist critics for confusing aesthetics and sociology. Couldn't we tell art from women? This last position, which has continued to thrive in the nineties, in many ways announces the colors of the fifties: a return to a Cold War ideology that takes the form on the academic front of an intertwined belief in Art and the Individual.

4. AFTER FEMINISM? 1990–

> Bob Dylan is clearly the first rock-and-roller to reach 50
> as a meaningful artist.
> —Dave Marsh (*The New York Times*, May 19, 1991)

I became a feminist critic along with a certain history: as it was
being made around me. By this I mean that my decades of
intellectual formation coincided with those of another chronology, a chronology of social revolution. I said earlier that I
had missed '68. That's true if we think of '68 narrowly as a
single apocalyptic event, or even as a network of events with
specific locales: the Sorbonne, Berkeley, Columbia. But '68,
we know, can also be seen as a trope: the figure of diffuse
political movements, including feminism, that came to re-
structure the social repertoire of cultural images. In this sense
'68 didn't miss me.

Teresa de Lauretis has argued that feminism's unique method
was what in the United States we referred to as "consciousness
raising" and that she prefers to call, through translation back
from Italian, the practice of "self-consciousness." And certainly
it was in the space of this group work that I began for the first
time to make sense of my life as a good daughter of the patriarchy. What flowered from those moments and flashes of
insight were the elements of an analysis—a reading—that would
make a larger kind of sense when articulated collectively. The
decades of the seventies and eighties saw the invention of new
social subjects, critics and readers who, in the cultural aftermath
of '68, created the feminism we now look back on. Whether
one calls this the institutionalization or, as I prefer, the tex-
tualization of feminism, what matters is the fact of that construction: the library of feminism's literatures.

But, you may say, this sounds so elegiac, as though what
matters to you were solely the invention of feminism's noble
past or, worse, its future anterior: what feminism will have
been. It's true. . . . At fifty, like Lot's wife, I seem rigidly turned
toward the past. What have I left behind? Despite the fashion
look-alikes, it's not the sixties and I don't have to worry about

M. Souilliez's hand down my blouse. It's not the seventies and
I don't have to hide my rage in writing from my judges. It's
not the eighties and I'm not running a Women's Studies Program. Still, you point out, sexual harassment is an ever-present
feature of academic life for students, and like Charlotte Brontë's
feisty heroine Lucy Snowe (not to mention Anita Hill!), our
younger colleagues continue to find their authority challenged.
You're just giving us a personal narrative of escape from certain
penalties of youth and more vulnerable professional location.
What is it exactly that you miss?

I confess: I look back wishfully to the seventies and the
extraordinary conjunction of structuralism and feminism that
fed both my writing and my life. But, most of all, I miss the
passion of community (what we took for community), and our
belief that things would change. In *Conflicts in Feminism*, Evelyn
Fox Keller comments on her attachment to this period: "If I
were to name one feature of feminist theorizing in the seventies
for which I am openly nostalgic, it is the conviction then widely
held that there was important work to be done—work that
could be supported in the name of feminism not because all
feminists held the same priorities, but because that work had a
radical thrust from which, we believed, feminists—and
women—would generally gain some benefit." The loss to contemporary feminism of the energy that emerged from that conviction cannot be underestimated, even if the reasons for it are
important. Keller adds: "We have learned well the lesson that
differences can be suppressed; I suggest we need also to learn
that commonalities can be as facilely denied as they were once
assumed." Perhaps this is what "lumber" for the coming decade
in feminism will entail: a rebuilding of alliances on new grounds.
Reconstruction after our civil wars.

Having arrived at this point, I should now adopt a more
confident, visionary tone and scan the cultural firmament for
signs of things to come: portents for feminism in the nineties.
(In pre-election 1992, they talk—again—of The Year of the
Woman.) But that would require that I feel either prepared to
speak for feminism, or willing, as I have been so often in the

past, to predict what its next moves might and should be. I seem instead to be more at ease reviewing (even teaching) the history of a feminist past than imagining its future; waiting, as the decade unfolds, to see what the critical subjects we have created in our students will bring about. The nineties in this sense are theirs and lumber what they make of it.

EXPANDING HUMANISM

AN INTERVIEW BY MARK EDMUNDSON WITH

Edward Said

Edward Said has achieved wide distinction both as a literary critic and as a political commentator and activist. Educated at Princeton and Harvard, Said teaches—and has taught from the beginning of his career—at Columbia University, where he is now university professor. His books include Beginnings/Intention and Method; Orientalism; The Question of Palestine; *and* Culture and Imperialism, *to be published by Alfred A. Knopf in February 1993.*

INTRODUCTION

THOUGH EDWARD SAID holds the position of Old Dominion Professor of the Humanities at Columbia University, he is anything but a standard American academic. Born in Jerusalem in 1935, Said was educated in the United States, taking his undergraduate degree at Princeton and his doctorate at Harvard. In 1963 he accepted a position as junior professor at Columbia, where his colleagues included F. W. Dupee, Steven Marcus, and Lionel Trilling. Said's first book, *Joseph Conrad and the Fiction of Autobiography*, was published in 1966.

During the early years of his academic life, Said also traveled back and forth to the Middle East, where most of his family resided. He had, as he says in the pages that follow, a pair of different and disconnected lives. That discontinuity came to a sudden end in the late sixties when, confronted by the results of the Arab-Israeli War in the Middle East and by the American movement against the Vietnam War, Said saw an opportunity to fuse his intellectual life and his cultural identity as a Palestinian. One result of that coalescence was *Beginnings*, a book Said discusses extensively here, in which he reflects on the necessity for people living in threatening political times to assume the burden of their destinies by declaring new starts. A key measure of human dignity, Said argues, lies in the power to initiate new political and cultural orders in the face of harsh events.

This faith in the human will, and in particular the political will of groups, sets Said apart from many of the Continental theorists, such as Foucault and Derrida, whose work he has read with interest. To Said, the great value of these thinkers is their ability to describe the resistance to productive change imposed by Western culture. Central to Said's thought is Foucault's notion of how various intellectual disciplines, such as anthropology, psychoanalysis, economics, and historiography, work to confirm oppressive power, often without the awareness of their practitioners. This idea informs what is probably Said's most important book, *Orientalism*, where he describes the manifold ways in which the Western world depicts the Orient, the better to justify its blindness and cruelties toward it.

But Said does not believe that power, and discourses invested with power, are impervious to human resistance. Just as a group can, through struggle, claim a fresh beginning, so a society can see its own intellectual and political errors for what they are and work to change them. This sense that men and women are responsible for the shape of their world, and have the powers to improve it, is central to the line of intellectual humanism that goes back at least as far as Rousseau.

A similar sense of hope also informs Said's more direct reflections on contemporary politics, such as *Covering Islam* and *The Question of Palestine*. Both books attempt to tell the story of the Middle East from the Arab side, and to counter the current results of Orientalism. Said's desire is to have a palpable effect, to intervene to some purpose in the affairs of the world—thus the centrality in Said's work of the term "worldliness."

Said is a humanistic intellectual in the line of Lionel Trilling, his great predecessor at Columbia. He departs from that tradition only in his hope that humanism might become an international doctrine, rather than a set of ideals applied racially or geographically to some chosen few while others are treated according to the dictates of expediency. If Trilling's constitu-

ency included all of the American reading public, Said aspires
for his to be global.

INTERVIEW

MARK EDMUNDSON: Can we begin with *Beginnings*?

EDWARD SAID: Yes. The book, I suppose, has an autobiographical root, which has to do with the '67 War. Nineteen
sixty-seven was a watershed in my life because up until then I
had been two people: on the one hand teaching at Columbia,
doing English and comparative literary studies with some theory and so on, and on the other going back and forth to the
Middle East, where my family lived.

The war happened while I was here in America. And it was
a shattering experience for me, partly because of the distance
and partly because of the tremendous upheavals, the consequences of which we are still living with today. I mean, the rest
of Palestine was gone; the Arab armies were destroyed; Abdel
Nasser resigned on June 9, then returned to power a few days
later by popular acclaim. I found myself trying to come to terms
with those events, and that is where I hit upon the importance
of beginnings, which, as opposed to origins, are something you
fashion for yourself.

I had recently reviewed Frank Kermode's *Sense of an Ending*.
I wrote about it in the old *Herald Tribune* when it came out,
and I liked it. I've liked a lot of his stuff. But I noted there that
it seemed to me more important in human life to be concerned
about beginnings than about ends. And I said it was a situational
thing. He tried to universalize matters and argued that the ending was always the most important thing.

I said, no, beginnings sometimes are more important, and
I tried to give examples: revolutionary periods, for instance,
certain moments in the life of the mind and of general consciousness. The main point was that certain periods, and this
was clearly one of them, required a redefinition of one's own

situation. And that in order to project where one was to go, one needed a sense of beginnings as starting points.

A major theme of the book was the act of will required: You had to say, "That is my beginning and I am going to go in this direction." And there, the great influence was Vico.

The book went on to try to bring this to bear upon literature and criticism. By that time I had absorbed a great deal of recent Continental theory, and in it I noticed an interest in the same kind of redefinitions, in the importance of refashioning in order to do something new. In other words, the whole idea was associated with novelty, revolution, the inauguration of a new stage, and so on.

So all these things came together, and I found that this new thinking opened up a lot in the study of literature—the novel, for example, which is really about inaugurations. It is a thought that has never left me since then because I keep coming back to it—you know, Daniel Defoe, the whole Robinson Crusoe project, which is central to the history of the novel.

And then the notion of what a text is and how one thinks about texts and how texts very often are associated with particular kinds of conventions and particular kinds of forces, some of which have to be associated with beginnings and breakings off and starting points.

I also took up the criticism that was coming out at the time, especially Derrida and Foucault.

M.E.: You are generally much more optimistic about the possibilities for beginnings than they are, aren't you?

E.S.: Yes, absolutely, absolutely. All of us, including them, were very much under the influence of 1968—that is, the startling events of 1968. The irony for me of course is that I was like Fabrizio at the Battle of Waterloo. I was a member of the Columbia faculty, and at the greatest moment of upheaval in its life I was not here. I was on leave. I was at the University of Illinois, in 1967–68, where I had gotten a fellowship at the newly established Center for Advanced Studies.

In the middle of the spring of '68, when the revolution broke out here, I got a telegram signed, I think, by Grayson Kirk, telling me that there was to be an important faculty meeting and "Would you come?"

So I flew to New York. The meeting was being held at the Law School, and I got to 116th Street and Amsterdam, where the entrance to the Law School is, and I noticed that there was a police barrier. I could not get through because I didn't have a valid I.D. So I had come all the way to New York, could not attend the meeting, and of course went back rather forlorn to Urbana.

But the point was that it was part of the period of upheaval. It was also a moment of upheaval on my Arab side, which was deeply depressing. And then there was the student upheaval, which was very optimistic. Theoretically anyway, it was like a new dawn.

And above all, intellectually, it was very important because it allowed me to break out of this rigid double structure that I had found myself in and to think in terms of new, and above all *intellectual*, paths—but intellectual in a wide sense. I do not mean professional. I have never been interested in the professional at all. But I saw the intellectual potential to fashion a different kind of life and production for myself, given the sort of capsizing of one life—my Arab life—and the turbulence in the other—my American one. And that is what set me off.

Now, this is where I found problems in some of the French theorists: First of all, it struck me—and this is absolutely central to what I did in *Beginnings* and to what I have done ever since—that even those theorists like Derrida, who appear to be breaking away from all the structures and the orthodoxies, logocentrism, phallocentrism, etc., etc., in time became prisoners of their own—I would not call it "system," but I would certainly call it their own "manner."

And I became even more disillusioned with Foucault because at least in parts of Derrida there is wit; sometimes there is almost an aspect of triviality because there is so much of it. There is a lot of circling around, a lot of meandering, a lot of, finally, dismissal of stuff, with some interesting insights, particularly in his earlier work.

I felt that Foucault had this initial idea based upon the notion of confinement—confinement and the challenge to the confinement, the breaking loose—which we now know has a lot to do with his own biographical trajectory. A man named James Miller is doing a kind of revisionist biography of Foucault, and Miller's point is that Foucault was always dealing with sado-masochistic impulses, including an early attempt at suicide. So this idea of confinement was very important to sort of getting it down and then breaking it open, hence the early importance to him of figures like De Sade.

But in time, what I think happened—and it was certainly true of Lacan and Althusser—to Derrida, Foucault, and some of the others is that they became prisoners of their own language, that what they were really doing was producing more work in fidelity to what they'd done before. They were maintaining the integrity of their work and, above all, maintaining a kind of loyalty to their readers, who expected more of the same.

In other words, I think Derrida has been very interested in having disciples and followers.

M.E.: He's founded a school.

E.S.: The most elite of schools. And I have never been interested in that because it seemed to me to be somehow imprisoning, and finally uninteresting. For me, it has always been a matter of exploration, of self-criticism and constant change in trying to surprise myself as well as my readers.

So I found that to be deeply problematic in their work. And above all, I found—the last point—I found, especially in the early seventies and thereafter, that they were fantastically Eurocentric. They were interested only in Europe—not even Europe, really. They were Franco-centric.

And I have always been opposed to any kind of centricity —as opposed to eccentricity—whether it is Afrocentric or Eurocentric or American-centric or whatever. It strikes me as very much the opposite, for temperamental and even ideological reasons, of what I want to do.

And it was at this point in the late sixties and early seventies that for me the notion of beginning also meant, really, the beginning of a fairly deep political and moral affiliation with the resurgence, after 1967, of the Palestinian movement. It happened altogether, you know, between '67 and, say, '71 and '72, and led to the publication, in 1975, of *Beginnings*.

For the first time I felt that it was possible to integrate these two aspects of my life, so that my returns to the Middle East in the summer and during the year and so on were no longer just visits with my family but part of an active political life. Members of my family, schoolmates of mine, acquaintances, friends were all beginning to be part of the movement. And I got into that.

And for the first time in my life, in 1972–73, I found myself restudying Arabic, which I had learned as a kid. It was my first language. But I had never studied in Arabic except when I was in school. But it was an English school, and whatever courses we had in Arabic were marginal. The main thing was to study English history, English literature, and that sort of thing.

In 1972–73 I was on a sabbatical leave in Beirut, and I took daily tutorials in Arabic from an eminent philologist at the American University of Beirut. I began to be aware of, in a serious way, Arabic and Islamic culture.

It was that experience, you see, that began to make me very critical of these theoretical pronouncements because they did not seem to respond to what a large part of the world was experiencing in the aftermath of imperialism, the problems of neocolonialism and, for me above all, the problems of Palestine.

M.E.: One way to think about *Orientalism*, the book you published in 1978 and for which you are probably best known, is that it both is, and in dramatic ways is not, in line with Foucault and his sense that intellectual discourses merge with power to create modes of human oppression that are virtually impossible to challenge. In Foucault, there isn't much that can be done. Your sense is that more awareness of the confining structures can lead to relative freedom. If I understand you correctly, Orientalism is pervasive, imposing, confining, but finally can be thrown off?

E.S.: Yes. It was about that time, while I was working on the final sections of *Orientalism* (which I really began to write, I would say, probably in the aftermath of the '73 war), that it seemed to me that, although it was certainly short-lived, there was some real hope. I'm thinking of the attempt by the Syrians and the Egyptians and, to a lesser extent, the Palestinians to break down the Israeli hold on the occupied territories.

Do not forget that the Egyptians had gone through the holding of the Suez Canal. The Syrians had broken through the Israeli lines on the Golan Heights when it was apparent that they could not do anything, just as almost twenty years later the *Intifadeh* broke out when everybody said the Palestinians were finished.

That has always interested me the most. I mean how—given the domination of one or another powerful system, whether economic, social, or political—one can break through. That is the most interesting thing, I think, about human behavior—that and the way people try to build on it, that oppositional quality.

So that is what I found about Orientalism—that you could study it and oppose it.

M.E.: At the beginning of the book, you offer a characterization of *Orientalism:*

Taking the late eighteenth century as a very roughly defined starting point Orientalism can be discussed and analyzed as the corporate institution for dealing with the Orient—dealing with it by making statements about it, authorizing views of it, describing it, by teaching it, settling it, ruling over it: in short, Orientalism as a western-style for dominating, restructuring and having authority over the Orient. I have found it useful here to employ Michel Foucault's notion, as described by him in *The Archaeology of Knowledge* and in *Discipline and Punish*, to identify Orientalism. My contention is that without examining Orientalism as a discourse, one cannot possibly understand the enormously systematic dis-

cipline by which European culture was able to manage
—and even produce—the Orient politically, sociologi-
cally, militarily, ideologically, scientifically, and imaginatively during the post-Enlightenment period.

E.S.: Right. Yes. I would only add that in the modern version
that most interested me in the book, Orientalism is associated
with imperialism. In other words, it is a style of knowledge
that goes hand in hand with, or is manufactured or produced
out of, the actual control or domination of real geographical
territory and people.

So Orientalism is not just a vicarious experience of marvels
of the East; it is not just some vague imagining about what the
Orient is, although there is some of that there. But it really has
to do with how you control actual populations; it is associated
with the actual domination of the Orient, beginning with
Napoleon.

M.E.: Yes. But in a passage like this there is the Foucaultian
sense that discourse can initiate domination.

E.S.: Yes. And I find that it is, in a certain sense, much more
mysterious than simply a kind of causal phenomenon. You
know, there is domination. Then there is this or there is that.
There is discourse, and then there is, you know, invasion.

But the difference is that Foucault always seems to align
himself with Power. He is like a scribe of a kind of irresistible,
ineluctable power. And I was writing in order to oppose that
power, so it was written out of a political position. At the end,
although it got to be rather helter-skelter, I tried to show the
lineaments of a kind of counter-Orientalism.

M.E.: How do you come out with a more optimistic view
than Foucault does? Is it a temperamental difference between
the two of you?

E.S.: No, I think the real difference is . . . I think it is
temperamental, but if you wanted to put your finger on one
particular thing and one particular style of thought, I think it's
the Gramsci factor.

I read the English translation of Gramsci's *Notebooks* shortly after it appeared in the early 1970s and found it intriguing but unsatisfying. There were too many ellipses; there were too many difficulties in understanding, literally, what Gramsci was about. It took reading the Italian to see what he was actually getting at. There is a very important passage in *Orientalism* where I cite Gramsci's observation that "the starting point of critical elaboration is the consciousness of what one really is, and is 'knowing thyself' as a product of the historical process to date, which has deposited in you an infinity of traces, without leaving an inventory."

Now, that is all the English translation says. But actually, in the original, which I then looked up, Gramsci said, "Therefore, it is imperative at the outset to compile such an inventory." You see? That was the difference. It is saying not just, "There it is," but then, "By *you* making an inventory"—and this is where the influence of Vico was very important—"you give it a kind of structure that allows you then to confront it, dismantle it." And that is what was terribly important for me in *Orientalism*.

But I could not possibly foresee, in writing *Orientalism,*—in fact, it has never ceased to amaze me—the incredible transformations of the book thereafter, because it has now been translated into seventeen or eighteen languages. It has been in print for thirteen years and it's selling in all the languages into which it has been translated. I was informed over the weekend that there is a Chinese translation that has not been published yet, but it has been completed. It is also in Japanese.

M.E.: Is there a relationship between the Orientalism book and your next work, *The Question of Palestine*?

E.S.: *Orientalism* was published in '78, and I had become more directly involved in politics. But expatriate politics have a downside to them. That is to say, you are always at a distance. And even in the days when I was much younger, I could travel a lot, but I was still teaching.

Nevertheless, in 1977 I became a member of the Palestine National Council, and it then occurred to me that it would be very important to continue *Orientalism*, which is a general book, and to look at particular cases—you might say, the other side, since *Orientalism* did not say anything about what "the Orient" genuinely was all about.

I wanted to write a political essay that was fully engaged— I mean, I never pretended that it was anything but that. If you remember, in the beginning I take up many of the same points that I did in *Orientalism*, though this time with specific reference to Palestine. I wanted to show Palestine from the point of view of the victims.

And I think I coined this idea of an alternative history, an instance of which I gave in *The Question of Palestine*. So it is directly related to *Orientalism*.

In fact, I wrote the three books—*Orientalism, The Question of Palestine*, and *Covering Islam*—more or less right after each other. And they appeared within a year of each other. Two of them, I think, appeared within the same year.

The objective of *The Question of Palestine* was to put the Palestinian case before an American audience. It was not meant to be written for an Arab audience, but a Western readership, given that the West had played a very important role in the formation of Palestine. That is to say, the Zionist movement came largely out of the West. It was supported by the West.

I wanted to give Americans a sense of what the dispossession and the alienation of Palestine meant from the Palestinian point of view. It was the first time I was able to write about this from my own experience, and I tried to reach a larger audience with it. In fact, I had a lot of trouble getting the book published.

M.E.: What happened?

E.S.: I had been approached by several publishers, actually, in the middle to late seventies, to write a book about Palestine. And the first one shied away after they approached me. Then the second one, or the third one, or the fourth one, gave me a contract.

And when I turned the book in to Beacon Press in the summer of 1978—I remember this very well; I had pneumonia that summer—I got a very long letter back from them, signed by the woman who had commissioned me to do it. She wanted me to write another book, in effect. And, of course, I was tremendously angry.

And so I said, "In that case, you are canceling the contract!" She said, "No."

And I realized that it was a way of getting me either to write another book or to give her back the advance. So I gave her back the advance.

Then I looked around some more. I went to the publisher of *Orientalism*, Pantheon, and showed it to André Schiffrin, and he refused to publish the book. He said it was not historical enough.

And I said, "What does that mean?"

And he said, "Well, you don't talk about oil."

And I said, "Oil is hardly at the center of the controversy, of the struggle over Palestine between Israelis or Jews and Arabs."

And I realized it was an ideological argument he was making.

So I went to two or three other publishers. And finally, by a chain of circumstances, in the fall of 1978, New York Times Books accepted it and it was published.

And then Random House, and in particular, Schiffrin, bought the book in paperback. That was ironic. They would not publish it originally, but they wanted it when it was successful.

M.E.: Presumably the resistance to publishing it bears out the thesis of *Orientalism*?

E.S.: Exactly—that was the whole point. They did not want the *other* person to speak. They did not want me to say these things. And what I was saying had never been said before in English in a mainstream publication. In the late seventies there was hardly anything. Palestinians were already quite clearly terrorists, and they wanted to keep it that way.

That was the point of *The Question of Palestine*. And, if I may say so, it was the first time in English, the first time in a clear way, that a Palestinian had said, "We must live together with the Israeli Jews." I made the point of coexistence, that there was no military option, in the final pages of the book. And these are things that are now echoed—many of them have been echoed not only in Palestinian writing but also in Israeli writing. But I think I was one of the first to actually say that in a clear way, from the Palestinian point of view.

M.E.: Are there tensions between being a literary scholar and being involved in political issues? Or do they work reciprocally?

E.S.: I think, on the whole for me, they work reciprocally. The tension lies in the fact that I have tended to resist the exigencies of politics—which have to do with authority, with power, with confrontation, with rapid responses—simply because I have always wanted to maintain privacy for my own reflections and so on. I have tried to remain outside of direct political office of one sort or another—God knows a good many have been offered me, or suggested for me—in order to be able to reflect in this literary way, which takes more time, requires more solitude.

Politics is the art of the gregarious, in a way. It is the art of being with a lot of other people. And I am not made that way, although I can be very personable and I can deal with people.

M.E.: Do you feel that the things you say in your political writing have ever compromised you?

E.S.: Well, I have had to deal with that problem a great deal since the late seventies because one has many constituencies. On the one hand, I am writing for an immediate audience, you know, which is not academic, which is engaged politically. So in America I have a constituency made up of people who count for me—let us say liberals—people interested in the Middle East, who are neither Arab nor Jew.

Then there are policymakers, and it is very important for me to be able to address them. And I take them into account, officials and so on. Then there are the ethnic and political constituencies. For example, when I wrote *The Question of Palestine*, I was dealing with a largely monolithic but not entirely monolithic so-called "Jewish community" in this country, and it was my interest to engage their attention and to draw things into

focus—which the book did, in part. Of course, it is not just
the book. You follow it up. You talk. I did an enormous amount
of speaking.

Always, I try to strike a balance between my literary and
cultural stuff on the one hand and my political work on the
other. And then there was a community of Palestinians. I mean,
I was very much writing to Arabs and Palestinians. But then,
of course, we are so fractionalized that I got many attacks. For
example, the Popular Front published a tremendous broadside
against me when *The Question of Palestine* came out, attacking
me for compromise, for—what is the word?—capitulationism,
all kinds of things. And other people praised it, you know. So
I am very much aware of the constituencies with which I'm
working.

M.E.: What is coming through to me is that, in certain ways,
your method comes out of the humanistic tradition of Arnold
and Trilling, and what you are asking people to do is to apply
humanistic values in ways that are much broader than Arnold
or Trilling ever maintained.

E.S.: Or more consistently. More consistently. You see, because there is nothing I disagree with in the broad, humanistic
tradition. One of the things I have spent the last seven or eight
years of my life doing is writing a kind of sequel to *Orientalism*.
There is a big book I have been working on called *Culture and
Imperialism* [which will be published in January 1993] that studies
the way in which the broad humanistic principles, the Western
principles in which I was educated and feel very much at home,
have always stopped short of national boundaries.

I will give you an example: De Tocqueville, right? His reflections on the United States in *Democracy in America* are, I
would say, very critical of the American treatment of the Indian
and of the black, of slavery in the South.

At the same time, or shortly after that, De Tocqueville—
because he was a member of the French Assembly—was very
involved in French colonial policy in North Africa. He justified
worse abuses by the French in Algeria, massacres of people,
and so on and so forth. And then you realize that what prevented

him from being consistent was a kind of nationalism that says
it is all right to criticize them, but when it comes to *us*, we are
always right.

I have always hated that. That, I would say, is the number
one idol of the tribe that intellectually and morally and politically
I have always been against. I mean, the idea that there should
be three or four sets of principles for the behavior of people
toward each other strikes me as one of the most difficult concepts
to dislodge.

You see it in John Stuart Mill, the great apostle of liberty
and freedom and democracy from whom we have all learned.
But he never advocated anything but continued dependence and
subjection for the Indians when he was in the India Office. And
I attempt, in my new book, to bring these things forward and
show how they really work.

And then I go on to talk about decolonization, which I did
not do in *Orientalism*. There I discuss it only from the European
side. A whole portion of my book concerns what I call opposition and resistance, how from the first moment the white man
sets foot in whatever part of the world it is—the New World,
Latin America, Africa, Asia, wherever—there is resistance. And
that gradually builds. It builds until it rises, of course, in the
great decolonization that occurs during the period after World
War II, to create a particular culture of resistance and liberation,
and I talk about that. You see, that is something I did not do
in *Orientalism*. Now I will try and show the other side.

And in the new book I advance a critique of nationalism—
its shortcomings as well as its necessity, because I grew up in
that very same world of postwar Third World nationalism. You
see, these are my two worlds: the world of the West and the
world of the Third World. Nationalism, which is necessary to
combat imperialism, then turns into a kind of fetishization of
the native essence and identity. You see it in countries like
Egypt. You see it in countries like Syria. You see it in Zaire,
in Iran, in the Philippines. And the climax of this is, of course,
reached in the war between the United States and Iraq last
spring—a battle of a kind of, in my opinion, decayed nation-

alism. Along with that go notions of identity, of essence, Englishness, Americanness, Africanness, Arabness, etc. Every culture that you could think of does more or less the same thing.

M.E.: Yes. It seems that hand in hand with your critique of nationalism or racialism is a lot of suspicion of religion, of transcendent philosophies.

E.S.: For me, religion is two things. I grew up in a land completely impregnated with religion. The only natural business of Palestine is the manufacture of religion. I mean, that is what we did, if you think about it for a minute, right? I grew up in the Arabic church, to which my great-grandfather was a major contributor. He translated the Bible into Arabic, and he was the first native Protestant. I come from Protestant stock, an offshoot of Greek orthodoxy. You see, the missionaries in our part of the world hardly converted any Jews and Muslims. The only people they converted were other Christians.

So my family on one side is converted from Greek orthodoxy to Episcopalianism, or Anglican Protestantism. And on my mother's side they are converts to Baptism and evangelicalism. My grandfather was a Baptist minister. So I grew up in that sort of religious environment, as well as bilingually, English and Arabic. I know both rites, and they mean a lot to me, the Book of Common Prayer, the Arabic Bible, hymns, and so on and so forth.

I have no misgivings about religion as a private autobiographical experience. And there is a sense of community among the small number of Christians in that part of the world. We are a small minority.

What I dislike is the hijacking of religion for political purposes, the second phenomenon. Fundamentalism—a term invidiously fastened only upon Islamics—certainly exists in Judaism and Christianity in our part of the world. And in America right now.

M.E.: Worldliness is central for you.

E.S.: Worldliness, secularity, etc., are key terms for me. And it is also part of my critique of and discomfort with religion that I am very, I have recently become very—how shall I put it?—ill at ease with jargons and obfuscations. I mean, special private languages of criticism and professionalism and so on: I have no time for that. It is much more important for me that people write in order to be understood rather than write in order to be misunderstood.

So the critique, such as it is, is not a systematic critique of religion. It really deals with religious fanaticism—that is to say, going back to some book and trying to bring it back to bear upon the present. That phenomenon is comparable to nativism, you know, the idea that there is some horribly troubling present-day situation from which you must escape and find solace in a pure essence back there in time. Then there's the organizational aspect, which has to do with any kind of guild, association, private fiefdom—which automatically, in my opinion, means tyranny and suffering for the designated others.

M.E.: Political criticism has now become very common in the academy, and recently, I know, you were involved in an exchange that probably sheds light on some of the new developments.

E.S.: Well, it was a funny kind of thing and the sort of experience, I suppose, that many of us have had. It was at Princeton, at the Davis Center, and I had sent about thirty or forty pages of the introduction to my new book on imperialism. You send on the piece in advance, and then there is a discussion. There were a lot of people there. I was impressed at how many turned up, mostly graduate students and faculty.

A summary of the paper was given by the director, and then I made a few comments, and the floor was opened to discussion. The first comment pointed out that in the first thirteen or fourteen pages of my manuscript I did not mention any living Afro-American women, etc. Most of the people I was quoting from, it was alleged, were dead white European males.

And since I was talking about the origins of a certain kind of global thought in strangely disparate fields like geography and comparative literature in Europe and America in the late nineteenth century, I said it was inappropriate for me to talk about living nonwhite females.

And then this woman said, "Yes, but then you talk about C. L. R. James."

And I said, "Yes. I mean, there you are. He is not European."

The only answer I got in response to that was a kind of dismissal of C. L. R. James, who is very important to me. I have written a lot about him. The problem was that he is dead. And that was all part of a kind of hostility toward me.

M.E.: It was a hostile question?

E.S.: Yes, very hostile. I mean, it was announced as hostile, even before it began. And later, at lunch, she gave me an even harsher treatment, accusing me of one thing and another.

Then I said, "Listen, I don't think you know who I am. I don't think you've read anything I've written, because the last thing I could be accused of is that sort of thing."

And then I was told by her that it was "time to be sent back." She said, "I am going to send you back to your white people now." And she got up from the table and sort of waved me off like that. I thought that was really outrageous.

Another interlocutor during the seminar was this retired professor, whom I have known most of my life (he is also an Arab), defending Orientalism and saying that Orientalism was a very good thing for us. Well, I don't think he spoke about us, he spoke about those people out there because, without the imperialism that produced Orientalism, *they* would not have been able to do anything, and so on and so forth, and the Europeans taught us how to read cuneiform and hieroglyphics and understand our own traditions, which we could not have done on our own.

It struck me as an absurd thing that academic discourse about the relations between cultures—which was really what I was talking about—and between different groups should always be either conflictual in a clearly marked way—you must be for one and against the other—or completely reductive in an equally caricatural way. You know, one says, "Well, it is all imperialism," and another says, "Without imperialism, we would have been nothing." And that I found very depressing.

One of the great problems is that the polemics on both sides in this stupid debate, about the canon, about culture, and about the university and all that, are so basically ill-informed. First, they do not seek to know much about the historical experience of the West, nor of the non-West.

Second, they are such poor readers that they think whole traditions can be reduced to caricatures, such as, "It is all racist," or "It is this, that, or the other thing." That, it seems to me, goes completely against the grain of the dissenting traditions offered up, say, by anti-imperialism or by feminism. It becomes silly and reductive. And it seems to me to reflect very poorly, not on the American academy—about which I have very positive feelings, because I would not want to exchange my life there for anything else—but on these manipulators of the academy who have become, in a certain sense, floor traders, who are deriving careers from it, like D'Souza and his opponents.

M.E.: Why do you think the controversies about the academy have risen up now?

E.S.: I don't really know. It's hard to tell. Probably . . . well, I could speculate. One reason is that, it does seem to me, there is a complete divorce between the academy and the world. The American academic in particular has a unique kind of arrogance, a presumption that he or she can talk about these general issues without any form of commitment to any social or political institution except the academy and the furthering of a career. I think that is one thing.

I think it is also the position of America in the world, where most of us are allowed to act that way because we are singularly untouched. I mean, look at the war in Iraq. It was one of the most horrible experiences of my life, and I did a huge number of interviews and speeches and I wrote a lot of stuff on it. Yet for most of us Americans it was little more than a remote television war. It was forgotten by those in the academy. There was no opposition to it.

So in that respect, I think it is the supreme luxury of the great imperial power to be untouched by things; that is, to talk about them the way in an Oscar Wilde play Ernest and Algernon can just babble on about whether they want to call themselves Ernest or not. It is that kind of thing.

And I think third is this idea of academic specialization. Academics have lost touch with the, shall we say, existential density of real human life, and they talk in these jargons.

I don't know. Those are just speculations. I don't know why it's happening now.

M.E.: Let me make a more challenging speculation that touches on your own work.

E.S.: Yes.

M.E.: If you look through academic literary history, what really tends to happen is that there are people who are extremely innovative in their field—like, say, Cleanth Brooks and W. K. Wimsatt among the New Critics—and what happens over the next couple of decades is that their students and their students' students, for all purposes, routinize the achievement.

E.S.: Yes.

M.E.: And that there arose in the American academy strong and innovative work, by you and a very few others, that was politically oriented. But that when any criticism occurs in the academy, it is inevitably going to be literalized.

E.S.: Yes.

M.E.: And reduced. And even turned against its initiators.

E.S.: And slenderized.

M.E.: Yes, and by dissertation writers who must have terms to get their theses written.

E.S.: No, I think that is true.

M.E.: Is that an argument against it? Here comes the hard part. Is that an argument against a politicized form of the criticism? Do you see what I am saying? If it is going to go through the dissertation mill and it is going to become—

E.S.: No, because it happens anyway. It is not the . . . Look, I think, rather than answering it directly, I first would like to draw your attention to the fact, for instance, that there is now a Conradian industry. There is a Joycian industry. There is a Yeatsian industry, a Dickensian industry. That has nothing to do with politics. There is, perhaps you might call it, a sub-discourse.

M.E.: Absolutely.

E.S.: But there are people who are doing routinized work on Dickens, Conrad, etc., all of these people we talked about. Now, that applies to all of the disciplines. It is, you might say, the professionalization of the discourse that we are talking about.

M.E.: But it seems to me to do no great harm that Joyce becomes an industry and is, for some critics, routinized. When the plight of African-Americans becomes an industry and is routinized and people stand up and denounce you for being a racist based on not having named X, Y, and Z, that does seem harmful.

E.S.: Yes. Okay. I see what you mean. But is the argument then to remove from academic scrutiny issues like race, like war, like the problematic of other cultures, relationships between cultures? I would say that that is not the solution.

I think what we need is a sense of what the university is about, you see? Here I think we have lost the spirit of the image that I keep referring to from C. L. R. James, who borrows it from Aimé Césaire: "No race possesses the monopoly of beauty, of intelligence, of force, and there is a place for all at the rendez-vous of victory."

In other words, I think the ethic implicit in a lot of current political criticism is that the academic world is a site of contest where you try to put yourself on top by bashing everybody around who does not agree with you. And that seems to me to be a mutilation of the academic quest, which is essentially not to try to resolve all of these contests in favor of one putting down all the others, but rather to try to accommodate by what I call "intellectual work," the intellectual process of research, discussion, etc., and to guard against the slenderizations, routinizations—efforts to push everybody else off the raft once you're on it.

Which I think can be done intellectually. I'm not talking about social or police work. I'm talking about intellectual work that suggests that the academy is not—this is the point I am trying to make—that the academy is *not* a place to resolve sociopolitical tensions. Perhaps it is a cliché to say the following, but it is a place to *understand* them, to understand them in their origin, to understand them in the way in which they are going, in which what is brought to bear is intellectual process. So, in that sense, I do not think the answer is to eliminate the politicized discussion, but to engage it in a rather more generous and open spirit.

M.E.: When people routinized the New Criticism, there were New Critics who said, "This is a good use of this particular method." And, "This is not such a good one." And it mattered, the subtlety, performance, the acumen of the individual critic. And that is possible to do, I think, with political criticism.

E.S.: But I don't think most of us, in the literary, humanistic field, have a very good sense of, let us say, the limits and the possible kinds of synchronizations that can occur between reading a literary text and politics in the national or international sense. These are very different things. And most people make the jump from a literary or intellectual argument to a political statement that cannot really be made. I mean, how do you modulate from literary interpretation to international politics? That is very difficult to do.

And most of the people who try it are so ignorant, as was manifest in the argument of the academic who told me, "But he is dead," in regard to C. L. R. James. That is not an argument! That is just silly, and needs to be exposed and dismissed.

M.E.: But I think that some of the people whom you are correctly characterizing would say that one of their major influences was Edward Said.

E.S.: Yes, I understand what you mean. Well, then I would say that they are stupidly misreading my books. For example, a review of *The World, the Text, and the Critic*, which I have somewhere, published by a kind of occasional journal of one of the major Jewish organizations, contends that when I talk about "secular criticism" I am using an esoteric method to advance the PLO goal of a secular democratic state to be achieved by killing all the Jews. That was actually said.

M.E.: That was a creative misreading.

E.S.: Exactly! A maliciously creative misreading. So one cannot always be blamed for one's misreaders, if you see what I mean, although one should, I think, probably be blamed to a certain degree. So you have to write more, explain more. Unlike Noam Chomsky, whom I admire a great deal, I am not a relentless answerer of letters or of misstatements, but I try, to a certain degree, to do it. But there is never enough time. I am always involved in something else that I want to do.

IN THE WAITING ROOM

CANONS, COMMUNITIES, "POLITICAL CORRECTNESS"

Judith Frank

for Sasha Torres

Judith Frank is a younger scholar with re-markable analytical powers and polemical verve. She received a B.A. from the Hebrew University in Jerusalem and an M.F.A. in fiction writing and a Ph.D. in English from Cornell. Frank is currently an assistant pro-fessor in the English department at Amherst College, where she teaches eighteenth-century English literature, women's studies, and cre-ative writing. She is at work on a study of eighteenth-century satirical fiction and its rep-resentations of the poor. Her essay that fol-lows is a revised version of a talk that was first published in Amherst *magazine.*

IN THE WAITING ROOM OF A STATE-OF-THE-ART FACILITY, on my first day of radiation therapy for breast cancer, the radiologist, who had heard that I was an English professor, asked me if colleges and universities weren't going too far with this political correctness thing. A close friend had come with me, and she sat glowering on a couch with a twelve-year-old *National Geographic* on her lap as I argued fiercely with him for fifteen minutes or so. I don't know why I let him engage me. Maybe, even at a point when I was involved so completely in the emergency of my own body, I knew that this issue would come to seem increasingly urgent; or maybe I was fighting just to feel myself fight something. I was grateful, though, when a young woman technologist finally interrupted us to take me into the simulation room to prepare me for the first treatment. As she made a mold of my upper body and marked my chest with five tiny tattoos ("How about a snake, or a heart that says MOM?" I asked, like, no doubt, hundreds of comediens before me), the radiologist came in and out to check, measure, and approve, and to continue our argument. But wasn't it true that the best works of art came from Western culture? And didn't I think it was a kind of useless tyranny when in the push for multiculturalism students demand courses like—and he mustered what was for

127

him the most ludicrous possible example—"The Puerto Rican Novel"?

It was in this very particular kind of public sphere, the waiting rooms of a variety of specialists, that I first encountered what was soon to become a vast sea of polemic against the academy in the popular press: in *Newsweek*, *The Atlantic*, *New York* and *The New Republic*, to name just a few magazines, and in every newspaper you can imagine. I didn't read it then, thinking of it as an irritant from which I was entitled to shield myself. As we left the radiation therapy department that morning, though, my friend cried in grief and vexation. She cried partly because she didn't think I should have to fight with a person who was supposed to be helping me get well. But she also cried, she said, because she thought I'd argued so badly.

I was wounded—I thought I'd done pretty well, considering the circumstances. Furious at each other, we fought all the way home, and then sat in the parked car arguing about the best ways to oppose this backlash against ideas we care about, until we grew chilled by the gray February morning. I take this essay as a chance for another effort—a better one, I hope.

I'm going to say some things here that seem to me very simple and self-evident. For the media has so successfully forged a kind of mainstream consensus, so successfully established the terms by which we discuss this topic, that sometimes we need to go back to the beginning. To, for example, the small matter that there is no such thing as "the movement for political correctness." There is, in fact, as far as I can tell, no such thing as "political correctness" without quotation marks around it. People who are political activists or write political criticism have generally used the term ironically, as a kind of check to *themselves* in their political zeal. The fact that people now use the term "political correctness" routinely without the quotation marks attests to the frightening success of anti-academic discourse. Here's another simple proposition: that the alleged chaos in the humanities is in fact an intellectual revolution. You get bad work as well as great work in this kind of climate; a revolution is liable to be messy. But what I'll loosely call political criticism

—and that covers a diverse group of critical practices—has constituted a kind of paradigm shift in the humanities, a shift that has enabled a wide and interesting variety of new work to appear over the past fifteen or so years.

This essay is divided into two interrelated parts: The first treats the revolution in the humanities; and the second, the alleged regime of left-wing intolerance at America's universities.

I. "GRAB A HARPOON!"

In this section I'm going to grit my teeth and spend some time with one of the most popular and widely read spokesmen against the paradigm shift in the humanities. In a column for *Newsweek* titled "Literary Politics" (April 22, 1991), George Will attacks the notion—advanced, he says, in the academy—that "all literature is . . . political." Here is his parody of contemporary literary criticism:

> Shakespeare's "Tempest" reflects the imperialist rape of the Third World. Emily Dickinson's poetic references to peas and flower buds are encoded messages of feminist rage, exulting clitoral masturbation to protest the prison of patriarchal sex roles. Jane Austen's supposed serenity masks boiling fury about male domination, expressed in the nastiness of minor characters who are "really" not minor. . . . Melville's white whale? Probably a penis. Grab a harpoon!

The arguments Will renders in their Classic Comics form sound pretty hilarious in their evocation of words like *imperialism, patriarchy,* and *sexuality*, and in their quarrelsome counterintuitiveness. They sound that way partly because of the success of Will's frenetic and strategic anti-intellectualism, which exploits the fact that academic arguments sound odd to those not practiced in them. Former Secretary of Education William Bennett—who apparently had trouble understanding one form of literary theory, deconstruction, when he was an academic—recently yucked it up on C-SPAN by telling a joke about the mafioso deconstructionist who says, "I'm going to make you an offer you can't understand." I don't believe in esotericism for its own sake, nor do I believe that the public can't understand what's at stake in academic debates. But Will seems to expect the humanities to be utterly transparent to the general population, when the truth is that for those of us who have gone through graduate training, the humanities are a profession, and that the people who practice a particular profession are trained in its language. If those of us who aren't scientists were to read scientific titles aloud to ourselves, we would laugh at how hard the words are to pronounce, how impenetrable and awkward they sound. But we'd assume we were lacking the tools to decipher them, not that there's something ludicrous about science.

Tellingly, Will's strategic buffoonery vanishes when the subject shifts to access to the academy by minorities, and to their potential impact on the university curriculum. Here is his next paragraph:

> The supplanting of esthetic by political responses to literature makes literature primarily interesting as a mere index of who had power and whom the powerful victimized. Thus does criticism dovetail with the political agenda of victimology. The agenda is the proliferation of groups nursing grievances and demanding entitlements. The multiplication of grievances is (if radicals will pardon the expression) the core curriculum of universities that are transformed into political instruments. That curriculum aims at delegitimizing Western civilization by discrediting the books and ideas that gave birth to it.

Whereas just a moment ago we were all sitting around with a six-pack, with the ballgame on in the background, chuckling "Grab a harpoon," now we quickly sober under the ice bath of Will's superciliousness. In an alarming increase of syllables-per-word, his diction has elevated to accommodate a discourse of beleaguered elitism. And well it might, because now he is no longer talking about professors, but about "groups nursing grievances and demanding entitlements"—the petty, the insolent, the uppity, women (presumably), and people of color. Evoking the demand for entitlement as though it were necessarily corrupt and intellectually bankrupt, rather than, say, an honored tradition in democratic societies, Will is worrying here about expanded access to the university.

The primary entitlement these new groups demand is the revision of what has counted as the Western civilization curriculum. And come to think of it, my own pedagogical practice illustrates Will's point. The semester before my cancer was diagnosed, I had taught, in a remarkable coincidence, not one but three literary works about breast cancer—none canonical, none, that is, traditionally part of the literature curriculum. In my eighteenth-century novel course, we read Maria Edgeworth's witty and overwrought 1802 novel *Belinda*, one of whose plots concerns a wealthy and giddy lady who believes she is going to die from a tumor in her breast, acquired when her gun backfires during a duel she undertakes as a lark; only when she is reformed into a loving wife and mother does the novel allow the doctors to discover it is a mere bruise. In that class we also read the novelist Fanny Burney's journal account of her mastectomy, an operation performed during the eighteenth century with only a wine cordial as anesthesia, while in my freshman English course we had a series of contentious conversations about the black lesbian-feminist writer Audre Lorde's 1980 account of her battle with cancer, *The Cancer Journals*.

Despite the picture Will paints of contemporary academic life, I did not whine to my colleagues that Shakespeare and Milton don't talk about breast cancer; nor did I, deciding that the lack of a poetic treatment of breast cancer in their works makes them bad writers, demand that my department replace our courses in Shakespeare and Milton with courses on Maria Edgeworth and Audre Lorde. Rather, like many of my colleagues, I taught the noncanonical alongside the canonical: Edgeworth and Burney, for example, alongside Defoe, Richardson, Fielding, Smollett, and Sterne. Will is anxious about

the wholesale destruction of Western civilization, I think, because canon revision reveals the canon to be a social institution
rather than a self-evidently sublime entity unsoiled by the grime
of human interest. The canon is changing (and has always
changed) because the kinds of people who read the canon are
changing. Which of the works I taught that semester constitutes
"great" art is not only a vexed question here (it seems quite
likely to me, for example, that *Belinda* is a "better" novel than,
say, Smollett's *Peregrine Pickle*, or even Sterne's *A Sentimental
Journey*) but also a necessarily partial one. For regardless of the
charged and invested idea of greatness, these works are inval-
uable documents of women's and literary history, demonstrating the richly complicated ways women have thought about
the relations between their bodies, their desires, the world
around them, and their art.

I doubt George Will is very interested in these issues; I doubt
they have much to do with what he thinks of as either history
or art. But for women (indeed, for many people), the literary
expression of female bodily experience is vitally interesting, on
both an intellectual and an emotional level. It is for that reason
that we demand entitlement: that is, access to and institutional
space in which to study works of literature of vital interest to
us. Not anticipating my own diagnosis, I did not choose to
teach these works specifically because they deal with breast
cancer. As powerful works can do, though, they later came to
my aid in a crisis, enriching my experience of illness immea-
surably, at times in quite immediate ways. Conjuring up Fanny
Burney lying on a bed surrounded by seven men in black robes
("Why so many? & without Leave?—But I could not utter a
syllable"), refusing to be held down, and feeling the knife scrape
her breastbone, rendered me, I must say, slightly more mature
than I might otherwise have been during my needle biopsy.
And with her bracing rage about the ways in which the institution of medicine colludes in the oppression of women, Lorde
had given me an expanded sense of both my medical and my
emotional options. My claim that women's literature helped me
when I was sick might sound vulgarly utilitarian. But isn't that,

after all, what many people think good literature should do: sustain us when we're weak, deepen our understanding of history, expand our sense of what it's possible to think and feel?

I am fairly certain Will believes something like this. He certainly believes in the deepening of historical understanding, warning us, later in the article, that

> . . . the transmission of the culture that unites, even defines America—transmission through knowledge of literature and history—is faltering. The result is collective amnesia and deculturation.

Few in the academy today would question whether literature and history are important, but many *would* ask what will *count* as literature and history, and about which events we will choose to be anmesiac. The revolution in the humanities seeks to restore to our cultural memory such texts as *Belinda* and Burney's journals, and such events as "the imperialist rape of the Third World"—an event that, for Will, clearly doesn't count as history, just as silliness. I think he knows that the "imperialist rape of the Third World" occurred, but he tries to trivialize its import with (interestingly enough) the word *rape* and implies that those whose bodies may have gotten in the way of such a rape are crybabies. I think he knows that it occurred; he just doesn't think it's a proper object of study.

The word *reflects* is also reductive here, suggesting that we literature professors teach *The Tempest* by drawing a simple equation on the board: "*The Tempest* = the imperialist rape of the third world." Now, over the past fifteen or so years, it has been very pleasurable for women and minority readers, among others, to say, "Our mostly white male professors told us *The Tempest*, or *Robinson Crusoe*, or *Heart of Darkness*, or *Women in Love*, was a triumph of Western culture, when they made *us* feel kind of weird in a way we couldn't quite define. But aha! They're really about the *brutality* of Western culture!" I myself have certainly experienced this pleasure, as works I was supposed to admire in college if I were to be a truly cultured person became accessible to me in new ways. Suddenly I got to trust

my intuition as well as my knowledge; I got to challenge received ways of reading and look more critically, in the strong
sense of that word, at the "great works." Whatever George
Eliot's intentions were, there *is* something a little creepy, it turns
out, about *Daniel Deronda*'s portrayal of Jews, not to mention
its representation of Palestine as uninhabited. But that pleasur-
ably rebellious moment is limited in itself; it is not where you
stop if you're a good critic. We don't trivialize "the political"
by saying it's a "mere index of who had power over whom."

Let me give you an extended example from a work I know
a little better than *The Tempest: Robinson Crusoe*, which, I might
say, if I were planning on being reductive, is "about the imperialist rape of the Third World." That Defoe's novel is about
English colonialism, its presence and violence in the Caribbean,
is, in the argument I'm going to present, supposed to be an
enabling insight, not a foreclosing one. We don't say, with Will,
that now that we've shown that Defoe's novel is about the
power of the English in the Caribbean, our reading is over. The
story of *Robinson Crusoe* is not reducible to the mere fact that
white European men had power over non-European native peoples; it's about their interaction, about how things got to be
that way, about what kind of fantasies were spun by a culture
to legitimize that order, about the curiously marvelous cultural
artifacts that arise out of such brutality.

Robinson Crusoe is the story of a young man from a middling
English family in the mid-seventeenth century, whose restless
nature hurries him "into the wild and indigested notion of raising my fortune," and who desires, against the instructions of
his father, to go to sea. After several disastrous voyages aboard
merchant ships, Crusoe ends up in Brazil, where he sets up a
sugar plantation. But after four years of subsistence farming,
Crusoe feels both lonely and in need of more laboring hands.
Indeed, his need for labor power is sometimes indistinguishable
from an almost metaphysical sense of loss: "I had no body to
converse with but now and then this neighbor; no work to be
done but by the labour of my hands; and I used to say I lived
just like a man cast away upon some desolate island, that has

no body there but himself." So he decides to leave Brazil on a slaving expedition to the Guinea coast. It is during that journey that the climactic shipwreck occurs, and Crusoe, the sole survivor, reaches an island that the novel situates in the estuary of the Orinoco, within sight of Trinidad. He is stranded there for twenty-eight years, about half of them with the companionship and labor power of a native Carib who offers to be enslaved, and whom he names Friday. A series of adventures involving a group of shipwrecked Spaniards allows Crusoe to finally leave the island, and to administer it from England as his own property, his own little colony. Meanwhile, during his thirty-year absence, his Brazilian plantation has flourished with the help of slave labor. At the end of the novel, Crusoe is a rich man.

In the hundred years after 1650, during the years in which Defoe's novel takes place, England had a lot to do with the Caribbean. It established an Atlantic economy in which English traders bought slaves in Africa, sold them in the West Indies (and later in the North American colonies), and returned to England with the sugar of the Caribbean slave plantations. The growth of this system in the late seventeenth and early eighteenth centuries was a crucial source of English prosperity. The sugar colonies benefited English trade in manifold ways. They supplied Europeans with a variety of exotic goods in growing demand; gave employment to fortune hunters, younger sons, and seamen; provided raw materials for processing and manufacturing industries; and generated the profitable trade in African slaves. In 1713 the Peace of Utrecht, concluding the War of the Spanish Succession with France, gave England the Asiento grant, a monopoly contract to supply 4800 slaves a year to the Spanish New World. This made England the major slave-trading nation in Europe. Six years later, *Robinson Crusoe* was published.

In Will's argument it would be ridiculous for me to claim that Defoe's novel is importantly about Europe and the Third World. But I wonder, how is it possible that the historical events I have recounted—events whose economic, social, and cultural effects were cataclysmic—would not have made it into *Robin-*

son *Crusoe* and other literature written at this time? Mid-seventeenth- and early-eighteenth-century English literature is in fact full of energy and anxiety about Britain's mercantile adventure; when it's not *explicitly* celebrating or excoriating it, it's busy being entranced by its products, such new exotic imports as coffee and pineapple. When Will attacks critics for claiming that literature is irreducibly political, he acts as though the perverse and willfull choice to ignore that Defoe's novel is about the historical and social events it purports to be about were *not* a political act. You need to do a lot of work to ignore the historical context of *Robinson Crusoe*, no matter how mythically it presents itself. And yet it has been read as being about anything *but* the social and historical: as a spiritual autobiography, as a parable of modern individualism, as the first true work of "realism," as the story of the solitary human spirit. Then, in 1986, under the impetus of the revolution in the humanities, enacting no doubt what George Will calls "the political agenda of victimology," a literary critic named Peter Hulme perversely insisted on dragging politics into it (Octave Mannoni had done so in French in the 1950s, in a book called *Prospero and Caliban: The Psychology of Colonization*, an English translation of which I'm told was given to Peace Corps volunteers in the 1960s). Hulme, like Mannoni, thought *Robinson Crusoe* might be a novel about the place in which it occurs, a novel about slavery, a novel about British colonialism.

Although slavery plays a relatively minor role in the novel, I would argue that it resonates throughout it. Crusoe lands upon his island, which the novel represents as an almost mythic site of solitary manual labor, because he was sailing to capture slaves. The novel never causally links the two in an explicit way, but consider the rich symbolism of Crusoe's punishment. You remember, I'm sure, those great images of Crusoe having to learn everything anew: making his dishes and ovens and his own clothes, planting his own crops with the use of laboriously handmade tools, making do with the raw materials given him. I'd suggest that we read this labor, a labor Crusoe calls "inexpressible," as the novel's expression of anxiety about the trade in slaves. Although it never explicitly condemns the slave trade, it arranges that Crusoe's punishment fit the crime. At the same time, Crusoe's labor is not only difficult; it's also a source of immense satisfaction, an almost utopian pleasure. With considerable self-irony, Crusoe compares his skill in making an earthen pot to that of children making dirt-pies; but when he finally succeeds in making a pot that can withstand being fired, he says, "No joy at a thing of so mean a nature was ever equal to mine." One might argue that in scenes like this the novel attempts to reattach value to labor, a labor that has become degraded in slave economies.

In Hulme's political reading, *Robinson Crusoe* also becomes a story about an English merchant adventurer's contact with native peoples. Even before Crusoe meets Friday, a crisis in the narrative occurs when he encounters a lone footprint in the sand, after being alone on the island for many years. Suddenly he is galvanized into a series of terrifying fantasies. Perhaps the cannibals will destroy him and his crops, turn loose his livestock, kill and, worse yet, devour him. The way Crusoe talks about these possibilities, Hulme argues, reveals a fear of utter self-dissolution. The footprint takes him "out of my self" and makes him "start at my own shadow," as his sense of bodily boundaries becomes compromised. In a moment that blurs the boundary between himself and the natives, he thinks that it may be his *own* footprint. This frightening loss of boundaries is magnified when, to his horror, he comes across the remains of a cannibal feast. He says, "My stomach grew sick, and I was just at the point of fainting, when nature discharged the disorder from my stomach, and having vomited with an uncommon violence, I was a little relieved." What a complicated moment that vomiting is! In its production of a body Hulme calls "alimentarily chaste," Crusoe's vomiting seems to assert his utter difference from the cannibal. But I would add to Hulme's observation that it's also a moment of keen and scary identification. It is, after all, the cannibals who have eaten human flesh, and Crusoe's stomach that is revolting. His "wild and *indigested* notion of

raising [his] fortune" indeed: the way Defoe represents the im-
petuosity of young Crusoe's decision to join the colonial enterprise foreshadows, it turns out, this moment—a moment in
which the threat to identity posed by native peoples is so unprepared for and so frightening it makes his stomach turn.

If you read the novel as being merely about the eternal
verities, or about the imagination, or about language, you can't
see any of this. Nor can you see that Defoe's novel is in fact
troubled about Britain's colonial enterprise. It endorses it, certainly, not least through a happy ending that has Crusoe rich
from the profits of the slave trade, but it also problematizes it
—through its long fantasy about building your plantation by
the work of your own hands, and through its portrayal of the
colonizer as full of self-doubt and apprehension about his relation to the colonized. If this is an appropriate reading—and I
happen to think it's a rather fruitful and creative one—George
Will should be *happy*. Because I'm reading *Robinson Crusoe* as
an artifact, as an imaginative cultural act, from a culture that
was talking to itself very seriously—if also self-servingly—
about what it was doing in Africa and the Caribbean. My reading suggests that rather than exploiting and butchering thousands of slaves while feeling good about itself, British culture
worried about it. Far from "discrediting" Defoe's novel, my
reading gives it credit. But perhaps such readings sound incoherent in a climate in which our own foreign policy decisions
are celebrated with a feel-good discourse that is utterly one-
dimensional. Maybe in such a climate, insights like these from
the humanities sound psychotic. Maybe that's why people think
the humanities are in chaos.

2. "THE NEW MCCARTHYISM"

Those following this issue have probably noticed that Smith
College gets mentioned a lot as, in the words of *The Wall Street
Journal* (November 25, 1990), "a hub of Political Correctness."
That's because Smith's Office of Student Affairs issued a well-
meaning if slightly sanctimonious worksheet on oppression,

trying to educate students during freshman orientation about the political valences of particular names we give to ethnic groups, and defining the various types of oppression that exist in our society. This worksheet, it is worth noting, was not a set of rules for what it is permissible to utter. The terms found particularly risible by *The Wall Street Journal* and *Newsweek* were, among others, *heterosexism, ableism* (which the sheet defined as "oppression of the differently abled, by the temporarily abled"), and *lookism*, the belief that appearance is an indicator of a person's value.

Whatever we think of the validity of these terms—from where I stand, *heterosexism* rings true while *ableism* does not, and *lookism* probably speaks to anyone who's been a teenager —it is worth noting that Smith College, an alleged "hub of Political Correctness," is in fact quite conservative curricularly. At nearby Amherst, meanwhile, our trustees are fretting about the faculty's repeated rejection of anything remotely resembling a core curriculum or distribution requirement, and "heterosexism" is being explored in an increasing number of courses in the emerging field of gay and lesbian studies. We at Amherst, however, appear somewhat differently in the popular press, when *U.S. News and World Report* annually trots us out at or near the top of their best college list, to the delight of everybody's parents. You've got to wonder why Amherst remains invulnerable to attack while Smith does not: I suspect is has something to do with the fact that Smith is a women's college—and therefore particularly vulnerable to ridicule— while "Amherst" still signifies, in the public imagination, an elite male college.

Using the Smith worksheet as a prime example, writer after writer has argued that free speech is under attack on campus. *Newsweek*, for example, refers to "political correctness" as "the new McCarthyism" (December 24, 1990), while in *The New Republic*, Eugene Genovese, who in fact has many leftist credentials, refers to the student "terrorists" and "storm troopers" who do such things as commit civil disobedience on campus on behalf of various leftist causes (April 15, 1991). Much has been made of the statistic that some 70 percent of campuses have codes restricting harassing and demeaning speech.

I don't want to discuss free speech in the constitutional sense here. If I did, I might mention that the line between free speech and hate speech, or actions intended to incite violence, is a time-honored tightrope in our society, walked most recently by those conservatives who, when the Supreme Court upheld the right to burn the flag under the First Amendment, proposed a new constitutional amendment to circumvent it. I might mention that many existing college speech codes are intended to *promote* First Amendment values—to prevent, for example, the shouting down of another speaker—and were instituted in the early 1970s as a conservative response to left-wing student activism, with academic conservatives arguing that "the life of the mind requires a higher standard of civility and respect for the views of others than could be tolerated in society at large" (Michael Kinsley, *New Republic*, May 20, 1991). I might mention that Congressman Henry Hyde, who has sponsored the bipartisan Collegiate Speech Protection Act of 1991, a bill that would provide legal assistance to students who succeed in challenging university codes aimed at regulating offensive speech, voted in the recent debate about the National Endowment for the Arts *for* the amendment restricting the content of federally funded art, endorsing a ban on any representation of homoeroticism and any statement that might be considered offensive to any religious group—or else to abolish the Endowment (Richard Goldstein, *Village Voice*, May 7, 1991). And I might mention that when the *New York Times* carried an article on President Bush's claim, in his University of Michigan commencement address, that "the notion of 'political correctness' " has led to "inquisition," "censorship," and "bullying" on some college campuses, there appeared *on the very same page* an article headlined "Long Series of Military Decisions Led to Gulf War News Censorship," which stated that these decisions originated with President Bush, who elected to "manage the information flow in a way that supported the operation's political goals and avoided the perceived mistakes of Vietnam" (May 5, 1991). I might mention these things if I were going to discuss the constitutional sense of free speech, but I won't, because the egregious hypocrisy and cynicism they betray enrage me too much. So instead, I'd like to discuss a different matter, one often blurred with free speech in the constitutional sense but actually quite different from it.

Genovese writes that universities "are merely doing their best to create an atmosphere in which professors who value their reputations and their perquisites learn to censor themselves." Similarly, in an article from the *Chicago Tribune* titled "The Death of Free Speech on Campus," Charles Sykes quotes a Wesleyan student as saying, "People are very reluctant to say what they feel if it doesn't mesh with the prevailing ideology. There is a form of self-censorship in which people can't say what they really think because of fear of being labeled insensitive or, even worse, racist or sexist."

Self-censorship is a word that makes our hackles rise, surely, evoking as it does—in its intentionally misleading way—the basic freedom from censorship provided by the first amendment. But self-censorship is not about free speech in the constitutional sense; it's about the commonsense meaning of speaking freely, without reserve, without worrying about reproach, without having to watch what you say, without having to think about it all the damn time.

Surely we watch what we say a lot. Students, regardless of their political orientation, watch what they say in class, because they know it's risky to offend the professor, if not their classmates. Junior faculty take care not to offend those senior colleagues who may end up sitting on their tenure committees—and not because we're chicken, either, not because we walk around in anything you would call fear, but because we almost unconsciously weigh the satisfaction of speaking our minds against the potential long-term injury to ourselves such free speech may cause. People like to pass their courses and keep their jobs, so they watch what they say. Watching what you say is a particularly well-internalized act for people who are subordinate to others. But our senior colleagues also watch what they say. They have long histories with one another, histories full of affection and camaraderie, as well as old grudges and disappointments. So if you sit in a department meeting, you will notice it is chock-full of people watching what they say. They are watching what they say because they are trying to be a community.

But some kinds of watching what we say, or "self-censorship," feel more natural than others. It feels, for example, pretty natural to most of us not to use the racial slurs *nigger*, or *kike*. But it didn't always. One of the instructive things about the PBS series *Eyes on the Prize* is the archival footage of white men and women not even hesitating to use the word *nigger* on television. You don't hear that word uttered on television anymore, although I suspect that the popularity of the seventies series *All in the Family* came not only from seeing such overt racism satirized but also from getting to hear those words once more on television, however ironically meant, before they disappeared. In a complicated way, Archie Bunker helped naturalize a heretofore unnatural form of "self-censorship." Do we suggest that television has curtailed free speech because it no longer tolerates particular racial slurs?

With new kinds of people populating the academic community—women, blacks, other ethnic groups, and gays and lesbians (who have always been in the academy but who have only recently made ourselves visible)—we have to censor ourselves in new and unfamiliar ways. In the old, men-only Amherst faculty club, faculty members presumably did not have to watch what they said about women. Now they do, because they understand it as a responsibility to participate in making this workplace, this community, livable for women. While some might welcome the opportunity for graciousness and civility afforded by new kinds of colleagues, this new self-censorship is doubtless difficult, even painful, for many. It makes you feel disoriented in a place that once seemed as familiar as your own home; it makes you have to think about yourself as a sexist, as a person who once sat around with your friends saying jokingly derisive things about women. It is that pain, and that disorientation, that make people lash out in the press about the curtailing of their freedom of speech. It has little to do with actual free speech.

And just when we got used to the women, along came the blacks, the Hispanics, the Asians, and the queers. In this kind of climate, a person might well ask, "How am I supposed to keep track of what I say to whom? Or of what I call people? Is it fair to call me a racist because I didn't know I was supposed to say *Asian* instead of *Oriental*, *Native American* instead of *Indian*? Such a fate apparently befell Professor Stephan Thernstrom at Harvard, a "preeminent scholar" of history whose story was written by John Taylor of *New York* magazine (January 21, 1991):

> "Racist."
> "Racist!"
> "The man is a racist!"
> "A *racist!*"
> Such denunciations, hissed in tones of self-righteousness and contempt, vicious and vengeful, furious, smoking with hatred—such denunciations haunted Stephan Thernstrom for weeks. Whenever he walked through the campus that spring, down Harvard's brick paths, under the arched gates, past the fluttering elms, he found it hard not to imagine the pointing fingers, the whispers. Racist. There goes the *racist*. It was hellish, this persecution.

Because I know none of the principals in this drama, I will bracket the issue of what actually happened at Harvard; I would, though, like to pressure the article's representation of these events. Thernstrom was guilty, the article claims, of using the word *Indian* instead of *Native American*, and *Oriental* instead of *Asian*, of assigning a book against affirmative action, and of endorsing the claim of the Moynihan report that the cause of black poverty is the black family. According to the article, Thernstrom's colleague Professor Bernard Bailyn was similarly challenged by his students for having them read from the diary

of a Southern planter without giving equal time to the recollections of a slave. He pointed out, the article claims, that "no
journals, diaries, or letters written by slaves had ever been
found"—a claim so ignorant I can only assume it is Taylor's,
not Bailyn's. Taylor writes, "But that failed to satisfy the complaining students." Now I'm only speculating, but that might
be because some of them knew that it wasn't true, knew that
out of some sixty thousand slaves who escaped to freedom
across the Ohio River and the Mason-Dixon line, over one
hundred wrote book-length narratives, and that between 1703
and 1944, some six thousand ex-slaves narrated the stories of
their captivity in interviews, essays, and books.

According to the article, the "vicious and vengeful" behavior
the students committed consisted of writing letters to the *Harvard Crimson*, as well as a six-page letter to Bailyn. You might
consider that vicious and vengeful—with his repetition of the
word *racist*, Taylor is clearly trying to make their accusations
sound like hate speech—but you might also consider it taking
charge of their education. But I can't avoid the sense that what
really galled John Taylor is that these accusations occurred as
Thernstrom walked "down Harvard's brick paths, under the
arched gates, past the fluttering elms," where "he found it hard
not to imagine the pointing fingers, the whispers." In Taylor's
phantasmagoric portrayal of white authority besieged at Harvard, charges of racism apparently ruined Thernstrom's view.
The haunting pointing fingers of his imagination—pointing
black fingers, perhaps, black *people*—soured Thernstrom's enjoyment of the aesthetic privilege Taylor lovingly dwells upon
in his representation of the elite institution's expensive landscape. Don't think that it isn't a problem for Taylor that students
of color walk those same brick paths.

The Taylor article, and many like it, present an innocent
and well-intentioned man getting attacked by thought police.
This hapless professor didn't know he was offending anyone.
It's easy, and maybe inevitable, to sympathize with particular
individuals at moments like that, but if you've been exposed
for much of your life to a more *systemic* ignorance—a racism,

say, that thrives on ignorance—you are much less likely to be sympathetic than you are to feel the blood rushing to your face. I will admit that this matter of not knowing, of saying the wrong thing—this can be an intensely painful matter when it involves people we should care about: good people, or older people who are not keeping up as well as they used to. I don't quite know how to prescribe appropriate behaviors in such excruciating circumstances. I do know, though, that the happy expansive pity we generally direct toward those we think of as ignorant comes from a soft spot we have for ignorance, even ignorance that hurts people.

Indeed, it is important to note that cultures promote and encourage ignorance, that ignorance is not a matter of individuals so much as an institutional practice. The literary critic Eve Kosofsky Sedgwick has argued that knowledge is not itself power, that ignorance competes with it for power in the creation of cultural meaning. She writes, "If M. Mitterrand knows English but Mr. Reagan lacks French, it is the urbane M. Mitterrand who must negotiate in an acquired tongue, the ignorant Mr. Reagan who may dilate in his native one." It is, she claims, "the interlocutor who has or pretends to have the *less* broadly knowledgeable understanding of interpretive practice who will define the terms of the exchange." Rather than being a kind of passive innocence, in other words, ignorance is often harnessed, licensed, and even promulgated, to particular political effects. The way the government has regulated funding for safe-sex education, in bills with obscenity-law riders attached, is an object lesson in the distribution of various knowledges and ignorances—some to the "community at large," some to the targeted communities who are not considered to belong to our society at large. It is a distribution that cares about preserving particular ignorances at least as much as it cares about preserving lives. You may also be thinking of the recent Supreme Court ruling on abortion counseling, Rust *v.* Sullivan, which by upholding the government's right to withdraw funds from federally funded family-planning clinics should their doctors mention abortion as a medical option—that is, should they dispense information—mandates the production of ignorance in these clinics.

Mary Louise Pratt discusses this kind of ignorance in an article about the 1988 Western culture debate at Stanford (*SAQ* 89). In the days that followed the final approval of the new curriculum, she writes,

> . . . A student was expelled from his dormitory after a year of disruptive activity directed especially toward a gay resident assistant, culminating in an assault on the resident and the vandalizing of the dormitory lounge. The following evening, ten fraternity brothers, in defense of the expelled student's freedom of speech, staged a silent vigil at midnight outside the dormitory lounge wearing masks and carrying candles, a gesture that seemed to deliberately invoke the customs of the Ku Klux Klan. The reactions of black students who assembled at the site ranged from terror to outrage, and the action was treated by the university as a serious racial and homophobic incident. The ten demonstrators, however, claimed complete ignorance of the associations their vigil invoked. They did not know, they said, that masks and candles at midnight had any connotations—it is just what they thought a vigil was.

Pratt comments on the climate of sanctioned ignorance that made this episode possible, claiming that "in pleading ignorance, the students were following the example of many of the country's own leaders, for whom ignorance had become an acceptable standard of public life. Throughout their high school and college years these students had looked to a president who consistently showed himself to be both ignorant and utterly comfortable with his ignorance."

Pratt also refers this spectacle of sanctioned ignorance back to the curricular debate that preceded it. If the students were not lying when they pleaded ignorance, young people can apparently leave the American educational system ignorant of the history of U.S. race relations—which, she adds, is *not* a part of standard Western culture curricula. Indeed, the traditional Western civilization curriculum is one institution whose job it is to foster specific kinds of ignorance. The narratives of ex-slaves were best-sellers in their time, so how is it that they fell into a kind of black hole of cultural consciousness until the 1970s? The claim that there exist no journals or letters written by slaves could only be made in a curriculum set up to make this writing invisible in a way that I must insist is not innocent. And this ignorance has material effects on peoples' lives. If white America thinks of African-Americans as people without writing, without ideas, without a culture, it's not very likely to treat them as fully human.

When people like my radiologist assume that the idea of the Puerto Rican novel is patently ridiculous, I want to ask, in the most seriously philosophical way possible, how does he know? Here's how he knows. His college courses never mentioned such a thing; he is ignorant of such an entity. It is precisely the ignorance encouraged by his culture—a culture that would tend to be incredulous at the placement of "Puerto Rican" and "culture" in the same phrase—that allows him to assert its unsuitability as an object of study with such insolent assurance. His confidence was so astounding it took my breath away at the time. Now, after some research, I have it back. It might, I've discovered, not make that much sense to create a course focusing on the genre of the novel, rather than dealing with Puerto Rican literature more generally; and it might not be altogether fruitful to focus only on Puerto Rico, which locates itself in relation to Latin American culture at large, and when Latin American literature courses are hardly plentiful to begin with. But if you did focus on the Puerto Rican novel, here's a rough draft of a packed fourteen-week syllabus: The course will study, to name just a few possible issues, the attempt to forge a national identity in the wake of Puerto Rico's colonial history; the effect of Puerto Rican multi-racialism, bilingualism, and popular traditions on novelistic technique and language; and representations of the diaspora to the New York or Chicago barrio. The syllabus is composed of writers both from the island and the mainland:

René Márquez, José Luis González Coiscou, Pedro Juan Soto, Luis Rafael Sánchez, Jaime Carrero, Tato Laviera, Victor Hernández Cruz, Piri Thomás, Nicholasa Mohr, Edward Rivera, Rosario Ferré.

Finally, Pratt's account of the Western culture debates and their violent backlash at Stanford also reminds us of something mentioned only in the most glancing way in the magazine accounts of campus speech codes and the attempt to regulate "hate speech"—that is, the hate that precipitates such attempts, a hate clearly on the rise since the Reagan years. Especially now, when we're in a recession, we are looking for scapegoats. Consider a white student who graduates from college and can't find a job. The culprit must be affirmative action—some person of color (or, to use a phrase considered by many to be a redundancy, some *unqualified* person of color) who got that job because of "political correctness." What the press systematically ignores is that the hate is not expressed only in genteel classroom debates. The frat boy at Stanford whose right to free speech was so indignantly defended by his brothers was not disciplined for saying "homosexual" instead of "gay," but for assaulting a gay student. Why do we not read in the mainstream press about the fact that people of color and gay people are routinely victimized by hate crimes both on and off college campuses? It is clearly not that newsworthy or controversial when certain kinds of people are harassed and assaulted.

It used to be, I know, that any self-respecting leftist criticized the university as a place that perpetuates privilege. Today things have turned around, and I find myself in an awkward position, summoning up as many resources as I can to defend the university against the blunt-edged polemic now wielded against it, not only by the mainstream press but also by the federal government, which is in a position to do serious material damage to it. I do this because although the academy is *still* a bastion of privilege, it now at least has a discourse in place to talk about that. And as the country pulls together in a frenzy of jingoistic self-congratulation, as our corporate intervention in the Third World becomes increasingly celebrated as a new world order, as (and I know this is boring, because so routine) the rich get richer and the poor get poorer, the university is one of the only places left in this country where there remains anything resembling a climate of dissent, anything resembling an analytical dissenting discourse about the nature of culture, institutions, and power. I say this in the understanding that we think dissent is a necessary and valued part of democratic society, whether or not we agree with it, whether it occurs in the waiting room or the classroom. I *refuse* to believe that the attempt to discredit it has been entirely successful.

THE
FALLS
OF
ACADEME

*William
Kerrigan*

William Kerrigan is a well-known Milton scholar who has published two major studies of the poet, The Sacred Complex *and* The Prophetic Milton. *With Gordon Braden, he co-authored the prize-winning volume* The Idea of the Renaissance, *which renews claims for the period's integrity and coherence. Kerrigan is a contributing editor to* Raritan, *Renaissance editor of* Hellas, *and director of the program in literature and psychoanalysis at the University of Massachusetts at Amherst. He has taught at the University of Virginia and the University of Maryland at College Park and holds degrees from Stanford and Columbia.*

THE MOVEMENT I CALL THE THEORY EXPLOSION began for me in the early 1970s when I was teaching Milton and Renaissance literature in the famously conservative English department at the University of Virginia. First came the French imports: structuralism, poststructuralism, deconstruction, postmodernism. There was (and still is) much confusion over the content of these movements and their proliferation of new jargons; makers of handbooks to guide the perplexed became famous for translating French obscurity into clear English prose. But for me the main excitement of those days lay not in the feeling that I now possessed wonderful new ideas capable of doing wonderful new things with literature. Theory exposed my ignorance. I needed to become a better intellectual historian if I was to benefit, in any serious way, from this sudden increase in the number of books from which literary critics might draw inspiration. To approach theory without a thick sense of its history was to surrender to the tedious regurgitations of the handbook makers.

For me, then, the most positive effect of the Theory Explosion was the encouragement to read forbiddingly difficult books that professors in graduate school had never recommended. At the beginning of this period I was regularly experiencing back pain, and decided that my best chance of beating surgery was daily exercise. So, during summers and vacations,

I would awaken to a regimen of calisthenics and weight lifting, then turn, all pumped up, to the toughest great books in the world. During the next decade I read Kant's critiques, Hegel's *Phenomenology of the Spirit*, Schelling, Feuerbach, Dilthey, Kierkegaard, Nietzsche, Wittgenstein, Saussure's *Course in General Linguistics*, Gadamer's *Truth and Method*, Blumenberg's *The Legitimacy of the Modern Age*, the works of Lévi-Strauss, Lacan, and Derrida, Ricoeur's attacks on them, most of Husserl, lots of Heidegger, and virtually all of Freud. It was like another education.

System-building philosophers proceed as if one's beliefs should be utterly consistent and logically integrated; I make do with a softer coherence. But a great deal of work, emotional as well as intellectual, was necessary to get this second education to feel at home with my first. James Earl, the Old English scholar at Virginia, made some of this labor coincident with building a friendship. On Thursday nights we would get together in each other's studies to discuss the new sorts of books we were reading and their application to literature, history, mythology—to everything under the sun. It says something about the Virginia English department of those years that its two most innovative thinkers were a Miltonist and a medievalist.

As I turned those dense pages, trying to figure out the debts and affinities, my intellectual life went into overdrive. No questions left me speechless. Around me unknown kingdoms shimmered, ready for conquest. One might hope to understand, not a specific literary work, but literature itself—language itself, mind itself, being and time and all that jazz.

Together with Joseph Smith, a Washington psychoanalyst, I began editing annual volumes for a series called Psychiatry and the Humanities. In these books, leading intellectuals of a Freudian bent would write on topics made fashionable by the Theory Explosion. Once a year we sponsored a lecture at the National Institute of Health given by the volume's main contributor. The appearance of Jacques Derrida, theory's brightest superstar, was a memorable occasion.

He had sent an advance text of his lecture. Joe and I figured that it would run about two hours, whereas our audience expected a lecture of half that length. It was decided that the text should be cut, and that I should be the one to work with Derrida in arriving at the pared-down American-sized lecture. The night before Derrida flew in from Paris, my wife dreamed of Jack the Ripper. This was taken as an ominous sign in our Freudian household: Jack was obviously Jacques, and Jacques was a ripper because he would have to cut his text. But what of me? Was I not to be a ripper as well? Over a congenial dinner, Derrida suggested that I come to his hotel room the following afternoon, the day of the lecture, and help him decide what to take out. Maybe the idea of murderous trespass in my wife's dream had seeded my mind with foreboding, but a steeliness in Derrida's smile as we made these arrangements sent tremors of anxiety through me. Yet everything went ahead smoothly the next afternoon. After several hours with Derrida, knocking the lecture into shape, I walked out of the elevator and into the lobby a relieved man with a full bladder. Standing in the men's room, I was thinking about what a successful afternoon it had been when I glanced down to see drops of blood falling into the water below from what appeared to be my penis. Jacques the Ripper had castrated me! As it turned out, I had somehow managed to cut my hand, perhaps on Derrida's text. In any case, I was not altogether surprised when, at the lecture that evening, Derrida read for two solid hours his text as originally composed. Nobody followed it.

The story suggests that theory and I were not getting along very well. It was fun to put favorite literary works under the lens of theory and see how they looked. It was fun to debate authorities on theory, fun to discuss whether various theories could be made compatible. All of us, it seemed at the time, could meet on the common ground of theory. The whole community of humanists was now talking to one another, transcending the provincialism of earlier intellectuals. Everything might be, in a favorite word of those early days, "rethought." We would expose the errors of our teachers, and pass on to our students an intellectual legacy better fortified against disillusionment.

But I was trained to be a scholar. Scholarship may arrive at grand generalizations, yet its methods are painstaking. One slowly builds a case. Evidence is beautiful, footnotes are beautiful. The speed possible in literary theory was both exciting and alarming to me. With Lacanian psychoanalysis in mind, one could zip into a poem, name the telling illustrations, play around with the jargon, and mount soaring conclusions about the "laws of desire" or the "exclusions of the imaginary." For me the sense of dizzying triumph was always threatened by the suspicion that it had been a lead pipe cinch. Nabokov, in a famous lecture, told students to caress the "divine details." Literary theory, for all its abstraction, was not above details, but far from caressing them, it wanted to manage them, transforming them straightaway into allegorical instances of its own ideas. The scholar in me wanted to slow down. Even as a theorist I was drawn to the work of the Christian philosopher Paul Ricoeur, whom others find slow, pedantic, and given to wooden dialectics. His work is all of that, but I think it was in some measure the pace that attracted me. Reading Ricoeur on phenomenology, structuralism, psychoanalysis, or religious symbolism, one at least had the sense that the matter under discussion had been carefully defined and weighed.

The violence of rapid and unending self-confirmation in literary theory was troublesome on other grounds. Theory's disposition toward literature was of course that of mastery. It was precisely in the mastery that its attraction lay. I was hardly immune to the pleasures of intellectual conquest, but I also wanted to be *inspired* by literature. A long time back I had hoped to be a writer, and in my undergraduate days took a number of courses in "creative writing." Perhaps their intellectual content was questionable. But it was suggested to us in these courses that the critic's primary disposition should be intuitive and unprogrammatic, not theoretical. That left its mark. I remember Wallace Stegner telling us a story about Ken Kesey, his most illustrious pupil. During an office conference, Stegner had informed Kesey that the concluding pages of his recent story were bogged down in wordy explicitness. Suddenly Kesey reached across the desk, seized the manuscript from Stegner's hand, and, clearly in a fit of high inspiration, struck out the last three pages, replacing them with a single new sentence: "My salvaged heart rang like a jackpot." Now, *that's* writing.

A theorist might offer a Freudian analysis of the elations of gambling, might compare this ecstasy to the chemical highs that the author is known to have cultivated, might expatiate on the semiotics of the slot machine, the modern imagery of fate, the Cartesian background of the idea that a heart is a machine, or whatever. But isn't the theorist in effect reproducing the earlier and inferior ending, the one deadened by exposition? For the goodness of the sentence is rooted in another kind of knowledge. You have to have been in a casino to know that ringing, and have to have been on a tight budget and a couple of hundred down to know that salvaging: The thrill of the sentence lies in offering us, imaginatively, just that jackpot. When I switched from writing fiction and poetry to writing literary criticism, I did not change my standards for good sentences. I still wanted to evoke the life in literary works and thereby, I suppose, testify to my own. Theory, by contrast, demanded (and got) impersonality. Mastery was won at the price of service to the system. It ran on willpower rather than sharp instincts. Its prose almost never hit the jackpot.

Imagine these objections to theory beginning as momentary doubts and tiny afterthoughts, then gradually, as the novelty wore off, taking center stage. One by one I lost my heroes in the theory movement. That was no small loss to me, for I have a history of hero worship. When I was in junior high school, the general awfulness of education dawned on me—those mindlessly repetitive homework assignments, those stupid tests, those empty A's doled out to the most obedient sheep, those honor roles and VIP societies. I loved to read, but in the classroom I was mostly surrounded by, in Milton's phrase, "readers of no empyreal conceit." I dealt with the scorn by finding superb teachers to idealize. As an undergraduate at Stanford, I came under the sway of Yvor Winters, a brilliantly eccentric poet and scholar. As a graduate student at Columbia, I was helped immensely by one of the finest and most honored teachers in America, Edward Tayler, who gave me perspective on Winters, liberated my sense of humor, and taught me a scholar's love for the past on its own terms. This defense mechanism serves me still: I need heroes as I need food. But I could not for long sustain my willingness to fall in step behind the new French celebrities.

Jacques Derrida, for one. Geoffrey Hartman wrote a book defending Derrida as a great writer the likes of James Joyce; Richard Rorty maintained that Derrida was not contributing to philosophy but, like a poet, giving us new metaphors (writing, mail, voice, presence) to try out. No one seemed willing to confess that the works of this Joycean logophile, this supposed poet, were dreadfully, awesomely overwritten, in a prose style so dedicated to self-awareness that reading it was like watching someone study his facial tics in a mirror. Derrida offered portentous generalizations about Western metaphysics that boiled down, in the end, to a particularly arduous variety of skepticism. Some of his most outlandish claims were laid to rest in John Ellis's devastating *Against Deconstruction*. Yet I suspect that the tiresome style is responsible for Derrida's having become, for today's critics, passé. A handful of his early essays are still *de rigueur*, but few contemporary theorists could tell you the titles of his last two books. Derrida was the quintessential phenomenon of the Theory Explosion—little known through direct contact, well known through handbook expositions.

Jacques Lacan, for another. I found some use in my own work for the psychoanalysis of Lacan. Today my allusions to him seem to me disposable: I took nothing from Lacan that I might not have taken from Freud. It was always my assumption that one could dig out the best ideas in Lacan and toss aside his arrogance and surreal pseudo-rigor. But it became increasingly clear that this lessened Lacan would not satisfy prominent exponents of his thought; they offered tortured apologies for the worst aspects of his work. One day in the early 1980s I realized that it was immoral to go on pretending that I thought he made sense, and I wrote an essay, "Terminating Lacan," to save graduate students from the time lost in trying to read him. Then there was Michel Foucault. I received no enlightenment whatsoever from the paranoid Foucault.

If Derrida, Lacan, and Foucault were of uncertain value, not even that could be said for the likes of Paul de Man. His former students at Yale gave him rave reviews, but this seemed to me a clear "you had to be there" case, and I hadn't been. On paper he looked to me, long before the revelations of his early fascist period, a second-rater, someone whose examples never quite meshed with his abstract contentions; I defy anyone to make good sense of his application of "metaphor" and "metonymy" to the bit of Proust discussed in his incoherent essay "Semiology and Rhetoric."

I kept hoping that a powerful American thinker would emerge from the Theory Explosion, but I could not bear the weak imitations produced by native disciples of the Parisian giants. Later on I would discover, with great pleasure and admiration, the work of the American philosopher Richard Rorty. But his mind was formed before the Theory Explosion. It seems true to me that there is not a single American intellectual of genuine stature whose mind was shaped by the ideas of this movement. We settled for derivative—and in a big way. Today I wonder if there is not a parallel between the American professoriate's eagerness to duplicate the work of others and the lack of creative direction in the American economy during the last twenty years.

From their beginnings in the Italian Renaissance, humanists have always been vulnerable to the occupational hazards of great vanity and its counterpart, an almost mysterious self-loathing. One of the attractions of teaching lies in its opportunities for adulation, the joys of being thought an authority; as for the self-loathing, one must pay a price for never having gotten out of school, and never being able, in an ordinary social situation with people from other walks of life, to explain or justify exactly what one does and why it should matter. (Outside the profession, adulation ceases pretty quickly.) Something in the new theories spoke to the latent grandiosity of the profession, perhaps their promise of a new cure for the self-loathing, and soon professional gatherings became platforms for preening know-it-alls. There were more gatherings than ever, as if professors had suddenly realized how much fun it was to sit in chairs all day long and listen to other professors revile previous generations of professors for their lack of theoretical sophistication. We had found our own version of the pleasures of the Rotary Club. The rhetoric of self-congratulation had never been exercized so unrelievedly in the university.

Ben Jonson spoke of the decadence of preferring words to matter: "You may sound these wits, and find the depth of them with your middle finger. They are *Creame-bowle*, or but puddle deep." Such were the wits, their superficiality masquerading as depth, that brought theory to every corner of the English department. Soon there was feminist theory, gay theory, gender theory, black theory, composition theory, narrative theory, postcolonial theory—all of it humorless, sexless, and without much feel for the reality of politics. In part because the new French masters were themselves breaking away from a generation of existentialists, most of the theorists detested individualism. Foucault did not even want to mention the names of the "authors" of the various tracts he distorted to reach resounding banalities about "classic" *mentalité*. Prose style, one of the mediums of individualism, went into decline. Although the philosophical concept of essence was ritually attacked, academic prose began to sprout poisonous blossoms like "narrativity" and "intertextuality." People got tenure for writing about the imperialist fantasies of Marvel Comics or the gender rules in Harlequin Romances—ideas that might have made decent articles for *High Times* but, driven by theory, got seriously out of hand. Instead of quick takes on ephemeral subjects, we wound up getting solemn treatises on the universe viewed from a trashy perspective. People who had never written anything of any interest about a literary work suddenly became renowned in the profession as authorites on theory or the history of literary study. The revelations of junior high had not prepared me for this sudden falling off in intellectual health.

Even in what resembled old-fashioned historical scholarship I began to notice that footnotes were thinning, that large assertions were being mounted on the basis of evidence as flimsy as an anecdote, that an ellipsis in quotations, indicating that something had been left out, had now to be checked out, because one could no longer suppose on the basis of professional courtesy that the quotation meant what it was characterized as having meant. Good scholarship and criticism continued to be written; fine courses were taught. A few good professors saw what was happening and spoke out against the theorists. But they were gentle souls, men and women whose knowledge came from an ability to lose themselves imaginatively in the massive entanglements of history. They had no will for a real fight, and their opposition was ineffective.

While I was reading difficult books, the new cream-bowl theorists, content with handbook-deep knowledge, went into serious professionalism, jerry-building "programs" and "concentrations" onto the traditional structure of academic majors, setting up "institutes" to secure their unearned self-importance, arranging conferences and starting journals. Graduate students were told that the profession was now the site of the Theory Explosion, and those who did not champion a theory, or at least show themselves "theory-literate," would not get jobs. One began to hear in tenure cases the argument that appearances at conferences and institutes should be counted as equivalent to publications. Professional dossiers swelled with lists of slide-show presentations, conferences organized, occasions where the visible young professor had served as "respondent" on panel discussions with titles like "Getting Licked: Lesbian Exchanges in the Mother Tongue." As in Borges's mordant fable of "Tlön, Uqbar, Orbis Tertius," a mad and minutely detailed counter-world had managed to displace reality.

For a time in the early 1980s Richard Rorty kept me on an even keel by supplying a practical American map to the madness. *Someone* had managed to go on making sense. What had

happened, he explained, was that philosophy—the Enlightenment queen of disciplines, once the arbiter of the ultimate sense
of other disciplines—was dying before our eyes. She had no
self-evident or logically necessary truths. There was nothing
left but to declare bankruptcy, go out of business, and turn to
"conversation." Philosophical texts naturally became the province of every intellectual. All of us could handle the sacred
documents of metaphysics; they had been democratized. The
notion that we professors were now having a "conversation"
in which no one possessed ultimate truth seemed ecumenical
enough, but also likely to turn, in hands less steady than those
of Rorty himself, into an exaltation of chitchat. Rorty also fore-
shadowed the most recent phase of the Theory Explosion by
showing that the only truths we do have to guide our behavior
are contingent products of history. And these are ultimately
political.

In a way, it was inevitable that the next phase of the Theory
Explosion would fasten onto the concept of ideology, since
what passed for theoretical knowledge was obviously no longer
disinterested or empirical. Major reputations had been staked
on the respectability of the new intellectual systems. It was no
longer (if it ever had been) a matter of theory's credibility.
Leading thinkers, who had begun as exponents of structuralism,
went on to newer concepts such as "aporia" and (today's magic
bullet) "power" without admitting that they had in earlier in-
carnations proven vulnerable to fad and mystification. The theorists were swimming in "ideology," not agreeing on what it
meant but agreeing to keep the disagreement under wraps for
a while. By the middle of the 1980s the whole enterprise had
turned into politics.

English professors still knew everything—where Kant went
wrong, why Freud misunderstood women, why encyclopedic
knowledge was the product of industrial capitalism. But now
all the answers to the questions were political. Marxism enjoyed
a resurgence. (Frank Lentricchia once suggested that the problem with Foucault is that he was mourning the death of liberalism; since liberalism is far from dead in the real world, I

suggest that a more serious problem in the profession today is an inability to mourn the death of communism.) Feminism, postcolonialism, and multiculturalism approached literature like brutal religious fundamentalisms, posing standardized questions in order to reach predictable answers. The categories of race, gender, and class became boring fixations.

Theorists maintained that the love of great literary works was a refuge for political conservatism. "What is so special about poetry and about lyric poetry in particular," wrote a famous Renaissance scholar, "that we should read it to the exclusion of other forms of discourse and with such minute attention to detail? What can it display about the seventeenth century that could not be better understood by reading Donne's letters to his friends, Thomas Hobbes's *Leviathan*, or the records of parliament of 1628–29?" Philistines could get just that proud. What used to be called "aesthetic experience" or "imaginative experience" was now declared to be an ideological delusion, meant to supply the imaginative aesthete with the false but no doubt comforting belief that he had escaped from politics. All knowledge, the theorists now revealed, is political—a way of claiming dominance, insinuating that someone else has no knowledge and is, because of this ignorance, inferior. The point of such ugly arguments, a pragmatist might say, is what they allow you to do: These made it seem appropriate at any time in any intellectual pursuit to change the subject to politics.

More locally, in the English department, the theorists in their political incarnation joined forces in urging the overthrow of the traditional "canon" of great literary works. These books should no longer be the objects of study in undergraduate majors and graduate training. We should instead teach books that were politically congenial, books by or about women, homosexuals, oppressed minorities, victims.

I should say immediately that I did not enter this profession to listen to the political opinions of my colleagues (I thought we might talk about books) and debate politics with them (I thought we might debate about books) in order to preserve the centrality of Western civilization in American education. I grew up middle class in Southern California. Politics? The best book I read as a teenager was less thrilling than coming off the lip of a good wave at Corona Del Mar. As a youth I had no idea—and I mean *not a clue*—that a judgment on the long process of my education would some day boil down in the minds of many professors to the character of my political opinions. In graduate school I participated in the infamous riots at Columbia University. (Whatever happened to that gym?) I went to all the Washington marches protesting the Vietnam War. I spent a summer in South Carolina teaching in the Head Start program. During these years the quarrels in my family took on a political form. But I never ceased to love great works of literature, and I never supposed for a moment that my contribution to understanding them would be political. The political attitudes I have developed in my lifetime lack the systematic and historical rigor found in the political circles of big cities, where the factions are many, their evolution complex, and memory is long, vendettas intricate. I like to think—though of course it is self-serving—that such political outlooks are mind games of a particularly demonic kind, able to bind an intellect once and for all. Politics that allow no concept of the apolitical are the worst kind.

But these are the politics of the academy today, hard-core politics, unwilling to let the attention of others wander beyond race, gender, and class. I should have seen from the beginning that many of the theorists hated literature. Attacks on the "elitist" idea that our profession should encourage the best criticism on the best books have made that hatred self-declared.

As a critic, I have always been drawn to major authors. I entered the profession to teach, study, and write about major authors. Milton is a discipline unto himself. Off-the-cuff opinions count for nothing in the minds of Miltonists. I think that literary interpretation makes sense only within the context of a tradition of commentary. The aim of it is to say something that, in view of this tradition, seems original, plausible, and interesting. My dissertation began in some intuitions about the importance of the role of prophet in Milton's works; by the time

I was done I had traced the idea of prophecy from the Bible and the Greeks, through the Middle Ages and the Renaissance, to Milton himself, who makes the story of this idea both surprising and coherent. Milton makes a lot of stories surprising and coherent: The history of English literature would be utterly different without him. When the Theory Explosion went into politics, I tuned out, wrote a book with my friend Gordon Braden about the period concept of the Renaissance, and undertook another project of reeducation, aiming to make myself a Shakespeare scholar. That is my response to theory at this point: to love literature and learning, with contempt for anything less.

Current attacks on the literary "canon"—an unfortunate word that evokes a list of books dropped from heaven above —suggest all sorts of good reasons for studying overlooked works by women, nonwhites, and postcolonial authors. The reasons do sound good to me, but I cannot overcome the heartfelt conviction that the educational program they support is a prescription for mediocrity. Nothing I have ever read or heard has made me doubt for a moment that the greatest figures in English literature are Chaucer, Shakespeare, Donne, Milton, Swift, Pope, Johnson, Austen, the Romantic poets, Dickens, Emerson, Melville, Whitman, and so on. Doing something like justice to some few of these writers is work enough for an English major. Really doing justice to one of them is work enough for a doctorate. But mine may be the first generation of American literary critics who are simply not up to the challenge and will prefer instead to spend their days in the sun finding principled reasons for resenting the fact that they should have been challenged in the first place.

The new decentered curriculum, which has infected even the elementary schools, would rather teach a little bit about a lot of things than go into depth about some few things. The result is that everything is reduced to political sermonettes about race, class, and gender that make contemporary people feel good, feel sympathetic and tolerant and superior to the evil past. *We* know that white settlers committed genocide on Native

Americans. But didn't the French send Indians to attack British colonists? *We* know that colonialism was a great evil. But what about all those hospitals and schools? *We* know that there is an inherent bond between capitalism and slavery. But didn't Adam Smith argue on purely economic grounds that slavery was the most expensive form of labor? *We* know that gender is socially constructed. But is there in fact no element of biology, of what Shakespeare would have called "nature," in gender? *We* know that Orientalism was an academic discipline expressing Western fear and loathing of an alien culture. But how much did Islamic scholars know about us? (Answer: next to nothing.) There's no time for the details and the nuances, because getting into them means tarrying with a subject, working past the easy attitudes and entering into long, disciplined arguments. It means not having educational time for all the other occasions for feel-good learning.

Attacks on the traditional curriculum confuse education with integration. America is of course a "culturally diverse" nation, and we need powerful antidotes to racism. But an undergraduate education that saddles students with "cultural diversity" requirements, encourages them to flit incoherently from this concentration to that program, and asks them to drift through the empty prescriptions of departmental majors, is not the answer. The new educational fundamentalisms treat representation in the curriculum as the symbolic equivalent of sharing in political power. At all levels of education in the humanities, we need the courage to say, "These are the best books. Our culture should be centered on them until better ones come along. You shall study them, and our degrees will certify that you have." It is argued that blacks perform poorly on SAT tests because they are "culturally biased." One can adduce a tradition in which testing has indeed been the vehicle of racial exclusion. But if the SAT tests are biased toward being able to read and draw logical inferences from fairly complex texts written in Standard English, then the bias is altogether appropriate. This is exactly what they are, and should be, testing. Black and Hispanic students must be taught the language of the British and American intelligentsia, since integration will never succeed on any other terms. Asian students, who might be thought to face a severer linguistic adjustment when learning Standard English, are the last to complain and the first to succeed. As I see it, liberal educators have become pathologically sensitive to complaints of ethnocentrism. Rather than elevating the minds of students from historically oppressed groups, the whole educational system is sinking. The decentered multicultural curriculum is just the particular way in which the upper tier of this system is now collapsing.

Such sentiments are not politically correct. In some universities I would be shouted down for giving voice to them. The media sometimes treats the atmosphere of "political correctness" on the American campus today as a joke, and it is funny to observe, for example, the neurotic shifts in preferred designations—not "blacks" anymore, but "African-Americans," and, doing away with hue altogether, the drab rainbow of "persons of color" rather than the once popular, now odious, "colored persons." But the everyday tolls of political correctness are, I assure you, quite wearisome. A friend of mine in the Business School recently drew stares of horrified disbelief from his colleagues when he confessed at lunch that he was in favor of capital punishment. Is this not a controversial issue? Is it incredible or appalling that someone in a university could hold the incorrect opinion? Well, one could get along without lunch with one's colleagues. The more alarming fact is that great literature is becoming unreadable in this climate of indulged offense-taking.

No doubt there are scandalous pages in most of our great English authors, pages that are deeply offensive by the standards of enlightened sensibility in contemporary America. Shakespeare's misogyny knows no bounds; Milton's hatred of Catholicism never ends. But these attitudes are part and parcel of visions of the world, ways of organizing Western traditions, that have no rivals in our language for amplitude and clarity, not to mention literary originality. To dismiss writers because their myths are not our myths is a sign of small-minded intolerance—a lack of faith in the historical imagination, and an act of insufferable condescension, as if we would tolerate all differences except the ones that might really matter. It is possible to treat the hatreds and self-deceptions of the past in sympathetic depth, as aspects of a larger vision, without taking any position whatsoever on contemporary political issues. In fact, that is how they should be studied.

But the idea that the young ought not to study these scandalous old masters, or be free not to study them, has at least the virtue of intellectual honesty. Defenders of the canon sometimes say that it is not the fact that particular books are taught, but how they are taught. I fear that they are right. The deliberate misinterpretation of past literature to make it palatable to politically correct stomachs has to be among the worst of our academic sins. *Henry V* is not a patriotic masterpiece about a warrior-priest-king who reverses the Norman Conquest; it is an ironic exposure of the mystifying ideologies of monarchical power. *The Tempest* is not the story of Prospero putting forgiveness above revenge, abjuring his rough magic, and handing the world over to the next generation; it is the story of Caliban, victim of colonial oppression. Such interpretations are offered in the name of "revisionist" history, but in fact deny history and project our own smug correctness on the face of the past. Last year I heard a prominent scholar lecture on the value of the computer. Shakespeare's comedy *The Taming of the Shrew* was, she declared, deeply offensive. No problem: An inferior but politically correct version of the play already exists; it is not by Shakespeare, of course, but having his and related works on a computer disk allows you to produce designer versions of the plays, and with a single keystroke the feel-good *Shrew* can forever supplant the troubling *Shrew*. O brave new world, that has such scholars in it!

I believe that I have experienced a fuller range of American English departments than other contributors to this book. As a teacher, I went from the University of Virginia to the University of Maryland, and from there to the University of Massachusetts. I have also taught at Middlebury College and for a semester at Johns Hopkins. In deliberations about hiring and tenure, the professors of Charlottesville never discussed a candidate's politics. We spoke instead of "quality of mind" and "intellectual distinction." Often this language masked vicious and asocial passions, a hidden world of rivalrous vanity. But it did allow us, sometimes, to assess the intellectual abilities of our personnel. At other schools, I have learned, "quality of mind" language counts for nothing. When it comes to professional judgments on tenure, few people care to render an honest opinion of what the Assistant Professor thinks, writes, or teaches. If the candidate belongs to a particular category—is female, third world, or Marxist—he is automatically supported by an alliance of newly arrived theorists. At some point in the process quality of mind must be invoked, yet only because convention still demands that professional judgments appear to be apolitical. It seems to me a sad state of affairs when the language of intellectual merit has become a species of disinformation.

I expect that most of the other contributors to this book feel that recent attacks on the humanities are misguided. Our media critics have mistaken for decadence a golden age of intellectual pluralism, bursting with fresh ideas and utopian visions. For what it's worth, I thought Roger Kimball's *Tenured Radicals* a prim and undiscerning performance; I doubt whether there is a meaningful correlation between positions taken twenty-five years ago on the Vietnam War and the current politics of literary theory. On the other hand, I thought David Lehman's *Signs of the Times* did a pretty good job on Paul de Man and his apologists, who certainly had it coming. Generally speaking, I welcome the attention. Maybe such books are being read by parents who must refinance their homes and go into debt to send their kids to college. If so, this audience has every right to hear about some of the high-powered foolishness to which their children may be exposed. There is certainly a lot of political teaching going down. This semester, walking a hallowed hall, I heard from behind a closed office door a professor browbeating a student at the top of his lungs: "Where do you think the homeless go when the shelter is closed!" The hectored student probably thought it was going to be a course in composition.

For the time being, my love of literature and learning, with contempt for anything less, is out of fashion. The humanities temporarily belong, in the phrase of Harold Bloom, to "a pride of displaced social workers." But I'll be back with students at my side. Quality will out. Great literature, I guarantee, will one day bury theory, and its scandals will outlive all the political correctness in this confused world. Imagination, which had the first word, will have the last.

DISCIPLINE
AND
THEORY

*Michael
Bérubé*

Michael Bérubé's rebuttals to Kimball, D'Souza, and Company, published in the Village Voice *and the* Yale Journal of Criticism, *have helped to establish him as a leading young critic (he recently turned thirty-one). His first book, an original study of the hows and whys of academic canonization, focuses on Pynchon and the African-American writer Melvin Tolson.* Marginal Forces/Cultural Centers *came out from Cornell in 1992. Bérubé holds a B.A. from Columbia and a Ph.D. from Virginia; he teaches English and cultural studies at the University of Illinois at Urbana-Champaign.*

Scorn the sort now growing up
All out of shape from toe to top.
                              —W. B. Yeats,
                          "Under Ben Bulben"

IT'S A BEASTLY ROUGH CROWD I RUN WITH. No doubt about it, junior faculty are getting out of shape and out of hand. "The grimmest and most orthodox partisans of 'political correctness,' " writes Louis Menand in *The New Yorker*, "are junior professors, most of whom are under forty and many of whom are under thirty." Mind you, this line doesn't come from George Will or Lynne Cheney, or any of the usual suspects who routinely accuse us of being gleeful nihilists and/or humorless ideologues; it comes from the pen of a fellow English professor, a guy who's been one of the sharpest *critics* of Dinesh D'Souza, Roger Kimball, and the rest of the purveyors of PC polemics. Even to the enemy of our enemies, it seems, we look something like a cross between Johnny Rotten and Cotton Mather: Just take the Sex Pistols' political tact and respect for authority, toss in the Puritans' good cheer and sense of rhythm, and presto, you've got Rotten Mather, assistant professor of English, thirty years old and not to be trusted.

How did I let myself in for this? I'm not sure. Applying to graduate school in English, ten years ago, was as much the result of a process of elimination as of a positive decision: I had already worked in journalism and advertising during college, and I didn't much like what I'd seen. Law paid notoriously well, but I knew from proofreading and word processing at one of the country's largest law firms that law generally isn't much fun to read or write. Besides, it was 1981, the lawyer glut was upon us, and the competition promised to be intense and nasty. I didn't think resignation or ambivalence would get me very far.

Among these options, then, I supposed that graduate school in English would surely be the most intellectually fulfilling way to spend my early twenties—and late twenties, too, since most graduate students keep being graduate students for the better part of a decade. But I didn't know that then; actually, I didn't have any specific idea of what graduate school would entail or how long it would entail it for. All I knew for sure was that I would be taking a vow of poverty for an indeterminate period of time, and that it wouldn't make much sense to defray tuition by taking out more loans. In 1981 assistant professors were making about $17,000; those were the lucky ones, the ones who got jobs. And since I'd spent most of my undergraduate career learning to play drums, I didn't think I'd earned myself a realistic shot at fellowship support. All the schools I applied to agreed.

The way I figured it, either I would earn a fellowship later on or I'd leave the academic life after a year of graduate school, twenty-two years old and still less than $10,000 in debt. Attracted as I was to a life of teaching and learning, I had no silly idea that the professoriat (if and when I ever entered it) would look like an endless *Times Book Review* symposium, full of tweedy people sitting around the faculty lounge jawing about the Joyce centennial. I'd had the benefit of watching my father go from being a researcher and policy analyst to being a professor of education; and consequently, I'd had the benefit of watching him fall under Abe Beame's budget ax in 1975, when New York City pruned itself of nonessential personnel like college teachers. So I knew fairly well what it was like to grade papers, sit on faculty committees, negotiate with deans, and look for academic employment at a moment's notice, but I knew comparatively little about the world of literary criticism and interpretive theory.

For most twenty-year-old aspiring textmongers, "criticism"

means things like book and movie reviews. My guess is that that's what "criticism" means to much of the rest of the culture, too: Even though both my parents have written plenty of book reviews, they had no idea what professional literary criticism looked like. Once when my father and I were discussing my plans, he told me I'd better begin thinking about a dissertation *now* (rather than, say, next week), and he asked me whom I intended to do. I had not thought I'd have to *do* somebody, but I said "Faulkner" anyway. My father shook his head. "Faulkner's been done. Who else were you thinking of?"

My father, it turned out, imagined that the culmination of one's graduate work in literature would naturally be the writing of a critical biography. But what else would he think? He reads the general intellectual journals most often read by general intellectuals, chiefly the *Times Book Review* and the *New York Review of Books*, and like a lot of literate nonspecialists, he'd considered critical biographies the predominant scholarly form of criticism, more arduous and painstaking than movie and book reviews, necessary foundations for further "interpretive" work. Even today, in fact, my parents can read the *Times Book Review* and come away believing that not much has changed in the small world of professional litcrit, as if critical biographies remain the only academic-press books of general interest to the literate public.

As for me, I knew even then that there was more to academic life than the writing of critical biographies; I assumed that the business of criticism was interpretation, and that critics spent their time arguing one interpretation over another—that is, when they weren't grading papers, sitting on faculty committees, negotiating with deans, or looking for academic employment. I had, for example, heard of Roland Barthes. But I had no clear idea that Barthes wasn't really a "critic" like, say, Edmund Wilson or the *Times*'s Christopher Lehmann-Haupt, and that his *S/Z* isn't an "interpretation" of Balzac's short story "Sarrasine," but a "rewriting" (brilliant, maddening, and immensely fascinating) of realist narrative in terms of the plurality and reversability of its "codes." I read *S/Z* in graduate school, of course. But not right away: Well into my third semester of graduate study in 1984, I was still wandering around randomly, churning out interpretations on demand. When one of my younger professors praised my reading of narrative ruptures of "desire" in William Thackeray's *History of Henry Esmond* by saying I had read the novel as a profoundly self-contradictory text without falling into the usual deconstructionist traps, I appeared at her office within twenty-four hours, wanting to know *what* deconstructionist traps I had avoided and how I'd avoided them. I felt rather like Chance the Gardener, and not for the last time.

What I was ignorant of, in short, was literary theory—the bodies of diverse, interdisciplinary writing that generate not interpretations but interpretive modes. Yes, I'd heard of things like Marxism, feminism, and psychoanalysis, but I hadn't yet seen them at work *as interpretive theories*. When it came to reception theory, structuralism, hermeneutics, reader-response criticism, New Historicism, deconstruction, and the like, I was just about as much at sea as anyone.

Why rehearse my ignorance at such length today? I can think of three immediately pressing reasons.

First, fear of "literary theory" continues to provoke the most hysterical and embarrassing outbursts, both in the profession and outside it. Peter Shaw, for instance—one of Lynne Cheney's recent appointees to the National Council on the Humanities —has actually written in a recent *Chronicle of Higher Education* that " 'theory' of any kind is at present a code word for the politicization of literature." Nor is Shaw alone; indeed, public professions of such Know-Nothing credos—whereby ignorance of theory represents itself as a form of moral probity— are becoming more commonplace with each passing day.

Second, the foes of theory tend to portray themselves either as lonely keepers of the flame beset by hordes of swarming thought police, or as friends of the common reading man who can't be bothered with impenetrable French neologisms or radical-lesbian-feminist-extremist cant: "We just love literature," they say, "and we don't want to ruin it by thinking about it too much, like all those *theoreticians* with their *slide rules* and *hidden agendas*, who twist *our books* to fit *their schemes.*" (It happens, by the way, that many of these folks love literature only so long as it allows them to believe in the characters or the images, and only if it doesn't get too silly or experimental. But this is a fine point.)

Third, graduate school in English seems to have a very bad effect on people who don't like theory. One prominent ex–graduate student left Yale and became managing editor of *The New Criterion*, where he's been sniping at academics ever since, most notably in *Tenured Radicals*, a book about tenured radicals; another picked up a Columbia Ph.D. but was scarred by a postdoc year of exposure to deconstruction at Cornell and has spent the past few years writing poetry and a book called *Signs of the Times*, whereby he's tried to bury deconstruction once and for all; and every so often the profession of literary studies manages to alienate a few of its would-be apprentices, and students sign off, telling anyone who'll listen that they just love literature, but they can't put up with all that theoretical gobbledygook and poststructuralist shilly-shallying, not to mention the slide rules and the hidden agendas. Actually, considering how poorly most graduate students get paid for the amount of teaching they do, it's a wonder the humanities haven't produced many thousands of jaundiced, embittered ex–graduate students by now, "theory" or no "theory."

What with reasons like these, it's become something of an article of faith among the Lovers of Literature that today's graduate students don't read literature anymore—just a little Barthes here, a little Foucault there, some Derrida now and then, and a smattering of post-crypto-neo-Marxists; no Lawrence, no Dickens, no Spenser, no Pope. It's even been said that some of these brave new students don't *care about* literature at all; no, they don't care about fine writing of any kind—that's why they're reading that theory gunk instead.

Well, I went to graduate school in English in the 1980s; I swam, I hiked, I encountered interpretive theory for the first time. And so far as I can tell, I *still* love that literature, I think.

But then again, I always did like the playful, labyrinthine stuff anyway, the kind of writing that's always already chock full o' theory, Beckett and Borges and Joyce and Gide and Sterne and Spenser. So maybe you shouldn't go by me.

Yet surely it's as anti-intellectual to embrace all of "theory" indiscriminately as it is to dismiss it all out of hand; after all, the many varieties of contemporary literary theory have numerous opponents who are themselves contemporary theorists. As Henry Louis Gates has written, "To become aware of contemporary theory is to become aware of one's presuppositions, those ideological and aesthetic assumptions which we bring to a text unwittingly." Likewise, to be engaged by "theory," I think, is largely to be engaged by *conflict among* theories, and that's one reason why debates in the humanities are so hard to keep track of. It's also why I find it hard to think of my own theoretical training as some sort of conversion experience. I do, however, recall my most pronounced resistances: I was especially skeptical about psychoanalysis, reader-response criticism, and deconstruction. Psychoanalysis, because I was leery of its claims to interpretive certainty; reader-response, because I didn't think it was possible or useful to talk about "what happens" when readers read; deconstruction, because I didn't care for the way it represented itself by insisting that it could not be represented, that it was always someplace else. Once I finally found my way around deconstruction's enumerations of "conditions of impossibility," though, I found myself engrossed and energized by the ways it interrogates "representation"—in narrative, in literary canons, and in political or pedagogical practice.

Not everyone has the necessary patience (or time) for such things. Certainly I can't deny that academic literary criticism and theory generally presume an intimate acquaintance with academic literary criticism and theory, and I can't deny that theory's surface noise can be distracting, or worse; people who complain that theoretical work is opaque to "general readers" aren't necessarily lazy readers. But then again, opacity is in the eye of the beholder. Many professors in the humanities these days are working on projects that bridge disciplinary boundaries, and it's quite ordinary to find "English" professors conversant in branches of anthropology, sociology, history, philosophy, linguistics, psychology, law, and political science. The same opaque "critical jargon" that doesn't seem to speak to "general readers," therefore, may also be the only critical language that can speak across a spectrum of disciplines to scholars in the social sciences as well as the humanities.

My first theoretical work wasn't all that interdisciplinary; it had to do with narratologists, people like Tzvetan Todorov, Gerard Genette, and Roland Barthes. At the time this seemed a natural extension of my fascination with James Joyce: Joyce's narratives reproduce the minutiae of mental events, and Genette reproduces the minutiae of Proustian narrative; Joyce's texts flaunt their own artifice and their infinite capacity for formal elaboration, and Barthes's texts recast criticism as a creative enterprise with infinite capacities for formal elaboration. Forbidding modernist narratives, whether Joyce's or anyone else's, simply *are* narratological. And though narratology can surely be one of the most arcane and jargon-ridden branches of interpretive theory, it did impress upon me, in meticulous and admirable detail, the conviction that storytelling is one of the most complex and significant forms of human behavior, too complex to be dealt with in catchall terms like "point of view" or "third-person narration."

Still, not until I read Mikhail Bakhtin's *The Dialogic Imagination*, particularly the very long final essay, "Discourse in the Novel," did I have any sense of what the larger purpose of careful narrative analysis might be. For in Bakhtin's model, narrative isn't a question of how much a narrator "knows" or who sees what from what "point of view"; Bakhtin starts, instead, from the position that language is a profoundly social phenomenon, that our social lives are composed of myriad, competing dialects and idiolects, and that a language's or a word's meaning is radically dependent on its social context and social use—and not on a presumedly straightforward relation between "words" and "reality." From this position, it follows for Bakhtin that the novel is the most capacious, the most fluid of literary genres, because it can re-present so many different subgenres and social idiolects, dramatizing their conflicts and their concordances. Novels, according to Bakhtin, aren't privileged sites of narrative "realism" so much as language labs in which various "sociolinguistic points of view" get stirred together into a polyphonic chorus that he calls "heteroglossia."

For me, Bakhtin's work was positively liberating, in two important ways: First, because he defined the novel—a genre notoriously resistant to "definition"—not in terms of the elements all novels have in common (for there are no such common elements), but in terms of the novel's linguistic voraciousness, its very willingness to "raid" other, more stable genres in the process of composing new and complex multigeneric molecules. This crucial insight that "definition" need not hinge on the assertion of a form's "essential" characteristics is what led me, eventually, to read Ludwig Wittgenstein's *Philosophical Investigations*, and to espouse the Wittgensteinian position that genera of objects—novels, games, nations, races, genders, classes, tables, chairs—are constituted by "family resemblances" rather than by their common "essences." Wittgenstein's analogy is this: Think of a cord of many overlapping fibers in which no one fiber runs the whole length of the cord. Now think of objects many of which have a number of significant features in common, but not all of which possess all the "significant features" under discussion. That's more or less what "family resemblances" look like in Wittgenstein's family.

My second Bakhtinian liberation was this: Bakhtin's emphasis on narrative *discourse* (as distinct from narrative epistemology) manages to combine narratology's emphasis on narrative minutiae with a sophisticated account of the social contexts in which different forms of language operate. According to Bakhtin, then, the same word—oh, let's take a good one, like *liberty*—gets rearticulated, refashioned, and redefined by diverse social groups, and these groups' struggles over the meaning of words (think of "peace through strength") consti-

tute the social life of narrative forms. This position, too, I
wound up glossing by means of Wittgenstein, who maintains
that "the meaning of a word is its use in the language." Sounds
commonsensical enough—until you realize how thoroughly
anti-Platonic a position it is, how much it goes against our sense
that words *refer to* something. But what do words like *however*
and *actually* refer to? And why do we think we can look up
words' meanings on a reference table, absent the social context
in which they are used? As for words like *table*, which are, as
we know, less subject to social contestation than words like
terrorist, their meaning too resides in their use in the language,
not in any linguistic essence; it's just that most people tend not
to see any need to argue about their use.

In a word, then, upon reading Bakhtin and Wittgenstein I
became an anti-essentialist, and to this day, sure enough, there's
a little anti-essentialism in everything I do. In my next close
encounter of the mid-1980s, I came up against Thomas Kuhn's
Structure of Scientific Revolutions, and took a seminar on Martin
Heidegger with Richard Rorty, and from that point on I've
been an "antifoundationalist" as well. For thanks to Kuhn's
refusal to believe that science "progresses" in some linear, in-
cremental way, and Rorty's refusal to believe that philosophy
is the "foundation" of human knowledge, I've come to believe
and argue that our social practices and identities are "contingent" rather than "grounded"—that there are no final, universal, transhistorical standards for the production or value of
human knowledge and understanding.

It's been a mild shock to me to discover how disturbing this
position is to many traditionalists in the humanities. Scientists,
by contrast, seem largely untroubled by it; Kuhn himself draws
most of his examples from the "foundational" sciences of chem-
istry and physics, both of which have taken stock of Kuhn's
account of "normal science" and have kept right on conducting
normal science as Kuhn understands it. Fairly recently, in the
fall of 1991, I presented the case for antifoundationalism at an
interdisciplinary conference at which I was asked to speak about
"new directions in knowledge" in my field; I talked mostly

about the effects of "theory" on the way we do literary history, and along the way, I invoked the names of Kuhn and Wittgenstein, and Michel Foucault, too. To my surprise, I was met with questions from physicists and psychologists who demanded to know what was so "new" about the propositions that humans perceive things through interpretive paradigms and that human knowledge, like all things human, is historically conditioned and socially constructed. Why, I was asked, would anyone disagree with such things? I had to admit I didn't really know: It all made sense to *me*, once I became acquainted with the relevant arguments. It seems, I said, that physicists and mathematicians are unthreatened by ideas like "indeterminacy," but that some of us in the humanities cannot contemplate the notion that *meaning* is indeterminate without declaring that the sky is falling; and many cognitive psychologists work well with the assumption that all perception is a form of interpretation, whereas in some "traditionalist" circles, you still can't say such a thing about literary texts without being accused of some horrid thing like moral relativism.

Stanley Fish, for example, has gotten a good deal of grief for arguing that "there is no such thing as intrinsic merit." Fish is adept at concocting such memorable, provocative formulae, and accordingly, he's been subjected to the kind of media treatment usually reserved for Afrocentrists and day-care Satanists. In this case, however, he's merely saying that nothing just *has* merit in and of itself—things have only the merit that we ascribe to them. People like Dinesh D'Souza have claimed that Fish's position undermines all possibility for ethical judgment; but my guess is that stamp collectors, spin doctors, stockbrokers, writers, and other working folk won't be too surprised or upset by the suggestion that "merit" and "value" are human inventions.

In other words, antifoundationalism is not a relativism; it doesn't say that every interpretation, every historical epoch, every value system or every form of government is "equal." On the contrary, it says we don't have access to the kind of historical omniscience that would enable us to equalize or rank everything in the first place. We can look back and say we're grateful that we now conduct trials by jury instead of trials by ordeal, but we shouldn't conclude from this that our current beliefs are the culmination and fulfillment of all human history. As Kuhn concludes, we may have evolved away from certain beliefs and practices (like geocentrism or witch burning), but we're not necessarily evolving *toward* anything in particular; there's no "goal" to human history, no secure and self-evident criterion for the human understanding of notions like *gravity, matter, liberty,* or *justice.* Even when it comes to things that pre-exist humans, like gravity and matter, the point remains that humans in every epoch have interrogated those things as they knew best: Aristotle's or Thales's understanding of "matter" isn't as comprehensive as ours, but it isn't quantifiably "less scientific," either. It proceeded from utterly different assumptions about what science is, assumptions that themselves were part of a worldview every bit as complete and internally coherent as our own (though not as good, in retrospect, at understanding the things it did not have the means to conceive of, like heat transfer or unstable isotopes).

Does antifoundationalism imply that "the history of Western civilization" (whatever that phrase means to you) is nothing more than a series of choices, and not the slow triumphant march of eternal, universal virtues such as democracy and individualism? Yep, it sure does. It implies that *all* histories—literary histories, too—are profoundly up for grabs and always have been, having been made by humans in social contexts, making human and social choices. It insists that there's no sense in which all of Western culture was always somehow slouching from the *agora* in Athens (or from the banks of the Nile, or the Tigris) toward the United States, no sense in which our current forms of life were foreordained by heavenly or historical forces. But foundationalism makes strange bedfellows, as they say, and it's probably fitting, though of course not inevitable, that today's strongest "foundationalists" would be religious fundamentalists, unreconstructed Brezhnev-era Marxists, right-wing libertarians, and traditionalists in the humanities.

Bakhtin, Wittgenstein, and Kuhn weren't the last writers to

influence the way I think about language, life, and literature, but they've more or less set the terms on which I now read theorists who differ from them. The little Foucault I know, for instance, is the Foucault of *The Archaeology of Knowledge*, who examines what he calls "discursive formations"—involving the hierarchies within which different sorts of knowledge are ordered, by the various institutional sites within which discursive "authority" has historically been constructed. Or, reading Derrida by way of Wittgenstein, I'm engaged most by things like "Signature Event Context," in which Derrida takes on speech-act theorist J. L. Austin, whose theory of "performative utterance" is itself a powerful exception to most Western thinking about language. Some sentences, says Austin, don't "describe" things at all; they perform them. (Think of "I now pronounce you husband and wife.") And, in their repeatability (or "iterability"), they demonstrate vividly, for Derrida, how *all* utterances are radically dependent on contexts: Thus "meaning" is never synonymous with or reducible to "intention." To make this point to undergraduates, ask them how they know what stop signs "mean." Then ask what kinds of "intention" we normally assume to be indispensable to "meaning," and what kinds of "intention" we normally assume are irrelevant to it. Then ask when and why we assume these things about stop signs, poems, or signatures. When you've done all this, you've earned your keep, and you can go collect your paycheck—whether or not its signatory "intended" to pay you.

The more practiced you become at "doing" theory, the more theory informs your practice. And by the spring of 1986, I had some practical matters on my mind. In April, my wife, Janet Lyon, had our first child, Nicholas; and because Janet was also a graduate student—worse yet, a graduate student about to take her Ph.D. qualifying oral exams—I wound up being a full-time house-husband. However generally sympathetic I'd been to feminism up to that point, it really wasn't until I cared for an infant that I began to see what feminism had to do with the smallest details of my daily life. (I'm always amused at the claim that feminism is bad for the family; I find it hard to believe my family would be better off if I left all the material child care to Janet, contenting myself with the dispensation of money, justice, and sound moral observations.) I thought I knew something about the worlds of women and children—but as Bakhtin would say, I had to hear the *sound*, the *language* of that world before it could be my world, too. In daytime TV, in the ads in *Parents* magazine, in the "children's" aisles of major supermarkets—the gendering of child care became palpable to me, and not because I was especially sensitive; only because I was a graduate student, and didn't have a day job . . . and, most of all, I was the wrong gender. No one knows or cares what lousy brand of peanut butter choosy fathers choose.

I'm not sure when it was, precisely, that I began to see "gendering" everywhere I looked; maybe it was the day I had to take my four-month-old from the supermarket to the "home-improvement center" (lumberyard), and realized that the latter had shopping carts with no child seats. Or maybe it was the day I realized that I wasn't one of the men I saw in floor-cleaner ads, because unlike them I *knew* the floor wasn't wet— just shiny, thanks to my application of amazing Miracle Wax. No matter. What matters to me now is that I learned to read supermarkets, child care, and advertising anew, and I didn't (and don't) see any substantive difference between my interpretations of such "social texts" and my interpretations of "literary" texts. On the contrary, the analytical tools I'd honed in the academy sharpened and gave point to my reading of the semiotics of supermarkets—and vice versa.

I don't mean to suggest that I suddenly became Feminist Man because my working wife had to take a test and left me with the kid. For that matter, I don't consider feminism a chart that men can consult to find out how feminist they were today. Personally, I'm most at home with poststructuralist feminisms that contest the very idea of "Woman" while acknowledging that the category "Woman" is constitutive of patriarchy (that is, that patriarchy will oppress women, as a category, regardless of the internal differences among women, as social subjects). I am least at home with some feminists' sense that male feminism is a form of cross-dressing, ventriloquism, impersonation—or, at worst, a false embrace, a co-optive enterprise that seeks to establish what media theorist Tania Modleski calls "feminism without women." I tend to believe, instead, that male feminism is what happens when feminism begins to persuade nonfeminists of the urgency and substance of its ethical claims. Perhaps predictably, I take most to feminisms that interrogate all forms of gendering, all manifestations of differences between and within categories of subjectivity and sexuality. But what else would you expect from a fledgling Wittgensteinian with an infant on his arm?

And then, the week before Nicholas was born, I had to come up with a presentation in my graduate seminar in the American long poem—a presentation on Melvin Tolson's magnum opus, *Harlem Gallery: Book I, The Curator*, published a year before his death in 1966. The poem *is* magnum: 170 pages long, and much of it's about as dense and clotted as anything you'd expect to see from Ezra Pound or Hart Crane. I didn't understand *Harlem Gallery* then, and I didn't understand it six or eight months later, either, what with all that daytime TV monopolizing my interpretive frequencies. But I was flabbergasted by it nonetheless, and flabbergasted that no one I knew, save for Charles Rowell and Raymond Nelson among the Virginia faculty, had ever heard of it; flabbergasted to find no mention of Tolson whatsoever in literary histories, in "American" anthologies, in collections on modernism this and modernism that. (He can, however, be found in the comprehensive African-American anthology—a genre that flourished from 1965 to 1975 and has been moribund ever since.) I kept at the poem, and the poem continued to unknot itself, and almost before I knew it, I was consumed not only by the poem and its enigmatic author but by the question of how all literary works are read, understood, misunderstood, neglected, canonized, and culturally transmitted.

Just as it took Nicholas to bring feminism home to me, it

took Melvin Tolson, at last, to make "canonicity" and "neglect" visible to me. And between feminism and Tolson, I began to take more seriously revisionists' claims that the profession of English literature had been working for some time with a severely impoverished idea of its potential materials for study. I had been mildly suspicious of "canons" as an undergraduate, but only in the sense that I'd wondered vaguely about all the stuff one never reads or hears of in survey courses; each survey came to me with the implicit message that the selection process was done with, the works on the syllabus had been weighed in time's scales and found to be great, and the only business left at hand was for us to discover more and more ways in which these great works were indeed great works, great enough to be texts in core curricula. In fact, having met my "distribution" and "coverage" requirements a few times over, in college and in graduate school, I'd thought I was as cored as they come. Now here I was confronted with Tolson and, simultaneously, with the challenge of composing my own "canon," in the form of readings for my orals in twentieth-century literature (all of it). My preliminary conclusion, from which I have not yet backed off, is that when we talk about "periods" in literary history, we confront the vastest reaches of our ignorance. All I'd been taught about modernism, it seemed—and all I'd been taught about "American literature"—rested on the claims of about a dozen or so "representative" texts, and I had taken their "representativity" more or less for granted. Now, I would have to go back over all the literary history that wasn't in my synoptic literary histories, and this time I'd start with African-American poetry and fiction.

I wound up writing a somewhat long dissertation, half on Tolson and his neglect, half on the academic reception of the work of Thomas Pynchon, and over the course of five years the thing became my first book, *Marginal Forces/Cultural Centers.* The purpose of the study wasn't to find putatively "hidden" biases in canon formation by juxtaposing one neglected black poet and one newly canonical white novelist. Instead, I wanted to examine the terms under which disparately "marginal" writers become available for institutional attention, and the ways "gatekeeping" literary critics decide that certain writers aren't worth our further institutional attention. I found it quite interesting that Tolson went to extraordinary lengths to get the attention of the conservative white literati of his time (such as Allen Tate), and that Pynchon is so averse to publicity and criticism as to prohibit his publisher from publishing books about his work; but I found it much more interesting to examine what Tolson and Pynchon suggest to academic literary critics about their own roles as agents of cultural reproduction.

To many prominent Pynchon critics, academic literary criticism appears to be a gravely suspect enterprise, the central means whereby the "avant-garde" gets appropriated and co-opted into the mainstream; to the few Tolson critics in the country, academic criticism seems to be the guarantor of last resort, the only potential audience for otherwise "neglected" writers, and the only potential economic means for keeping marginal writers in print. Needless to say, Tolson and Pynchon gave me different takes on "race" in recent American literature, and differing perspectives on what constitutes academic "co-optation." And the further along I got, the more it became evident to me that canonicity and neglect were themselves historically specific phenomena involving variable margins and centers. It's been said that writing reception history modifies or undermines "traditional" literary history, and to a large extent that's so; but writing a history of *neglect* forced me to ask what kind of reading practices we consider to be part of a text's "reception" in the first place.

My long engagement with Melvin Tolson, then, served in part to lead me to re-examine my chosen profession, its politics, its social functions, its canons, and its relation to the nonacademic literary culture around it. And though I came up with an almost unteachable book—I can't imagine a seminar devoted exclusively to Tolson, Pynchon, and the practices of professional literary criticism—I've managed to spin the book into a variety of courses (thankfully, I teach in a department that gives me great latitude in course design and teaching assignments): a graduate seminar on reception theory; a course in twentieth-century African-American narrative; an "honors" course in postmodernism, critical theory, and recent American fiction; and a course I'm winding up as I write, a graduate seminar on recent African-American literature and literary theory.

In this seminar we've gone from the late Addison Gayle's 1971 anthology, *The Black Aesthetic*, to poststructuralists such as Houston Baker and Hazel Carby, by way of poets and novelists like Michael Harper, Audre Lorde, Toni Morrison, and Trey Ellis. Funny thing is, though, that fourteen of my fifteen students are white, and you can bet that whiteness (theirs and their instructor's) has been among our topics of interrogation in the past few months. This is all to the good in many ways, since most white Americans don't often see themselves as having the attribute of "race," any more than most men see themselves as being "gendered": Gender and race are usually O.P.P., other people's problems (and therefore, say the traditionalists, "divisive" things to talk about). But it makes my white students anxious all the same, especially when they wonder about whether they have the requisite cultural purchase on African-American literature and culture. In the past few decades, African-American literature has not lacked brilliant white critics, such as Kimberly Benston, Barbara Johnson, Eric Lott, and Robert Hemenway; regardless of the scope of one's brilliance, however, one can't very well be a white critic of African-American literature without reflecting on the political, historical, and institutional conditions of one's existence, and the sources of one's cultural "authority." That my own course is predicated explicitly on the aftermath of the civil rights movement makes my imperative to institutional self-scrutiny all the more urgent in this regard, since one of the legacies of the movement was the creation of courses in African-American literature in "mainstream" American universities, like Illinois.

To put this another way, I might point out how dangerous it is for white folks to assume that African-American literature is the sole province of African-American critics. For one thing, this assumption does no favors to the African-American critic who wants to specialize in Romanticism. And for another thing, even black African-Americanists don't have unmediated access to African-American texts simply because they're black; my access to such texts is thoroughly mediated, too, but here we're talking about differences of degree and not differences in kind. Well-meaning white critics may claim not to "know enough" about "the black experience" to teach African-American stuff, but I know full well that I never allowed my distance from turn-of-the-century Irish culture to prevent me from writing about Joyce and Yeats. My students, reflecting on their own institutional conditions daily if not hourly, ask whether they can "speak for" African-American writers and theorists; I tell them that if they become academic critics they'll be "speaking for" writers and texts whether they want to or not. Those writers and texts won't always be flaunting their skin colors for all to see, and as critics they'll be speaking for them anyway; besides, one does not inquire about "race" only when one is teaching a "nonwhite" text.

Still, it's impossible to broach this discussion without noting the dearth of African-American graduate students in literary study. Ninety years ago, in *The Souls of Black Folk*, W. E. B. Du Bois replied to Booker T. Washington's disparagement of liberal arts education in black colleges by arguing that the supply of black teachers *of any kind* would rely on the presence of black Americans in nonvocational higher education. More generally, Du Bois insisted that the cultural reproduction of African-American literature and history *in toto* would depend on the creation and maintenance of a professional class of African-American intellectuals; white American academics, by Du Bois's lights, couldn't be trusted with doing the job all by themselves, out of the goodness of their hearts. We've known for some time now that Du Bois was entirely right on this count, and what few black academics this country produced were (like Du Bois himself, despite his degree from Harvard) hired exclusively at small black colleges, or authorized to speak only about "black" issues. Given this legacy of apartheid in our institutional history, then, critics like myself can't, in good conscience, keep their hands off the cultural reproduction of African-American literature in the name of ethnic and ethical purity.

I have had undergraduates, of varying skin tones, who've told me they were surprised (and suspicious) that their African-American narrative class would be taught by me. To such students I usually offer as much of a three-part answer as they want to hear: I acknowledge that (1) the course will no doubt be "different" with me than it would be with a black instructor, but that (2) my whiteness is not the only thing I bring into the classroom (the course will also be "different" because I'm male, married with two kids, a New Yorker for my first twenty years, and a card-carrying anti-essentialist to boot), and, finally, that (3) I have to try to keep points (1) and (2) from degenerating into glibness by listening to African-American writers who have a few cautionary words for white anti-essentialists: As Toni Morrison puts it, "the people who invented the hierarchy of 'race' when it was convenient for them ought not to be the ones to explain it away, now that it does not suit their purposes for it to exist." Meaning, of course, that deconstruction, even the deconstruction of "race," can paradoxically work to further white male privilege, too. About that possibility I think it's best to be theoretical—which is to say, in my language, it's best to be *explicit*.

In ten years I've had a lot done to me. I've been gendered, I've been racinated, I've become grim and orthodox, I've turned thirty, and, worst of all, I've been disciplined by theory again and again, and it keeps showing me my interpretive presuppositions, making me stay after class and write fifty times on the board, "I will not take my interpretive presuppositions for granted." In one way I haven't changed from the person I was ten years ago: I still think the business of criticism is interpretation. I just no longer believe that interpretive criticism is transparent, or that it sees the world steadily and sees it whole. Nor is interpretation properly "supplementary" to its object, like reader's guides and *Cliff Notes*. I believe instead that interpretation is always partial, that it never "fills up" its object, and

that its "partiality" needs to be interpreted in its turn. For literary criticism, too, is written, just like the writing that occasions its writing, and there can be no final writing that clarifies
everything, no final reading that obviates all further reading.
I've heard tell that this is precisely the kind of thing literary
critics say to keep themselves in business, but I hold fast nonetheless to the conviction that reading, writing, and interpretation are historical processes, and that historical processes do not
end until history does. And if "theory" does nothing more—
or less—than make explicit such interpretive variables as races,
genders, and historical processes, well, then, it's not just a discipline I can live with; it's something I can no longer do without.

AUTHORITY
AND
ORIGINALITY

AN INTERVIEW BY
ANTONIO WEISS
WITH

Harold
Bloom

Harold Bloom is America's best-known and most controversial literary critic. Bloom's early books, such as Shelley's Mythmaking *and* The Ringers in the Tower, *were central in establishing the value of Romantic poetry in the face of dismissals by T. S. Eliot and the New Critics. His most famous work,* The Anxiety of Influence *(1973), proposed a fresh theory of poetic creation that has had a bearing on virtually all subsequent Anglo-American criticism. Bloom's last two books have been studies of the Bible's J author and of the Gnostic undercurrents in American religion. He is at work now on a book that will be called* The Western Canon. *Bloom received his doctorate from Yale and his B.A. from Cornell and is now University Professor at both Yale and NYU. What follows is excerpted from an interview conducted by Antonio Weiss and first published in* The Paris Review.

INTRODUCTION

BORN IN NEW YORK CITY on July 11, 1930, the son of Russian and Polish immigrants, Harold Bloom attended the Bronx High School of Science, where he did poorly, and Cornell, where he finished at the top of his class. After spending a year at Pembroke College, Cambridge, as a Research Fellow, and receiving a Ph.D. in English from Yale in 1955, he joined the Yale faculty and has remained there ever since. No critic in the English language since Samuel Johnson has been more prolific. Aside from providing the introductions to some five hundred volumes in the Chelsea House Library of Literary Criticism, of which he is General Editor, he has written over twenty books. The best known: *The Visionary Company* (1961) helped restore English Romantic poetry to the canon and to the syllabi of college courses in literature. Part of a tetralogy, *The Anxiety of Influence* (1973) attempts to redefine poetic tradition as a series of willful "misreadings" on the part of "strong," ephebe poets, of their precursors. Taking its title from the Greek word for "struggle," *Agon* (1982) further explores the subject of influence and originality and provides some illustrations. *Ruin the Sacred Truths* (1989) looks broadly at the continuities and discontinuities of the Western tradition, from the Bible to Beckett, insisting that the distinction between sacred and secular literature is a wholly societal one, with no literary consequences whatsoever: From a literary standpoint, the Bible can be no more sacred than Beckett. *Poetics of Influence* (1988), edited with an introduction by John Hollander, provides a fine selection of Bloom's work.

Among other prizes, Bloom has received a MacArthur Grant and the Christian Gauss Award for the best book of literary criticism (*Ruin the Sacred Truths*). He has spent sabbaticals teaching at Hebrew University, Jerusalem, the Universities of Rome and Bologna, and, most recently, giving the Flexner Lectures at Bryn Mawr College. Simultaneously residing at Yale and at Harvard, where Bloom was Charles Eliot Norton Professor of Poetry in 1987, was, in some sense, a warm-up for his current act: twin appointments as Sterling Professor of the Humanities at Yale (he broke with the English department there in 1977) and Berg Professor of English at New York University.

The interview was conducted at the homes he shares with his wife, Jeanne, in New Haven and New York—the one filled with four decades' accrual of furniture and books, the other nearly bare, although stacks of works-in-progress and students' papers are strewn about in both. If the conversation is not too heavy, Bloom likes to have music on, sometimes Baroque, sometimes jazz. (His New York apartment, which is in Greenwich Village, allows him to take in more live jazz.) The phone rings nonstop. Friends, former students, colleagues drop by. Talk is punctuated by strange exclamatories: "Zoombah," for one—Swahili for "libido"—is an all-purpose flavoring particle, with the accompanying adjectival "zoombinatious" and the verb "to zoombinate." Bloom speaks as if the sentences came to him off a printed page, grammatically complex, at times tangled. But they are delivered with great animation, whether ponderous or joyful—if also with finality. Because he learned English by reading it, his accent is very much his own, with some New York inflections: "*You* try and learn English in an all-Yiddish household in the East Bronx by sounding out the words of Blake's *Prophecies*," he explains. Often, he will start a conversation with a direct, at times personal question, or a sigh: "Oh, how the Bloomian feet ache today!"

INTERVIEW

ANTONIO WEISS: What are your memories of growing up?

HAROLD BLOOM: That was such a long time ago. I'm sixty years old. I can't remember much of my childhood that well. I was raised in an Orthodox East European Jewish household where Yiddish was the everyday language. My mother was very pious, my father less so. I still read Yiddish poetry. I have a great interest and pleasure in it.

A.W.: What are your recollections of the neighborhood in which you grew up?

H.B.: Almost none. One of my principal memories is that I and my friends, just to survive, had constantly to fight street battles with neighborhood Irish toughs, some of whom were very much under the influence of a sort of Irish-American Nazi organization called the Silver Shirts. This was back in the 1930s. We were on the verge of an Irish neighborhood over there in the East Bronx. We lived in a Jewish neighborhood. On our border, somewhere around Southern Boulevard, an Irish neighborhood began, and they would raid us, and we would fight back. They were terrible street fights, involving broken bottles and baseball bats. They were very nasty times. I say this even though I've now grown up and find that many of my best friends are Irish.

A.W.: Do you think your background helped in any way to shape your career?

H.B.: Obviously it predisposed me towards a great deal of systematic reading. It exposed me to the Bible as a sort of definitive text early on. And obviously, too, I became obsessed with interpretation as such. Judaic tradition necessarily acquaints one with interpretation as a mode. Exegesis becomes wholly natural. But I did not have very orthodox religious beliefs. Even when I was quite a young child I was very skeptical indeed about orthodox notions of spirituality. Of course, I now regard normative Judaism as being, as I've often said, a very strong misreading of the Hebrew Bible undertaken in the second century in order to meet the needs of the Jewish people in a Palestine

under Roman occupation. And that is not very relevant to matters eighteen centuries later. But otherwise, I think the crucial
experiences for me as a reader, as a child, did not come reading
the Hebrew Bible. It came in reading poetry written in English,
which can still work on me with the force of a Bible conversion.
It was the aesthetic experience of first reading Hart Crane and
William Blake—those two poets in particular.

A.W.: How old were you at this point?

H.B.: I was preadolescent, ten or eleven years old. I still
remember the extraordinary delight, the extraordinary force
that Crane and Blake brought to me (in particular Blake's rhetoric in the longer poems), though I had no notion what they
were about. I picked up a copy of the *Collected Poems* of Hart
Crane in the Bronx Library. I still remember when I lit upon
the page with the extraordinary trope, "O Thou steeled Cog-
nizance whose leap commits / The agile precincts of the lark's
return." I was just swept away by it, by the Marlovian rhetoric.
I still have the flavor of that book in me. Indeed, it's the first
book I ever owned. I begged my oldest sister to give it to me,
and I still have the old black-and-gold edition she gave me for
my birthday back in 1942. It's up on the third floor. Why is it
you can have that extraordinary experience (preadolescent in
my case as in so many other cases) of falling violently in love
with great poetry . . . where you are moved by its power before
you comprehend it? In some, a version of the poetical character
is incarnated and in some like myself the answering voice is
from the beginning that of the critic. I suppose the only poet
of the twentieth century that I could secretly set above Yeats
and Stevens would be Hart Crane. Crane was dead at the age
of thirty-two, so one doesn't really know what he would have
been able to do. An immense loss. As large a loss as the death
of Shelley at twenty-nine or Keats at twenty-five. Crane had
to do it all in only seven or eight years.

A.W.: Did you read children's stories, fairy tales?

H.B.: I don't think so. I read the Bible, which is, after all, a
long fairy tale. I didn't read children's literature until I was an
undergraduate.

A.W.: Did you write verse as a child?

H.B.: In spite of my interest, that never occurred to me. It must have had something to do with the enormous reverence and rapture I felt about poetry, the incantatory strength that Crane and Blake had for me from the beginning. To be a poet did not occur to me. It was indeed a threshold guarded by demons. To try to write in verse would have been a kind of trespass. That's something that I still feel very strongly.

A.W.: How was your chosen career viewed by your family?

H.B.: I don't think they had any idea what I would be. I think they were disappointed. They were Jewish immigrants from eastern Europe with necessarily narrow views. They had hoped that I would be a doctor or a lawyer or a dentist. They did not know what a professor of poetry was. They would have understood, I suppose, had I chosen to be a rabbi or a Talmudic scholar. But finally, I don't think they cared one way or the other.

When I was a small boy already addicted to doing nothing but reading poems in English, I was asked by an uncle who kept a candy store in Brooklyn what I intended to do to earn a living when I grew up. I said I want to read poetry. He told me that there were professors of poetry at Harvard and Yale. That's the first time I'd ever heard of those places or that there was such a thing as a professor of poetry. In my five- or six-year-old way I replied, "I'm going to be a professor of poetry at Harvard or Yale." Of course, the joke is that three years ago I was simultaneously Charles Eliot Norton Professor of Poetry at Harvard and Sterling Professor of the Humanities at Yale! So in that sense I was prematurely overdetermined in profession. Sometimes I think that is the principal difference between my own work and the work of many other critics. I came to it very early, and I've been utterly unswerving.

A.W.: You are known as someone who has had a prodigious memory since childhood. Do you find that your power of recall was triggered by the words themselves, or were there other factors?

H.B.: Oh no, it was immediate and it was always triggered

by text, and indeed always had an aesthetic element. I learned early that a test for a poem for me was whether it seemed so inevitable that I could remember it perfectly from the start. I think the only change in me in that regard has come mainly under the influence of Nietzsche. It is the single way he has influenced me aesthetically. I've come to understand that the quality of memorability and inevitability which I assumed came from intense pleasure may actually have come from a kind of pain. That is to say that one learns from Nietzsche that there is something painful about meaning. Sometimes it is the pain of difficulty, sometimes the pain of being set a standard that one cannot attain.

A.W.: Did you ever feel that reading so much was an avoidance of experience?

H.B.: No. It was for me a terrible rage or passion which was a drive. It was fiery. It was an absolute obsession. I do not think that speculation on my own part would ever convince me that it was an attempt to substitute a more ideal existence for the life that I had to live. It was love. I fell desperately in love with reading poems. I don't think that one should idealize such a passion. I certainly no longer do. I mean, I still love reading a poem when I can find a really good one to read. Just recently, I was sitting down, alas for the first time in several years, reading through Shakespeare's *Troilus and Cressida* at one sitting. I found it to be an astonishing experience, powerful and superb. That hasn't dimmed or diminished. But surely it is a value in itself, a reality in its own right; surely it cannot be reduced or subsumed under some other name. Freud, doubtless, would wish to reduce it to the sexual thought, or rather, the sexual past. But increasingly it seems to me that literature, and particularly Shakespeare, who is literature, is a much more comprehensive mode of cognition than psychoanalysis can be.

A.W.: Who are the teachers who were important to you? Did you study with the New Critics at Yale?

H.B.: I did not study with any of the New Critics, with the single exception being William K. Wimsatt. Bill was a formalist and a very shrewd one, and from the moment I landed in the first course that I took with him, which was in theories of poetry, he sized me up. His comment on my first essay for him was, "This is Longinian criticism. You're an instance of exactly what I don't like or want." He was quite right. He was an Aristotelian; as far as I was concerned, Aristotle had ruined Western literary criticism almost from the beginning. What I thought of as literary criticism really *did* begin with the pseudo-Longinus. So we had very strong disagreements about that kind of stuff. But he was a remarkable teacher. We became very close friends later on. I miss him very much. He was a splendid, huge, fascinating man, almost seven feet tall, a fierce, dogmatic Roman Catholic, very intense. But very fair-minded. We shared a passion for Dr. Samuel Johnson. I reacted so violently against him that antithetically he was a great influence on me. I think that's what I meant by dedicating *The Anxiety of Influence* to Bill. I still treasure the note he wrote me after I gave him one of the early copies of the book. "I find the dedication extremely surprising," he said, and then added mournfully: "I suppose it entitles you to be Plotinus to Emerson's Plato in regard to American neo-Romanticism, a doctrine that I despise." Oh, yes, we had serious differences in our feelings about poetry.

A.W.: I wanted to ask you about a period of time in the mid-sixties, which you have described as a period of great upheaval and transition for you. You were immersed in the essays of Emerson.

H.B.: Yes, I started reading him all day long, every day, and pretty much simultaneously reading Freud. People would look at me with amazement, and say, "Well, what about Thoreau? He at least counts for something." And I would look back at them in amazement and tell them what indeed was and is true, that Thoreau is deeply derivative of Emerson, and very minor compared to him. Emerson is God.

A.W.: You were in analysis during this period. How did that go?

H.B.: As my distinguished analyst said to me at the end, there had never been a proper transference.

A.W.: You were unable to accept his authority?

H.B.: I thought and still think that he is a very nice man, but as he wryly remarked, I was paying him to give him lectures several times a week on the proper way to read Freud. He thought this was quite self-defeating for both of us.

A.W.: Can a successful therapy ever be so closely allied to a reading of Freud?

H.B.: I take it that a successful therapy is an oxymoron.

A.W.: It's always interminable?

H.B.: I do not know anyone who has ever benefited from Freudian or any other mode of analysis, except by being, to use the popular trope for it, so badly shrunk that they become quite dried out. That is to say, all passion spent. Perhaps they become better people, but they also become stale and uninteresting people with very few exceptions. Like dried-out cheese, or wilted flowers.

A.W.: Were you worried about losing your creativity?

H.B.: No, no. That was not the issue at all.

A.W.: You were having trouble writing at the time.

H.B.: Oh, yes. I was having all kinds of crises. I was, in every sense, "in the middle of the journey." On the other hand, this has been recurrent. Here I am sixty years old and as much as ever I'm in the middle of the journey. That is something that goes with the territory. One just keeps going.

A.W.: Do you see yourself as a difficult critic, in the sense that you qualify certain poets and prose fiction writers as "difficult"?

H.B.: I would think, my dear, that most people these days might be kind enough to call me difficult. The younger members of my profession and the members of what I have called the School of Resentment describe me, I gather, as someone who partakes of a cult of personality or self-obsession rather than their wonderful, free, and generous social vision. One of them, I understand, refers to me customarily as "Napoleon Bonaparte." There is no way of dealing with these people. They have not been moved by literature. Many of them are my former students, and I know them all too well. They are now gender and power freaks.

A.W.: How do you account historically for the "School of Resentment"?

H.B.: In the universities, the most surprising and reprehensible development came some twenty years ago, around 1968, and has had a very long-range effect, one that is still percolating. Suddenly all sorts of people, faculty members at the universities, graduate and undergraduate students, began to blame the universities not just for their own palpable ills and malfeasances, but for all the ills of history and society. They were blamed, and to some extent still are, by the budding School of Resentment and its precursors, as though they were not only representative of these ills, but, weirdly enough, as though they had somehow helped *cause* these ills, and even more weirdly, quite surrealistically, as though they were somehow capable of ameliorating these ills. It's still going on—this attempt to ascribe both culpability and apocalyptic potential to the universities. It's really asking the universities to take the place that was once occupied by religion, philosophy, and science. These are our conceptual modes. They have all failed us. The entire history of Western culture, from Alexandrian days until now, shows that when a society's conceptual modes fail it, then willy-nilly it becomes a literary culture. This is probably neither good nor bad, but just the way things become. And we can't really ask literature, or the representatives of a literary culture, in or out of the university, to save society. Literature is not an instrument of social change or an instrument for social reform. It is more a mode of human sensations and impressions, which do not reduce very well to societal rules or forms.

A.W.: How does one react to the School of Resentment? By declaring oneself an aesthete?

H.B.: Well, I do that now, of course, in furious reaction to their School and to so much other pernicious nonsense that goes on. I would certainly see myself as an aesthete in the sense advocated by Ruskin, indeed to a considerable degree by Emerson, and certainly by the divine Walter and the sublime Oscar. It is a very engaged kind of mode. Literary criticism in the United States increasingly is split between very low-level literary journalism and what I increasingly regard as a disaster, which is literary criticism in the academies, particularly in the younger generations. Increasingly scores and scores of graduate students have read the absurd Lacan but have never read Edmund Spenser; or have read a great deal of Foucault or Derrida but scarcely read Shakespeare or Milton. That's obviously an absurd defeat for literary study. When I was a young man, back in the fifties, starting out on what was to be my career, I used to proclaim that my chosen profession seemed to consist of a secular clergy or clerisy. I was thinking, of course, of the highly Anglo-Catholic New Criticism under the sponsorship or demigodness of T. S. Eliot. But I realized in latish middle age that, no better or worse, I was surrounded by a pride of displaced social workers, a rabblement of lemmings, all rushing down to the sea carrying their subject down to destruction with them. The School of Resentment is an extraordinary sort of melange of latest-model feminists, Lacanians, that whole semiotic cackle, latest-model pseudo-Marxists, so-called New Historicists, who are neither new nor historicist, and third-generation deconstructors, who I believe have no relationship whatever to literary values. It's really a very paltry kind of a phenomenon. But it is pervasive, and it seems to be waxing rather than waning. It is a very rare thing indeed to encounter one critic, academic or otherwise, not just in the English-speaking world but also in France or Italy, who has an authentic commitment to aesthetic values, who reads for the pleasure of reading, and who values poetry or story as such, above all else. Reading has become a very curious kind of activity. It has become tendentious in the extreme. A sheer deliquescence has taken place because of this obsession with method or supposed method. Criticism starts —it *has* to start—with a real passion for reading. It can come in adolescence, even in your twenties, but you must fall in love with poems. You must fall in love with what we used to call "imaginative literature." And when you are in love in that way, with or without provocation from good teachers, you will pass on to encountering what used to be called the sublime. And as soon as you do this, you pass into the agonistic mode, even if your own nature is anything but agonistic. In the end, the spirit that makes one a fan of a particular athlete or a particular team is different only in degree, not in kind, from the spirit that teaches one to prefer one poet to another, or one novelist to another. That is to say there is some element of competition at every point in one's experience as a reader. How could there not be? Perhaps you learn this more fully as you get older, but in the end you choose between books, or you choose between poems, the way you choose between people. You can't become friends with every acquaintance you make, and I would not think that it is any different with what you read.

A.W.: Do you foresee any change, or improvement, in critical fashions?

H.B.: I don't believe in myths of decline or myths of progress, even as regards the literary scene. The world does not get to be a better or a worse place; it just gets more senescent. The world gets older, without getting either better or worse, and so does literature. But I do think that the drab current phenomenon that passes for literary studies in the university will finally provide its own corrective. That is to say, sooner or later, students and teachers are going to get terribly bored with all the technocratic social work going on now. There will be a return to aesthetic values and desires, or these people will simply do something else with their time. But I find a great deal of hypocrisy in what they're doing now. It is tiresome to be encountering myths called "The Social Responsibility of the Critic" or "The Political Responsibilities of the Critic." I would much rather walk into a bookstore and find a book called "The Aesthetic Responsibilities of the Statesman," or "The Literary Responsibilities of the Engineer." Criticism is not a program for social betterment, not an engine for social change. I don't see how it possibly could be. If you look for the best instance of a socially radical literary critic, you find a very good one indeed in William Hazlitt. But you will not find that his social activism on the left in any way conditions his aesthetic judgements, or that he tries to make imaginative literature a machine for revolution. You would not find much difference in aesthetic response between Hazlitt and Dr. Samuel Johnson on Milton, though Dr. Johnson is very much on the right politically, and Hazlitt, of course, very much an enthusiast for the French Revolution and for English Radicalism. But I can't find much in the way of a Hazlittian or Johnsonian temperament in life and literature anywhere on the current scene. There are so many tiresomenesses going on. Everyone is so desperately afraid of being called a racist or a sexist that they connive—whether actively or passively—the almost total breakdown of standards which has taken place both in and out of the universities, where writings by blacks or Hispanics or in many cases simply women are concerned.

A.W.: This movement has helped focus attention on some great novels, though. You're an admirer, for example, of Ralph Ellison's *Invisible Man*.

H.B.: Oh, but that is a very, very rare exception. What else is there like *Invisible Man*? Zora Neale Hurston's *Their Eyes Were Watching God* has a kind of superior intensity and firm control. It's a very fine book indeed. It surprised and delighted me when I first read it and it has sustained several rereadings since. But that and *Invisible Man* are the only full-scale works of fiction I have read by American blacks in this century which have survival possibilities at all. Alice Walker is an extremely inadequate writer, and I think that is giving her the best of it. A book like *The Color Purple* is of no aesthetic interest or value whatsoever, yet it is exalted and taught in the academies. It clearly is a time in which social and cultural guilt has taken over.

A.W.: I know you find this to be true of feminist criticism.

H.B.: I'm very fond of feminist critics, some of whom are my close friends, but it is widely known I'm not terribly fond of feminist criticism. The true test is to find work, whether in the past or present, by women writers which we had undervalued, and thus bring it to our attention and teach us to study it more closely or more usefully. By that test they have failed, because they have added no one to the canon. The women writers who mattered—Jane Austen, George Eliot, Emily Dickinson, Edith Wharton, Willa Cather, and others who have always mattered on aesthetic grounds—still matter. I do not appreciate Elizabeth Bishop or May Swenson any more or less than I would have appreciated them if we had no feminist literary criticism at all. And I stare at what is presented to me as feminist literary criticism and I shake my head. I regard it at best as being well intentioned. I do not regard it as literary criticism.

A.W.: Can it be valued as a form of social or political criticism?

H.B.: I'm not concerned with political or social criticism. If people wish to practice it, that is entirely their business. It is not mine, heavens! If it does not help me to read a work of aesthetic value, then I'm not going to be interested in it at all. I do not for a moment yield to the notion that any social, racial, ethnic, or "male" interest could determine my aesthetic choices. I have a lifetime of experience, learning, and insight which tells me this.

A.W.: What do you make of all this recent talk of the "canonical problem"?

H.B.: It is no more than a reflection of current academic and social politics in the United States. The old test for what makes a work canonical is if it has engendered strong readings that come after it, whether as overt interpretations or implicitly interpretive forms. There's no way the gender and power boys and girls, or the New Historicists, or any of the current set are going to give us new canonical works, any more than all the agitation of feminist writing or nowadays what seems to be called African-American writing is going to give us canonical works. Alice Walker is not going to be a canonical poet no matter how many lemmings stand forth and proclaim her sublimity. It really does seem to me a kind of bogus issue. I am more and more certain that a great deal of what now passes for literary study of the so-called politically correct variety will wash aside. It is a ripple. I give it five years. I have seen many fashions come and go since I first took up literary study. After forty years one begins to be able to distinguish an ephemeral surface ripple from a deeper current or an authentic change.

A.W.: You teach Freud and Shakespeare.

H.B.: Oh yes, increasingly. I keep telling my students that I'm not interested in a Freudian reading of Shakespeare but a kind of Shakespearean reading of Freud. In some sense Freud has to be a prose version of Shakespeare, the Freudian map of the mind being in fact Shakespearean. There's a lot of resentment on Freud's part because I think he recognizes this. What we think of as Freudian psychology is really a Shakespearean invention and, for the most part, Freud is merely codifying it. This shouldn't be too surprising. Freud himself says "the poets were there before me," and the poet in particular is necessarily Shakespeare. But you know, I think it runs deeper than that. Western psychology is much more a Shakespearean invention than a Biblical invention, let alone, obviously, a Homeric, or Sophoclean, or even Platonic, never mind a Cartesian or Jungian invention. It's not just that Shakespeare gives us most of our representations of cognition as such; I'm not so sure he doesn't largely invent what we think of as cognition. I remember saying something like this to a seminar consisting of professional teachers of Shakespeare, and one of them got very indignant and said, "You are confusing Shakespeare with God." I don't see why one shouldn't, as it were. Most of what we know about how to represent cognition and personality in language was permanently altered by Shakespeare. The principal insight that I've had in teaching and writing about Shakespeare is that there isn't anyone before Shakespeare who actually gives you a representation of characters or human figures speaking out loud, whether to themselves or to others or both, and then brooding out loud, whether to themselves or to others or both, on what they themselves have said. And then, in the course of pondering, undergoing a serious or vital change, they become a different kind of character or personality and even a different kind of mind. We take that utterly for granted in representation. But it doesn't exist before Shakespeare. It doesn't happen in the Bible. It doesn't happen in Homer or in Dante. It doesn't even happen in Euripides. It's pretty clear that Shakespeare's true precursor—where he took the hint from—is Chaucer, which is why I think the Wife of Bath gets into Falstaff, and the Pardoner gets into figures like Edmund and Iago. As to where Chaucer gets that from, that's a very pretty question. It is a standing challenge I have put to my students. That's part of Chaucer's shocking originality as a writer. But Chaucer does it only in fits and starts, and in small degree. Shakespeare does it all the time. It's his common stock. The ability to do that, and to persuade one that this is a natural mode of representation, is purely Shakespearean and we are now so contained by it that we can't see its originality anymore. The originality of it is bewildering.

By the way, I was thinking recently about this whole question as it relates to the French tradition. I gave what I thought was a remarkable seminar on *Hamlet* to my undergraduate Shakespeare seminar at Yale. About an hour before class, I had what I thought was a very considerable insight, though I gather my students were baffled by it. I think that I was trying to say too much at once. It had suddenly occurred to me that the one canon of French neoclassical thought which was absolutely, indeed religiously, followed by French dramatists and this means everyone, even Molière and Racine—was that there were to be no soliloquies and no asides. No matter what dexterity or agility had to be displayed, a confidante had to be dragged onto the stage so that the protagonist could have someone to whom to address cogitations, reflections. This accounts not only for why Shakespeare has never been properly absorbed by the French, as compared to his effect on every other European culture, language, literature, dramatic tradition, but also for the enormous differences between French and Anglo-American modes of literary thought. It also helps account for why the French modes, which are having so absurd an effect upon us at this time, are so clearly irrelevant to our literature and our way of talking about literature. I can give you a further illustration. I gave a faculty seminar a while ago in which I talked for about two hours about my notions of Shakespeare and originality. At the end of it, a woman who was present, a faculty member at

Yale, who had listened with a sort of amazement and a clear lack of comprehension, said, with considerable exasperation, "Well, you know, Professor Bloom, I don't really understand why you're talking about originality. It is as outmoded as, say, private enterprise in the economic sphere." An absurdity to have put myself in a situation where I had to address a member of the School of Resentment! I was too courteous, especially since my colleague Shoshana Felman jumped in to try to explain to the lady what I was up to. But I realized it was hopeless. Here was a lady who came not out of Racine and Molière but in fact out of Lacan, Derrida, and Foucault. Even if she *had* come out of Racine and Molière, she could never have hoped to understand. I remember what instantly flashed through my head was that I had been talking about the extraordinary originality of the way Shakespeare's protagonists ponder to themselves and, on the basis of that pondering, change. She could not understand this because it never actually happens in the French drama; the French critical mind has never been able to believe that it is appropriate for this to happen. Surely this is related to a mode of apprehension, a mode of criticism in which authorial presence was never very strong anyway, and so indeed it could die.

A.W.: Can you explain how you came to notice this about Shakespeare's protagonists?

H.B.: Yes, I can even remember the particular moment. I was teaching *King Lear*, and I'd reached a moment in the play which has always fascinated me. I suddenly saw what was going on. Edmund is the most remarkable villain in all Shakespeare, a manipulator so strong that he makes Iago seem minor in comparison. Edmund is a sophisticated and sardonic consciousness who can run rings around anyone else on the stage in *King Lear*. He is so foul that it takes Goneril and Regan really to match up to him. . . . He's received his death wound from his brother; he's lying there on the battlefield. They bring in word that Goneril and Regan are dead: One slew the other and then committed suicide for his sake. Edmund broods out loud and says, quite extraordinarily (it's all in four words), "Yet Edmund was belov'd." One looks at those four words totally startled.

As soon as he says it, he starts to ponder out loud: What are the implications that, though two monsters of the deep, the two loved me so much that one of them killed the other and then murdered herself? He reasons it out. He says, "The one the other poison'd for my sake / And after slew herself." And then he suddenly says, "I pant for life," and then amazingly he says, "Some good I mean to do / despite of mine own nature," and he suddenly gasps out, having given the order for Lear and Cordelia to be killed, "Send in time," to stop it. They don't get there in time. Cordelia's been murdered. And then Edmund dies. But that's an astonishing change. It comes about as he hears himself say, in real astonishment, "Yet Edmund was belov'd," and on that basis, he starts to ponder. Had he not said that, he would not have changed. There's nothing like that in literature before Shakespeare. It makes Freud unnecessary. The representation of inwardness is so absolute and large that we have no parallel to it before then.

A.W.: So that the Freudian commentary on Hamlet by Ernest Jones is unnecessary.

H.B.: It's much better to work out what Hamlet's commentary on the Oedipal complex might be. There's that lovely remark of A. C. Bradley's that Shakespeare's major tragic heroes can only work in the play that they're in—that if Iago had to come onto the same stage with Hamlet, it would take Hamlet about five seconds to catch onto what Iago was doing and so viciously parody Iago that he would drive him to madness and suicide. The same way, if the ghost of Othello's dead father appeared to Othello and said that someone had murdered him, Othello would grab his sword and go and hack the other fellow down. In each case there would be no play. Just as the plays would make mincemeat of one another if you tried to work one into the other, so Shakespeare chops up any writer you apply him to. And a Shakespearean reading of Freud would leave certain things but not leave others. It would make one very impatient, I think, with Freud's representation of the Oedipal complex. And it's a disaster to try to apply the Freudian reading of that to Hamlet.

A.W.: You have mentioned you might write on the aesthetics of outrage as a topic.

H.B.: Yes, the aesthetics of *being* outraged. But I don't mean being outraged in that other sense, you know, that sort of post-sixties phenomenon. I mean in the sense in which Macbeth is increasingly outraged. What fascinates me is that we so intensely sympathize with a successful or strong representation of someone in the process of being outraged, and I want to know why. I suppose it's ultimately that we're outraged at mortality, and it is impossible not to sympathize with that.

A.W.: This is a topic that would somehow include W. C. Fields.

H.B.: Oh yes, certainly, since I think his great power is that he perpetually demonstrates the enormous comedy of being outraged. I have never recovered from the first time I saw the W. C. Fields short "The Fatal Glass of Beer." It represents for me still the high point of cinema, surpassing even Groucho's *Duck Soup*. Have you seen "The Fatal Glass of Beer"? I don't think I have the critical powers to describe it. Throughout much of it, W. C. Fields is strumming a zither and singing a song about the demise of his unfortunate son, who expires because of a fatal glass of beer which college boys persuade the abstaining youth to drink. He then insults a Salvation Army lassie, herself a reformed high-kicker in the chorus line, and she stuns him with a single high kick. But to describe it in this way is to say that *Macbeth* is about an ambitious man who murders the King.

A.W.: So in addition to being an outrageous critic, are you an outraged critic, in that sense?

H.B.: No, no. I hope that I am not an outrageous critic, but I suppose I am. But that's only because most of the others are so dreadfully tame and senescent, or indeed are now politically correct or content to be social reformers who try to tell us there is some connection between literature and social change. Outraged? No, I am not outraged. I am not outraged as a person. I am beyond it now. I'm sixty years and seven months old. It's too late for me to be outraged. It would really shorten my life if I let myself be outraged. I don't have the emotional strength anymore. It would be an expense of spirit that I cannot afford. Besides, by now nothing surprises me. You know, the literary situation is one of a surpassing absurdity. Criticism in the universities, I'll have to admit, has entered a phase where I am totally out of sympathy with 95 percent of what goes on. It's Stalinism without Stalin. All of the traits of the Stalinist in the 1930s and 1940s are being repeated in this whole resentment in the universities in the 1990s. The intolerance, the self-congratulation, smugness, sanctimoniousness, the retreat from imaginative values, the flight from the aesthetic. It's not worth being truly outraged about. Eventually these people will provide their own antidote, because they will perish of boredom. I will win in the end. I must be the only literary critic of any eminence who is writing today (I cannot think of another, I'm sad to say, however arrogant or difficult this sounds) who always asks about what he reads and likes, whether it is ancient, modern, or brand new, or has always been lying around, who always asks "How good is it? What is it better than? What is it less good than? What does it mean?" and "Is there some relation between what it means and how good or bad it is, and not only how is it good or bad, but why is it good or bad?" Mr. Frye, who was very much my precursor, tried to banish all of that from criticism, just as I tried to reintroduce a kind of dark sense of temporality, or the sorrows of temporality, into literary criticism as a correction to Frye's Platonic idealism. I have also raised more explicitly than anyone else nowadays, or indeed anyone since Johnson or Hazlitt, the question of "Why does it matter?" There has to be some relation between the way in which we matter and the way in which we read. A way of speaking and writing about literature which addresses itself to these matters must seem impossibly naive or old-fashioned or not literary criticism at all to the partisans of the School of Resentment. But I believe that these have been the modes of Western literary criticism ever since Aristophanes invented the art of criticism by juxtaposing Euripides with Aeschylus (to the profound disadvantage of Euripides), or indeed ever since Longinus started to work off his own anxieties about Plato by dealing with Plato's anxieties about Homer. This is the stuff literary criticism has always done, and, if it is finally to be of any use to us, this is what I think it must get back to. It really must answer the questions of good and bad and how and why. It must answer the question of what the relevance of literature is to our lives, and why it means one thing to us when we are one way and another thing to us when we are another. It astonishes me that I cannot find any other contemporary critic who still discusses the pathos of great literature, or is willing to talk about why a particular work does or does not evoke great anguish in us. This is of course dismissed as the merest subjectivity.

A.W.: Can essays like Hazlitt's or Ruskin's or Pater's still be written today?

H.B.: Most people would say no. I can only say I do my best. That's as audacious a thing as I can say. I keep saying, though nobody will listen, or only a few will listen, that criticism is either a genre of literature or it is nothing. It has no hope for survival unless it is a genre of literature. It can be regarded, if you wish, as a minor genre, but I don't know why people say that. The idea that poetry or, rather, verse writing, is to take priority over criticism is on the face of it absolute nonsense. That would be to say that the verse-writer Felicia Hemans is a considerably larger figure than her contemporary William Hazlitt. Or that our era's Felicia Hemans, Sylvia Plath, is a considerably larger literary figure than, say, the late Wilson Knight. This is clearly not the case. Miss Plath is a bad verse writer. I read Knight with pleasure and profit, if at times wonder and shock. These are obvious points but obviously one will have to go on making them. Almost everything now written and published and praised in the United States as verse isn't even verse, let alone poetry. It's just typing, or word processing. As a matter of fact, it's usually just glib rhetoric or social resentment. Just as almost everything that we now call criticism is in fact just journalism.

A.W.: Or an involvement with what you refer to as the "easier pleasures." What are these easier pleasures?

H.B.: Well, I take the notion from my friend and contemporary Angus Fletcher, who takes it from Shelley and Longinus. It's perfectly clear some very good writers offer only easier pleasures. Compare two writers exactly contemporary with one another—Harold Brodkey and John Updike. Updike, as I once wrote, is a minor novelist with a major style. A quite beautiful and very considerable stylist. I've read many novels by Updike, but the one I like best is *The Witches of Eastwick*. But for the most part it seems to me that he specializes in the easier pleasures. They are genuine pleasures, but they do not challenge the intellect. Brodkey, somewhat imperfectly perhaps, does so to a much more considerable degree. Thomas Pynchon provides very difficult pleasures, it seems to me, though not of late. I am not convinced, in fact, that it was he who wrote *Vineland*. Look at the strongest American novelist since Melville, Hawthorne, and James. That would certainly have to be Faulkner. Look at the difference between Faulkner at his very best in *As I Lay Dying* and at his very worst in *A Fable*. *A Fable* is nothing but easier pleasures, but they're not even pleasures. It is so easy it becomes, indeed, vulgar, disgusting, and does not afford pleasure. *As I Lay Dying* is a very difficult piece of work. To try to apprehend Darl Bundren takes a very considerable effort of the imagination. Faulkner really surpasses himself there. It seems to me an authentic instance of the literary sublime in our time. Or, if you look at modern American poetry, in some sense the entire development of Wallace Stevens is from affording us easier pleasures, as in "The Idea of Order at Key West," and before that "Sunday Morning," to the very difficult pleasures of "Notes toward a Supreme Fiction" and then the immensely difficult pleasures of a poem like "The Owl in the Sarcophagus." You have to labor with immense intensity in order to keep up. It is certainly related to the notion propounded by both Burckhardt and Nietzsche, which I've taken over from them, of the agonistic. There is a kind of standard of measurement starting with Plato on through Western thought where one asks a literary work, implicitly, to answer the question "More, equal to, or less than?" In the end, the answer to that question is the persuasive force enabling a reader to say, "I will sacrifice an easier pleasure for something that takes me beyond myself." Surely that must be the difference between Marlowe's *The Jew of Malta* and Shakespeare's *The Merchant of Venice*, an enigmatic and to me in many ways unequal play. I get a lot more pleasure out of Barabas than I do out of the equivocal Shylock, but I'm well aware that my pleasure in Barabas is an easier pleasure, and that my trouble in achieving any pleasure in reading or viewing Shylock is because other factors are getting in the way of apprehending the Shakespearean sublime. The whole question of the fifth act of *The Merchant of Venice* is for me one of the astonishing tests of what I would call the sublime in poetry. One has the trouble of having to accommodate oneself to it.

A.W.: Are you being fruitfully misread, as you would say, by anyone?

H.B.: I hope that somewhere in the world there is a young critic or two who will strongly misread me to their advantage. Lord knows, one is not Samuel Johnson or William Hazlitt or John Ruskin, or even Walter Pater or Oscar Wilde as critic. But, yes, I hope so.

You know, I've learned something over the years, picking up copies of my books in secondhand bookstores and in libraries, off people's shelves. You also learn this from reviews and from things that are cited in other people's books and so on, or from what people say to you: What you pride yourself on, the things that you think are your insight and contribution . . . no one ever even *notices* them. It's as though they're just for you. What you say in passing or what you expound because you know it too well, because it really bores you, but you feel you have to get through this in order to make your grand point, *that's* what people pick up on. *That's* what they underline. *That's* what they quote. *That's* what they attack, or cite favorably. *That's* what they can use. What you really think you're doing may or may not be what you're doing, but it certainly isn't communicated to others.

CRASHING
THE
PARTY

WOMEN IN THE
ACADEMY NOW

Susan

Fraiman

Susan Fraiman is a conspicuously talented member of the "second generation" of American feminist literary critics. She has published essays on George Eliot, Jane Austen, and Charles W. Chesnutt. Her critical study Unbecoming Women: British Women Writers and the Novel of Development *has recently been published by Columbia University Press in its Gender and Culture Series. Fraiman received her B.A. from Princeton University and her Ph.D. from Columbia. She teaches in the English department at the University of Virginia.*

I

WHEN I ARRIVED AT PRINCETON as an undergraduate in 1974, female students still felt a lot like guests, and many of our hosts were wondering uncomfortably how long we planned to stay. The first class of women, admitted in 1969, had graduated only the previous year, and we continued to be outnumbered three to one. A conservative alumni magazine, *Prospect*, was founded in 1972 largely to protest the opening of Princeton's doors to women and increasing numbers of blacks. These newcomers contributed, the magazine argued, to a loss of seriousness in the classroom and a general lowering of standards. Back in that experimental era, feminine muscles were not much more highly regarded than feminine minds. For a while I rowed with the fledgling women's crew team, but with few boats and no locker rooms we resembled the impoverished women's college of Woolf's *A Room of One's Own*—drinking water to the men's many shades of wine.

Our vintage was poor in the English department as well, where close to half the majors were female but none of the female faculty were tenured. One brave assistant professor taught a course called "Literature in a Man's World," a diagnosis she might well have made by glancing through *The Norton Anthology of English Literature* (3d edition), textbook for the department's required survey and for similar surveys around the country. At that time, the *Norton's* first volume swept from the Middle Ages up through the eighteenth century, pausing over a lone woman (Anne Finch, Countess of Winchilsea) for only three of its 2442 pages—unless, agreeing with Woolf that "Anon" was actually a woman crooning over a spinning wheel or cradle, we count its sections of anonymous ballads and lyrics. The second volume did better, but Woolf still got a scant eight pages to Joyce's eighty-seven, and of the forty authors representing the twentieth century, only three were women, leaving out such now obvious candidates as Dorothy Richardson, Edith Sitwell, Katherine Mansfield, Rebecca West, Jean Rhys, Elizabeth Bowen, and Stevie Smith. Most tellingly, the condensed "Major Authors" edition of the *Norton* had, in its 1974 incarnation, no women at all: among its many Williams and Johns, not a single Jane or pseudonymous George. Given the parade of masculine talent, is it any wonder I wrote my senior thesis on that flashiest of phallic writers, D. H. Lawrence? In those optimistic but confusing days of the mid-seventies, I would leave the Women's Center, consciousness newly raised, and lock myself into an underground study carrel. There I swilled Diet Pepsi and labored over an earnest if wishful defense of Lawrence's sexual politics, determined to see his gamekeeper and Lady Chatterley as the heralds of a new gender order.

As it turned out, while I was poring over my *Norton*, mastering the techniques of "close reading," and attempting to save D. H. Lawrence for women's liberation, feminist criticism was emerging onto the American literary scene, and calling attention to the contributions of women writers was one of its *raisons d'être*. By the time I got to graduate school in 1980, there was a growing body of work engaged in tracing out a female literary tradition: Patricia Meyer Spacks's *Female Imagination* (1975), Mary Helen Washington's *Black-Eyed Susans* (1975), Ellen Moers's *Literary Women* (1976), Elaine Showalter's *Literature of Their Own* (1977), Sandra Gilbert and Susan Gubar's *Madwoman in the Attic* (1979), and Barbara Christian's *Black Women Novelists* (1980), among others. At Columbia, I would have the chance to study with Carolyn Heilbrun and Nancy K. Miller, two important figures in the fast-growing field of feminist criticism and theory. And so I began to find my stroke in the academy just as feminist criticism's first great wave began to surge toward American shores. Yet this is not to say that women, female writers, and feminist approaches to literature were suddenly, painlessly welcomed into the university. In fact, Columbia College did not admit female undergraduates until as late as 1982, and its famous core course "Masterpieces of European Literature and Philosophy" would remain obliviously all-male until 1986. Even then, while finally agreeing to let Jane Austen scramble up into the treehouse, many Columbia faculty continued to doubt that *Pride and Prejudice* would really "stand up" by itself.

Sometimes it seems as though I move continually backward in time. In 1987 I found myself approaching the horse farms and classical facades of Charlottesville, Virginia, and somewhere south of Washington the years began to drop off one by one. When I began teaching at the University of Virginia, only two of the approximately fifty tenured English faculty were women. One of these was the first woman ever promoted from within; she would be the only one to come up through the ranks until 1991. The last five years have seen, by contrast, an impressive series of outside appointments, raising the number of senior female faculty to eight. My statistical preoccupations do not mean that all the women not hired or not tenured by the University of Virginia and institutions like it were victims of sex discrimination. Nevertheless, given the profound pool of female degree-holders in English, at a certain point numbers do tell the story. That story is one in which women, having been virtually excluded as writers from the canon and as scholars from the academy, began in the seventies and on through the eighties to make small but significant inroads into the man's world of literary studies and academic life generally.

Even now we are nowhere close to parity—we are still, typically, eight out of fifty—but there are enough of us so that new concerns and enthusiasms have been raised, and business cannot quite go on as usual. These recent gains need to be placed in relation to a larger demographic shift: a pattern of growth in the overall university population beginning in the early twentieth century, accelerating in the 1950s with the GI bill, peaking in the sixties with pressure from the civil rights and women's movements, and resulting by the seventies in a national community of faculty and students more than seven times as large as that of 1930, and far more heterogeneous. It is within this context of dramatic demographic change that I locate what I do as a second-generation American feminist critic—and also the resistance to what I do, so vehement of late.

When I began this essay, I was unsure about whether to address this resistance explicitly. On the one hand, I feared it would trivialize two decades of laborious and far-reaching feminist scholarship to hold it answerable to a rash of poorly researched attacks in the media. On the other hand, I know from experience that women demanding inclusion in the academy have always had to justify their cause to those who would keep them out. Imagine that for centuries you have been on the margins of scholarly production—like Milton's daughters, you have copied the great man's manuscripts, stirred his coffee and maybe, on a good day, his imagination. If one morning it strikes you that drinking the coffee and getting the byline yourself would make for a richer life, you had better be ready to answer some questions. And so my still-anomalous position as a female (and feminist) professor requires me, quite routinely, to explain myself—whereas those who habitually assume the legitimacy of their status and opinions have only recently been asked to account for what they do. It's no wonder that, used to authority, they panic in the face of recent changes: Being challenged feels strange and more threatening than actual circumstances warrant. The current debate just highlights the fact that from its inception feminist criticism has been involved in conflicts over power—conflicts between a majority snugly ensconced in the academy and a minority that has just, through difficult weather, come knocking on its door. A variation on the usual generational battle between fathers and sons, the struggle is intensified by long-standing inequities between white male professionals and the rest of us.

2

In *Tenured Radicals*, Roger Kimball goes off on a right-wing rant, claiming that all the respectable, tax-paying, solid citizens in the literary canon are getting squeezed out by weirdos. "Interest groups," as Kimball calls them, demand "more women's literature for feminists, black literature for blacks, gay literature for homosexuals, and so on." Belief in transcendent literary quality is down the tubes, he warns, replaced by views of literature as mere "popular entertainment," contingent on "race, gender, and the like." Gender *and the like*. Homosexuals *and so on*. Kimball leaves the rest to our lurid and alarmist imaginations.

Kimball is quite right that the inclusion of writing by women and other excluded groups in anthologies, in the curriculum, and in works of scholarship is one of feminist criticism's primary goals. There is frequently an archaeological and editorial aspect to this task: excavating forgotten works, sometimes best-sellers in their own time, dusting them off and getting them back into print. Feminist presses and special series at mainstream presses (such as the Black Women Writers Series at Beacon Press) play a crucial role in this project. As a result of such efforts over the last twenty years, hundreds of "lost" texts have been recovered, and many of them—Kate Chopin's *The Awakening* (1899) and Zora Neale Hurston's *Their Eyes Were Watching God* (1937), for example—have quickly achieved canonical status. Sometimes, by contrast, the task is to reconsider writers known and even taught, but relegated to literature's minor leagues (remember the "Major Authors" *Norton*). Edith Wharton, for example, long regarded as a lesser Henry James, emerges as an innovative novelist in her own right, once we refocus our critical gaze. Moreover, individual works must be reassessed in addition to authors; renewed attention to someone like Charlotte Brontë may suggest that her little-known last novel, *Villette*, is actually more interesting and ambitious than *Jane Eyre*.

Canon revision of this kind is emphatically not a matter of replacing the criterion of quality with the criterion of femaleness, blackness, or "the like." The common implication that to include women writers is necessarily to degrade standards—as if the highest quality and femaleness were mutually exclusive —is based on a naive view of what existing standards represent. For the feminist revisionist does not intrude upon a space in which objective judgments about literary value are calmly being made and forcibly impose a gender bias. Rather, since she has read so many works of obvious value by women, she recognizes their relative absence from literary histories as evidence of a gender bias already in effect. Our revisionist concludes from this that canonical texts do not nominate themselves, their inherent worth making them shine like so many stars in the firmament. They are, instead, selected by publishers, critics, and professors—then assiduously polished to such a gleam that the polisher can see his own reflection in their surface. That this business of selection depends upon the place and time as well as, say, the gender and race of those who run the culture industry would seem clear from the extreme fluctuations in literary taste from age to age. For the "traditional literary canon" by no means transcends historical vagaries, but proves instead to be highly reliant on them. Thus Milton, an exemplary figure for the Romantics, was disparaged by many of the Modernists and only fully regained his reputation among formalists of the early 1960s who admired his "grand style." Melville, to take another example, was largely ignored—along with American literature generally—until the 1920s, when a tiny band of white men from New England were suddenly hailed as the fathers of what came to be called the "American Renaissance." The opposition between "high" and "popular" works is similarly unstable. Two of the most esteemed figures today, Shakespeare and Dickens, were once widely enjoyed by popular audiences—the television of their times.

The point is therefore not "quality" versus "quotas," but rather who gets to decide what counts as quality. In *A Room of One's Own*, Woolf explains how judgments of quality are skewed by a society in which masculine values prevail, and offers the following example: "This is an important book, the critic assumes, because it deals with war. This is an insignificant book because it deals with the feelings of women in a drawing-room." Certainly it is also true, as Woolf argues at length, that social conditions have made it more difficult for women to write the plays of Shakespeare: Education has been lacking, domestic duties have called, and prohibitions have been severe. Yet women have written in spite of these obstacles, and if their work has been discounted this is partly because, as Woolf complains, "a scene in a battlefield is more important than a scene in a shop."

Even Jane Austen, though praised for her authoritative style, has suffered from the view that her subject matter—Catherine Morland's gothic fears, Emma Woodhouse's restless imagination—is incongruously slight, out of touch with the major events of her time; after all, she barely mentions the Napoleonic wars. Yet why should the story of women waiting, their marital prospects dimmed by the wartime shortage of men, be seen as any less significant than the story of men fighting? From the perspective of which interest group do women's lives appear less than "historical" and low on the scale of subjects deserving artistic representation? And what about Austen's commentary on class relations and women's education? What about her subtle insistence in *Mansfield Park* that genteel life is contingent upon urban squalor in Portsmouth and slave-owning in Antigua?

Questioning the universality of existing criteria for the canon, offering alternative criteria appreciative of women's concerns and values, does not mean throwing out traditional works altogether. In terms of actual course offerings, the claim that Shakespeare has been replaced by Jacqueline Susann, like the claim that radicals have overrun the university, is simply inaccurate. Such charges have been based primarily on the much-publicized curricular changes at Stanford; these changes, overstated and misunderstood, have then been taken as typical of trends nationwide. To confirm my sense that Shakespeare's place in the average curriculum is still secure, I did my own informal survey of English courses offered at the University of Virginia for the spring of 1992. (Compensating for the relative conservatism of Virginia's faculty, I included those generally more up-to-date courses designed and taught by graduate students.) Out of seventy-four courses, there were five on Shakespeare alone, and five others that featured him. Forty-four consisted primarily of canonical writers; another eighteen had a fair share of "greats" mixed in with less familiar names. Only twelve of the seventy-four were primarily "nontraditional," and here I included all courses centered on African-American and/or women writers, all those on contemporary theory, and all those on popular genres like the detective novel and film, even if taught from traditional perspectives. Surely these twelve out of seventy-four courses suggest little cause for alarm, and this ratio of new to old is typical. A 1989–90 Modern Language Association survey of works most frequently taught agrees with me in finding "no evidence that faculty members in English have abandoned traditional texts in their upper-division literature courses."

If it is not a fact that women and blacks have replaced white men in the canon, neither is it a goal. The hope, rather, is that reading *Moby Dick* in conjunction with Stowe's *Uncle Tom's Cabin* and Douglass's *Narrative of the Life of Frederick Douglass* will enable us to understand Melville and his moment in new ways. These two texts may, for example, by stressing the urgency of the slavery question for midnineteenth-century America, direct more of us to Melville's "Benito Cereno," his story of a slave rebellion at sea. It may also encourage us to read his best-known novel differently, seeing in the narrator's complex intimacy with Queequeg a meditation on white America's relationship to its racial Other. Stowe's domestic priorities may alert us further to Melville's estrangement from the domestic, not to mention the virtual absence of women from *Moby Dick*. Her record-selling novel may lead us to ask (following such critics as Nina Baym, Jane Tompkins, and Annette Kolodny) why American literature has been defined exclusively by books that hit the high seas, retreat to a pond, light out for the territory, or otherwise flee a sphere associated with the feminine—when popular novels by women were celebrating precisely this sphere.

A feminist take on the prevailing pattern runs something

like this. Critics have located the unique "Americanness" of American literature in its ability to replay a certain myth about our national origins and character. At the heart of this myth is a rugged individualist who struggles against the bonds of society and seeks freedom in the untrammeled wilderness. If you think this sounds like the story of male adolescence starring James Dean crossed with John Denver, you're on the right track. What's more, if its rebellious hero is by definition male, both the society he flees and the virgin land he seeks are generally imagined as female. So women do not exactly get speaking parts in this particular drama, and women writers, disinclined to give their female characters second-rate roles, are consequently marginal to the American canon. And speaking of women's absence from the canon as well as from Melville's whaling ship, Twain's raft, or Whitman's road, I would point out to Kimball and co. that it has hardly been necessary to *add* "gay literature" to the existing tradition. At least where men are concerned, revisionary critics have found more than enough gay texts to work with in the canon as it stands; their attention to ties between men (indulged and proscribed) has produced compelling new analyses of writers from Shakespeare to Henry James. The goal, as I say, is not to stop reading the works of such canonical figures but to read them again. It is not to substitute a new constellation of fixed stars for the old, but to recognize the subjective processes by which works rise and fall.

3

My guess is that Roger Kimball likes his women soft and docile; certainly he has no time for Princeton's Elaine Showalter, a leading feminist critic portrayed in *Tenured Radicals* as a kind of literary dominatrix. In Kimball's fantasy, the ruthless Showalter is "nothing if not ambitious" and will not stop at the inclusion of women in the curriculum. She seems to be wearing some kind of heavy boot in his picture of her quest for "nothing less than the triumph of feminist ideology over literature." We have just seen that Melville looks different when we recognize his maritime epic as a specifically masculine venture—not that he looks worse, but that his themes appear less universal, unable in and of themselves to define the "American." Moreover, his period, the American Renaissance, is also transformed when Melville et al. are situated among a host of other authors. So if Kimball is wrong that feminist critics want literature on its back, he is right in suspecting that our project goes beyond reconsidering what books we read to revising how we read them.

Let's take a closer look at what happens when gender becomes what Showalter calls, to Kimball's horror, "a fundamental category of literary analysis." And keep in mind that feminists do not triumphantly wrench literature from its normal impartiality, but simply attempt to identify the ways literary texts—and the critical frameworks used to interpret them—are already pulled to one side or another by various social factors, including gender. Often these frameworks are so familiar and taken for granted, so unthinkingly a part of our reading experience, that we don't even realize they are there. When, for instance, I teach a course on the British novel that starts with Fielding and ends with Joyce—a course in which all of the writers are male except Eliot and maybe a Brontë—my students inevitably assume they are taking an objective survey of "the" novel. Confident they are getting the real thing, no one asks me to explain why I chose the books I did or accuses me of having an interpretive ax to grind. The crowd before me is cheerful and contented, knowing that cultural literacy is just around the corner. When, on the other hand, I begin the course with Frances Burney and end with Woolf, and when half the writers in between are female, then suddenly a few heads stop bobbing in agreement, and certain young males start sulking in the back row. In this kind of class, discussions are sure to turn up disgruntled comments about having ordered a meat-and-potatoes novel course and gotten a *nouvelle* plateful of women. The indignant students behind these remarks have rightly noticed that by choosing some works over others I am mapping the genre's development in a particular way. They feel betrayed. But certainly this is no less true of the first version of the course, in which case, however, the map's familiarity rendered its gender partiality invisible. To many students (and some professors) the lineup of men seems only natural—although given the centrality to the novel of women as writers, readers, and protagonists, it is arguably the male sequence that cries out for rationalization.

This brings me back to Jane Austen, a novelist I have written about and frequently teach. We are used to thinking of biography as a nonfictional form, yet biographies, like canons, involve a process of selection and shaping, an argument about what a life means. In Austen's case this argument emerged one year after her death with her brother Henry's "Biographical Notice," published in 1818. The well-intentioned Henry began by describing his sister's life as lacking in "event," thereby illustrating what Carolyn Heilbrun sees as the paradox of women's biographies before 1970: the biographical endeavor assumes an exceptional subject, yet convention has assumed that a famous woman is a woman defamed, that a good woman has no past. Henry's insistence on what the author was not—she never spoke a harsh word, never thought of money or celebrity—is contradicted both by the merciless wit of her novels and by the interest in sales and reviews apparent in her letters. Yet the family myth of Jane's harmless modesty and piety would persist, and even now her name evokes a prim spinster, pouring tea and penning elegant tales in which everyone speaks well and everything interesting is totally repressed.

In criticism and biography alike, Austen has been admired for doing so little but doing it so skillfully; her greatest strength, scholars have said, was that she knew the limitations of her talent, and here they invariably trot out Austen's own image of her art as a "little bit (two Inches wide) of Ivory." They might, however, just as easily have cited the author's bold self-defense in *Northanger Abbey*, where she replies to those who would denigrate her genre: True, it is *only a novel*, "only some work in which the greatest powers of the mind are displayed, in which the most thorough knowledge of human nature, the happiest delineation of its varieties, the liveliest effusions of wit and

humour are conveyed to the world in the best chosen language."
Austen did not, it seems, belittle what she was about, nor did
she hesitate to challenge the critical truisms of her day. But this
has not kept her from being viewed as a charming conservative,
a good sport of an old maid, reining in her wayward heroines
and rewarding them with marriage. And even those who detect
a satirical edge to her treatment of Regency courtship and customs have tended to reduce her social criticism to a spinster's
sour grapes. Like Emily Dickinson—whose poems blaze with
bombs, volcanoes, and loaded guns, and whose image has been
that of a fragile poetess, naive in matters of sexuality and
punctuation—Austen has been read in terms constrained by
traditional views of the feminine.

So the first step in a feminist reevaluation of Austen is to
identify the myths of gender surrounding her. The second is to
reconceive her work in light of new critical frameworks. What
happens, for example, if we recall that Austen (born in 1775)
spent her impressionable teens with a monarchy rocking and
heads rolling just across the English Channel? Beginning with
this fact, Claudia Johnson sets Austen's work against the literature of the revolutionary era: when politics was an obsession
in England as well as France, when novels and tracts were
loosely interpenetrating forms. The result is to locate Austen's
cast of incompetent fathers—the despotic General Tilney, remote Mr. Bennet, invalid Mr. Woodhouse, and preening Sir
Walter Elliot—in relation to an ongoing cultural conversation
about whether patriarchs do in fact know best. Recovering the
muted but still implicit political agendas in Austen, Johnson
demonstrates that views of this writer as ahistorical are themselves historically insensitive.

Margaret Kirkham, also concerned to historicize her subject,
ties Austen to a rationalist tradition of feminism stretching back
to the polemicist Mary Astell (1666–1731). How does Kirkham
affect our understanding of *Pride and Prejudice*, for instance? Take
the funny scene in which the pompous and wordy Mr. Collins
proposes to Elizabeth Bennet and can't take no for an answer.
The heroine repeatedly turns him down flat, only to have Col-

lins come back with something like, Women are such teases; you know you want it and this may be your last chance—see you at the altar. Poor Elizabeth can only beg him to believe her "a rational creature speaking the truth from her heart," and Kirkham's genealogy enables us to hear this defense of female reason as an echo of Wollstonecraft's in *A Vindication of the Rights of Woman* (1792).

My own interest (for feminists do not always agree, on which more later) has been in those aspects of Austen apart from the rational or at least in excess of the measured and decorous. Her juvenile sketches, in particular, feature carriage accidents, drunkenness, theft, and various unseemly passions, and these may alert us to subtler degrees of violence in the later works. There is, for instance, the sordid drama of Lydia's shot-gun marriage to Wickham, erupting into and briefly taking over the last third of *Pride and Prejudice*. Why such an odd displacement of the central romance between Darcy and Elizabeth? Questioning the novel's "happy" end, I suggest that Lydia's seduction comments negatively on Elizabeth's courtship—that it acts out female vulnerability and loss in reference to the older as well as younger sister's fate. Sandra Gilbert and Susan Gubar have also brought out the protest in Austen against conventional female destinies, pointing to her many bossy matriarchs: Mrs. Ferrars, Lady Catherine De Bourgh, Aunt Norris, and Mrs. Churchill. According to Gilbert and Gubar, these women, though ostensibly vilified, have designs on the story and its characters much as Austen herself does, and we may read their rage for power as a covert expression of the author's own rage. None of the feminist revisions I have sketched would deny the elements of conservatism in Austen, that what she could say was limited by her status as a lady of the middling classes. Yet together such readings suggest a more complex and defiant figure than the gentle Jane of earlier eras—a writer more self-conscious about her project, more engaged by the political concerns of her day, and far less complacent about the darker aspects of the marriage plot.

4

Feminist critics, though located in English or other modern language departments, also contribute to and benefit from interdisciplinary women's studies programs. Dinesh D'Souza, once editor of Princeton's aforementioned *Prospect* magazine, has two major gripes about what he disparagingly calls the "studies" programs. First, he argues that they "balkanize" the academy, and finds it ironic that groups distressed about having been excluded should retreat into exclusive enclaves. Blacks segregate themselves by sitting together in the cafeteria and founding black organizations, or so this argument goes, and women are guilty of separatism when they establish a major intended to encourage teaching and scholarship about women's issues. But this line of reasoning has the cause and effect all wrong. Blacks and women did not create the situation that keeps them still on the margins of the community at large, a token presence on syllabi and in positions of power, undernourished at the predominantly white male table that is the university today. To blame these groups for compensating with social and scholarly communities of their own seems to me the height of unfairness.

Of course we would prefer women's history to be a central aspect of all history courses, instead of being left to women's studies professors and majors, a footnote to history "proper." But women's history is not just "out there," ready to be scooped up, added to existing courses, and tossed lightly—even assuming that most professors were willing to do this. It has to be assembled, piece by elusive piece, and its implications are often such that old theories must be refashioned or thrown out altogether. To take but one example, Joan Kelly's famous essay "Did Women Have a Renaissance?" suggests that the artistic, political, and economic growth of the Renaissance coincided with a contraction of sexual and social freedoms for women. Citing the new premium placed upon female chastity and dependence beginning in the fifteenth century, Kelly illustrates the way remembering women may challenge fundamental assumptions about historical periods. D'Souza's confidence that this kind of paradigm-shifting research concerning women and other neglected groups would happen all by itself, without the sponsorship of specialized programs, is simply not supported by institutional history. Women's studies programs have been and continue to be major forces behind the hiring of feminist faculty, the fostering of courses as well as research on women's issues, and the creation of a student population invested in women's materials and analyses. Only in this way can a body of knowledge be produced that can eventually be integrated into the curriculum as a whole. And as for those who ask, disingenuously I think, about "men's studies," it should be clear by now that feminist work begins by recognizing that so-called neutral scholarship has in fact amounted to the study of men by men.

D'Souza also charges women's studies programs with enforcing a party line, holding "the entire field" hostage to a "shared orthodoxy." If he means by this that antifeminist views are not included, he is right—but as I have just remarked, views indifferent if not hostile to feminism are adequately represented by the rest of the curriculum. To my mind, it makes no more sense to voice these in the context of women's studies than it does to make African-American studies a forum for racism. This said, however—that people in women's studies tend to favor women's liberation—I would argue that feminist scholarship is notable precisely for the diversity of its strategies and goals. For one thing, it is by definition interdisciplinary, and therefore takes in a dazzling range of methods, agendas, vocabularies, and viewpoints. Feminist literary critics alone come in an assortment of flavors, including the psychoanalytic, lesbian, poststructuralist, Marxist, African-Americanist, New Historicist, and tongue-twisting combinations of the above. From the mid-seventies to the mid-eighties we were split into national camps: glamorous French feminists, armed with wordplay and Continental theory, talking about a revolution; pragmatic Anglo-Americans marching for women writers and day care. Far from being grimly monolithic, we have been criticized for being theoretically eclectic, and our response to this criticism has, itself, been conflicted. In 1980, Annette Kolodny counseled us to embrace what she called our "playful pluralism," to be "responsive to the possibilities of multiple critical schools and methods, but captive of none." In 1981, Elaine Showalter called upon us instead to codify what we do, and began by setting off the practice of "feminist critique" (reading for the gender bias in masculine texts) from that of "gynocritics" (devising a new way of reading based on women's texts).

Showalter's useful distinction corresponds more generally to the one illustrated by my discussion of Austen: the dismantling of old models versus the rebuilding of new ones. It is also roughly parallel to another pervasive opposition in women's studies: between stressing the difficulty of conditions for women and stressing our resilient agency in spite of these conditions. But all of these differences of opinion pale beside the differences of social position—of race, sexuality, and class—that have fragmented the feminist community since the early eighties. Or perhaps I should say that, fragmented from the outset, the feminist community has only in the last decade begun to acknowledge the extent of its internal differences. For as African-American, lesbian, and Marxist feminists have long argued, feminism has claimed to speak for all women while in fact speaking largely for a highly specific group. The difficulty has been to admit that there is no universal "woman," but rather a multitude of local female constituencies, some more empowered than others. In this light, D'Souza's proposition that Betty Friedan's white liberal manifesto and Angela Davis's radical black one "reflect a similar, if not identical, understanding of gender difference" reveals itself as ludicrously uninformed. So painfully aware is feminism today of the dissimilarities between Friedan and Davis, that the question posed by the nineties is whether a coalition between the groups they represent remains possible—and given the present backlash, I can only hope that it is.

I say "backlash" because to me the so-called "crisis in the academy" decried by the likes of Kimball and D'Souza is essentially a period of transition from an era of elite higher ed-

ucation to one in which the walls of the university are somewhat
more porous to the general population. From my point of view,
the groaning that we hear is not Western culture collapsing but
a heavy door beginning to open—the same door that was closed
to Woolf's narrator in *A Room of One's Own*, shutting her out
of the library at Oxbridge. It is therefore disquieting to me and
other newcomers to academe that many are nostalgic for the
good ol' days when a genteel consensus about truth and beauty
was possible by virtue of our absence. It is naturally upsetting
to be told that the party is over because, at long last, you have
thrown off your coat and are heading toward the bar. Bringing
together Melville and Kimball, gathering up Hurston and Austen, I hope I have succeeded in suggesting that the party of a
more democratic culture is just now beginning.

QUEER

AND

NOW

Eve Kosofsky
Sedgwick

Eve Kosofsky Sedgwick is a distinguished practitioner of gay studies. Her books include Between Men *and* Epistemology of the Closet. *She holds a B.A. from Cornell and a Ph.D. from Yale; she has taught at Berkeley, Amherst, and Boston University and now teaches at Duke, where she is Newman Ivey White Professor of English. A collection of her essays,* Tendencies, *is forthcoming from Duke University Press.*

A MOTIVE. I think everyone who does gay and lesbian studies is haunted by the suicides of adolescents. To us, the hard statistics come easily: that queer teenagers are two to three times likelier to attempt suicide, and to accomplish it, than others; that up to 30 percent of teen suicides are likely to be gay or lesbian; that a third of lesbian and gay teenagers say they have attempted suicide; that minority queer adolescents are at even more extreme risk.[1]

The knowledge is indelible but not astonishing to anyone with a reason to be attuned to the profligate way this culture has of denying and despoiling queer energies and lives. I look at my adult friends and colleagues doing lesbian and gay work, and I feel that the survival of each one is a miracle. Everyone who survived has stories about how it was done

> —an outgrown anguish
> Remembered, as the Mile

> Our panting Ankle barely passed—
> When Night devoured the Road—
> But we—stood whispering in the House—
> And all we said—was "Saved"!

(as Dickinson has it).[2] How to tell kids who are supposed never to learn this that further along, the road widens and the air brightens; that in the big world there are worlds where our demand is plausible to *get used to it*.

EPISTEMOLOGIES. I've heard of many people who claim they'd as soon their children were dead as gay. What it took me a long time to believe is that these people are saying no more than the truth. They even speak for others too delicate to use the cruel words. For there is all the evidence: the preponderance of school systems, public and parochial, where teachers are fired, routinely, for so much as intimating the right to existence of queer people, desires, activities, children. The routine denial to sexually active adolescents, straight *and* gay, of the things they need—intelligible information, support and respect, condoms—to protect themselves from HIV transmission. (As a policy aimed at punishing young gay people with death, this one is working: In San Francisco, for instance, as many as 34 percent of the gay men under 25 being tested—and 54 percent of the young black gay men—are now HIV infected.)[3] The systematic separation of children from queer adults; their systematic sequestration from the truth about the lives, culture, and sustaining relations of adults they know who may be queer. The complicity of parents, of teachers, of clergy, even of the mental health professions, in invalidating and hounding kids who show gender-dissonant tastes, behavior, body language. In one survey 26 percent of young gay men had been forced to leave home because of conflicts with parents over their sexual identity[4]; another report concludes that young gays and lesbians, many of them throwaways, comprise as many as a quarter of all homeless youth in the U.S.[5]

Then there is the systematic denial of these truths among adults. The statistics on the triple incidence of suicide among lesbian and gay adolescents come from a report prepared for the Department of Health and Human Services in 1989. Under Congressional pressure, recommendations based on this section of the report were never released.[6] Under Congressional pressure, in 1991 a survey of adolescent sexual behavior is denied funding. Under the threat of Congressional pressure, support for all research on sexuality suddenly dries up. Seemingly, this society wants its children to know nothing; wants its queer children to conform or (and this is not a figure of speech) die; and wants not to know that it is getting what it wants.

PROMISING, SMUGGLING, READING, OVERREADING. This history makes its mark on what, individually, we are and do. One set of effects turns up in the irreducible multi-layeredness and multi-phasedness of what queer survival means—since being a survivor on this scene is a matter of surviving *into* threat, stigma, the spiraling violence of gay- and lesbian-bashing, and (in the AIDS emergency) the omnipresence of somatic fear and wrenching loss. But it also means surviving into a moment of unprecedented cultural richness, cohesion, and assertiveness for many lesbian and gay adults. Survivors' guilt, survivors' glee, even survivors' responsibility: powerfully as these are experienced, they are also complicated by how permeable the identity "survivor" must be to the undiminishing currents of risk, illness, mourning, and defiance.

Thus I'm uncomfortable generalizing about people who do queer writing and teaching, even within literature; but some effects do seem widespread. I think many adults (and I am among them) are trying, in our work, to keep faith with vividly remembered promises made to ourselves in childhood: promises to make invisible possibilities and desires visible; to make the tacit things explicit; to smuggle queer representation in where it must be smuggled; and, with the relative freedom of adulthood, to challenge queer-eradicating impulses frontally where they are to be so challenged.

I think that for many of us in childhood the ability to attach intently to a few cultural objects—objects of high or popular culture or both, objects whose meaning seemed mysterious, excessive, or oblique in relation to the codes most readily available to us—became a prime resource for survival. We needed for there to be sites where meanings didn't line up tidily with one another, and we learned to invest these sites with fascination and love. This can't help coloring the adult relation to cultural texts and objects; in fact, it's almost hard for me to imagine another way of coming to care enough about literature to give a lifetime to it. The demands on both the text and the reader from so intent an attachment can be multiple, even paradoxical. For me, a kind of formalism, a visceral near-identification with the writing I cared for, at the level of sentence structure, metrical pattern, rhyme, was one way of trying to appropriate what seemed the numinous and resistant power of the chosen objects. Education made it easy to accumulate tools for this particular formalist project, because the texts that magnetized me happened to be novels and poems. I am awed that others of my generation and since seem to have invented for themselves, in the spontaneity of great need, the tools for a formalist apprehension of other less prestigious, more ubiquitous kinds of text: genre movies, advertising, comic strips.

For me, this strong formalist investment didn't imply (as formalism is generally taken to imply) an evacuation of interest from the passional, the imagistic, the ethical dimensions of the texts, but quite the contrary: The need I brought to books and poems was hardly to be circumscribed, and I felt I knew I would have to struggle to wrest from them sustaining news of the world, ideas, myself, and (in various senses) my kind. The reading practice founded on such basic demands and intuitions had necessarily to run "against the grain" of the most patent available formulae for young people's reading and life—against the grain, often, of the most accessible voices even in the texts themselves. At any rate, becoming a perverse reader was never a matter of my condescension to texts, rather of the surplus charge of my trust in them to remain powerful, refractory, and exemplary. And this doesn't seem an unusual way for ardent reading to function in relation to queer experience.

———

WHITE NIGHTS. The first lesbian and gay studies class I taught was in the English Department at Amherst College in 1986. I thought I knew which five or six students (mostly queer) would show up, and I designed the course, with them in mind, as a seminar that would meet one evening a week, at my house. The first evening sixty-five students showed up—a majority of them, straight-identified.

Having taught a number of these courses by now, I know enough to expect to lose plenty of sleep over each of them. The level of accumulated urgency, the immediacy of the demand that students bring to them is jolting. In most of their courses students have, unfortunately, learned to relinquish the expectation that the course material will address them where they live and with material they can hold palpably accountable; in gay/lesbian courses, though, such expectations seem to rebound, clamorous and unchastened, in all their rawness. Especially considering the history of denegation most queer students bring with them to college, the vitality of their demand is a precious resource. Most often during a semester everyone will spend some time angry at everybody else. It doesn't surprise me when straight and gay students, or women and men students, or religious and nonreligious students, have bones to pick with one another or with me. What has surprised me more is how divisive issues of methodology and disciplinarity are: The single most controversial thing in several undergraduate classes has been *that they were literature courses*, that the path to every issue we discussed simply had to take the arduous defile through textual interpretation.

Furthermore it was instructive to me in that class at Amherst that a great many students, students who defined themselves as nongay, were incensed when (in an interview in the student newspaper) I told the story of the course's genesis. What outraged them was the mere notation that I had designed the course envisioning an enrollment of mostly lesbian and gay students. Their sense of entitlement as straight-defined students was so strong that they considered it an inalienable right to have all kinds of different lives, histories, and cultures unfolded as if anthropologically in formats specifically designed—designed from the ground up—for maximum legibility to themselves: They felt they shouldn't so much as have to slow down the Mercedes to read the historical markers on the battlefield. That it was a field where the actual survival of other people in the class might at the very moment be at stake—where, indeed, in a variety of ways so might their own be—was hard to make notable to them among the permitted assumptions of their liberal arts education. Yet the same education was being used so differently by students who brought to it sharper needs, more supple epistemological frameworks.

CHRISTMAS EFFECTS. What's "queer"? Here's one train of thought about it. The depressing thing about the Christmas season— isn't it?—is that it's the time when all the institutions are speaking with one voice. The Church says what the Church says. But the State says the same thing—maybe not (in some ways it hardly matters) in the language of theology, but in the language the State talks: legal holidays, long school hiatus, special postage stamps, and all. And the language of commerce more than chimes in, as consumer purchasing is organized ever more narrowly around the final weeks of the calendar year, the Dow Jones aquiver over Americans' "holiday mood." The media, in turn, fall in triumphally behind the Christmas phalanx: Ad-swollen magazines have oozing turkeys on the cover, while for the news industry every question turns into the Christmas question—Will hostages be free *for Christmas?* What did that flash flood or mass murder (umpty-ump people killed and maimed) do to those families' *Christmas?* And meanwhile the pairing "families/Christmas" becomes increasingly tautological, as families more and more constitute themselves according to the schedule, and in the endlessly iterated image, of the holiday itself constituted in the image of "the" family.

The thing hasn't, finally, so much to do with propaganda for Christianity as with propaganda for Christmas itself. They all—religion, state, capital, ideology, domesticity, the discourses of power and legitimacy—line up with one another so neatly once a year, and the monolith so created is a thing one can come to view with unhappy eyes. What if instead there were a practice of valuing the ways in which meanings and institutions can be at loose ends with each other? What if the richest junctures weren't the ones where *everything means the same thing?* Think of that entity "the family," an impacted social space in which all of the following are meant to line up perfectly with one another:

a surname
a sexual dyad
a legal unit based on state-regulated marriage
a circuit of blood relationships
a system of companionship and succor
a building
a proscenium between "private" and "public"
an economic unit of earning and taxation
the prime site of economic consumption
the prime site of cultural consumption
a mechanism to produce, care for, and acculturate children
a mechanism for accumulating material goods over several generations
a daily routine
a unit in a community of worship
a site of patriotic formation

and of course the list could go on. Looking at my own life, I see that—probably like most people—I have valued and pursued these various elements of family identity to quite differing degrees (e.g., no use at all for worship, much need of companionship). But what's been consistent in this particular life is an interest in *not* letting very many of these dimensions line up directly with one another at one time. I see it's been a ruling intuition for me that the most productive strategy (intellectually, emotionally) might be, whenever possible, to *dis*articulate them one from another, to *dis*engage them—the bonds of blood, of law, of habitation, of privacy, of companionship and succor—from the lockstep of their unanimity in the system called "family."

Or think of all the elements that are condensed in the notion of sexual identity, something that the common sense of our time presents as a unitary category. Yet, exerting any pressure at all on "sexual identity," you see that its elements include the following:

> your biological (i.e., chromosomal) sex, male or female;
> your self-perceived gender assignment, male or female (supposed to be the same as your biological sex);
> the preponderance of your traits of personality and appearance, masculine or feminine (supposed to correspond to your sex and gender);
> the biological sex of your preferred partner;
> the gender assignment of your preferred partner (supposed to be the same as her/his biological sex);
> the masculinity or femininity of your preferred partner (supposed to be the opposite[7] of your own);
> your self-perception as gay or straight (supposed to correspond to whether your preferred partner is your sex or the opposite);
> your preferred partner's self-perception as gay or straight (supposed to be the same as yours);
> your procreative choice (supposed to be yes if straight, no if gay);
> your preferred sexual act(s) (supposed to be insertive if you are male or masculine, receptive if you are female or feminine);
> your most eroticized sexual organs (supposed to correspond to the procreative capabilities of your sex, and to your insertive/receptive assignment);
> your sexual fantasies (supposed to be highly congruent with your sexual practice, but stronger in intensity);
> your main locus of emotional bonds (supposed to reside in your preferred sexual partner);

your enjoyment of power in sexual relations (supposed
to be low if you are female or feminine, high if male
or masculine);

the people from whom you learn about your own gender
and sex (supposed to correspond to yourself in both
respects);

your community of cultural and political identification
(supposed to correspond to your own identity)

and—again—many more. Even this list is remarkable for the
silent presumptions it has to make about a given person's sexuality, presumptions that are true only to varying degrees, and
for many people are not true at all: that everyone "has a sexuality," for instance, and that it is implicated with each person's
sense of overall identity in similar ways; that each person's most
characteristic erotic expression will be oriented toward another
person and not autoerotic; that if it is alloerotic, it will be oriented toward a single partner or kind of partner at a time; that
its orientation will not change over time. Normatively, as the
parenthetical prescriptions in the list above suggest, it should
be possible to deduce anybody's entire set of specs from the
initial datum of biological sex alone—if one adds only the normative assumption that "biological sex of preferred partner"
will be the opposite of one's own. With or without that het-
erosexist assumption, though, what's striking is the number
and *difference* of the dimensions that "sexual identity" is supposed to organize into a seamless and univocal whole.

And if it doesn't?

That's one of the things that "queer" can refer to: the open
mesh of possibilities, gaps, overlaps, dissonances and reso-
nances, lapses and excesses of meaning when the constituent
elements of anyone's gender, of anyone's sexuality aren't made
(or *can't be* made) to signify monolithically. The experimental
linguistic, epistemological, representational, political adventures attaching to the very many of us who may at times be
moved to describe ourselves as (among many other possibilities)
pushy femmes, radical faeries, fantasists, drags, clones, leath-

erfolk, ladies in tuxedoes, feminist women or feminist men, masturbators, divas, Snap! queens, butch bottoms, storytellers, transsexuals, aunties, wannabes, lesbian-identified men or lesbians who sleep with men, or ; . . . people able to relish, learn from, or identify with such.

Again, "queer" can mean something different: A lot of the way I have used it so far in this dossier is to denote, almost simply, same-sex sexual object choice, lesbian or gay, whether or not it is organized around multiple criss-crossings of definitional lines. And given the historical and contemporary force of the prohibitions against *every* same-sex sexual expression, for anyone to disavow those meanings, or to displace them from the term's definitional center, would be to dematerialize any possibility of queerness itself.

But a word so fraught as "queer" is—fraught with so many social and personal histories of exclusion, violence, defiance, excitement—can never only denote, nor even can it only connote; a part of its experimental force as a speech act is the way it dramatizes locutionary position itself. A hypothesis worth making explicit: that there are important senses in which "queer" can signify only *when attached to the first person.* One possible corollary: that what it takes—all it takes—to make the description "queer" a true one is the impulsion *to* use it in the first person.

CURRENT: PROJECT 1. *The Golden Bowl*, J. L. Austin, *Dr. Susan Love's Breast Book*, and Mme de Sévigné are stacked, open, on the chair opposite me as I write.

Project 1 is a book of critical essays about desires and identifications that move across gender lines, including the desires of men for women and of women for men. In that sense, self-evidently, heterosexuality is one of its subjects. But the essays are queer ones. Their angle of approach is directed, not at reconfirming the self-evidence and "naturalness" of heterosexual identity and desire, but rather at rendering those culturally central, apparently monolithic constructions newly accessible to analysis and interrogation.

The project is difficult partly because of the asymmetries between the speech relations surrounding heterosexuality and homosexuality. As Michel Foucault argues, during the eighteenth and nineteenth centuries in Europe,

> Of course, the array of practices and pleasures continued to be referred to [heterosexual monogamy] as their internal standard; but it was spoken of less and less, or in any case with a growing moderation. Efforts to find out its secrets were abandoned; nothing further was demanded of it than to define itself from day to day. The legitimate couple, with its regular sexuality, had a right to more discretion. It tended to function as a norm, one that was stricter, perhaps, but quieter. . . .
>
> Although not without delay and equivocation, the natural laws of matrimony and the immanent rules of sexuality began to be recorded on two separate registers.[8]

Thus, if we are receptive to Foucault's understanding of modern sexuality as the most intensive site of the demand for, and detection or discursive production of, the Truth of individual identity, it seems as though this silent, normative, uninterrogated "regular" heterosexuality may not function as sexuality at all. Think of how a culturally central concept like public/private is organized so as to preserve for heterosexuality the unproblematicalness, the apparent naturalness, of its *discretionary* choice between display and concealment: "public" names the space where cross-sex couples *may*, whenever they feel like it, display affection freely, while same-sex couples *must* always conceal it; while "privacy," to the degree that it is a right codified in U.S. law, has historically been centered around the protection-from-scrutiny of the married, cross-sex couple, a scrutiny to which (since the 1986 decision in *Bowers v. Hardwick*) same-sex relations on the other hand are unbendingly subject. Thus heterosexuality is consolidated as the *opposite* of the "sex" whose secret, Foucault says, "the obligation to conceal . . . was but another aspect of the duty to admit to."[9] To the degree that heterosexuality does not function as a sexuality, however, there are stubborn barriers to making it accountable, to making it so much as visible, in the framework of projects of historicizing and hence denaturalizing sexuality. The making historically visible of heterosexuality is difficult because, under its institutional pseudonyms such as Inheritance, Marriage, Dynasty, Family, Domesticity, and Population, heterosexuality has been permitted to masquerade so fully as History itself—when it has not presented itself as the totality of Romance.

Previous work in gay theory—other people's and my own—has been enabled by a refusal to accept codified definitions of "homosexuality" as a starting point; analogously, this project will adopt the strategy of refusing to take as a given the identity-definition "heterosexual."[10] One of the motives for this project is, indeed, to denaturalize any presumptive understanding of the relation of "heterosexual" to "homosexual" as modern sexual identities—the presumption, for instance, of their symmetry, their mutual impermeability, or even of their both functioning as "sexual identities" in the same sense. Accordingly, the essays are meant to embody and critique a variety of approaches to desires and identifications that cross gender; they don't assume cross-gender and same-gender relations to be mutually exclusive.

The part I am at work on now is proceeding under the provisional rubric of Queer Tutelage. Trying to open up the category of "the people from whom you learn about your own gender and sex," it is an argument against psychoanalytically based understandings of individual gender and sexuality, which see them as developing exclusively in relation to paths of desire and identification attaching to "the mother" and "the father": attaching, that is, by definition, to one man and one woman viewed exclusively through their roles in a procreative heterosexual couple. Little wonder, then, that heterosexuality, so installed at the origin of sexual development in psychoanalytic thought, should also so reliably emerge as its norm and telos.

In my work I use rich turn-of-the-century texts to argue that gender and sexuality (both hetero and homo) are also likely to be formed through similar choreographies of desire and identification involving same-sex pairs or groups, and frequently involving what were at the turn of the century nascent or newly crystallizing forms of gay and lesbian identity. It is my hope that with this project I will do theoretical justice to the heterogeneous adults who—often across boundaries of gender, of "sexuality"—offered so much to my own sense of self-recognition and possibility, in the years of acute adolescent depression when those seemed most threatened with foreclosure. In a discussion of Oscar Wilde's *The Importance of Being Earnest*, I'm suggesting that the customary (psychoanalytic and poststructuralist) critical focus on the father—whose identity is, after all, a blank until the next-to-last page of the play—might usefully give way to a focus on the play's ubiquitous uncle, aunt, and sibling relations, relations less tautologically structured by the presumption of procreative heterosexuality. In a reading of Henry James's *The Wings of the Dove*, I begin with some rhetoric in the novel that suggests that the father of one of the main woman characters should be understood as having been involved in a homosexual scandal; I speculate about how the itineraries of desire and identification among the characters may be read differently if one hypothesizes a (highly stigmatized) homosexual father at the origin of the novel's erotic identities and energies. And I want to look at Proust, and the very Oedipally centered Proust criticism, with an eye to arguing that the close couple into which the narrator has to insert himself in order to arrive at an individuated, gendered subjectivity is not actually, as the classic Oedipal account would have it, the one formed by his father and his mother, but rather the tighter one—modeled on the celebrated and strange bond between Mme de Sévigné and her daughter—formed by his mother and his grandmother. One of the impulses underlying this project is an impatience with the way available discourses, gay-affirming ones as well as homophobic ones, focus on homosexuality as a possible developmental outcome rather than as a developmental model. It is time for genetic narratives like psychoanalysis (and of course, all narratives are genetic narratives) to stop asking the assaultive and sinister question, Where do homosexuals come from? I see an urgency in understanding same-sex desires and queer people as not only *what the world makes* but *what makes the world.*

PROJECT 2. Here I'm at a much earlier stage, busy with the negotiations involved in defining a new topic in a usable, heuristically productive way; it is still a series of hunches and overlaps; its working name is Queer Performativity. It will consider the implications for gender and sexuality of a tradition of philosophical thought concerning certain utterances that do not merely describe but actually perform the actions they name: "*J'accuse*"; "Be it resolved . . ."; "I thee wed"; "I apologize"; "I dare you." Discussions of linguistic performativity have become a place to reflect on ways in which language really can be said to produce effects: effects of identity, enforcement, seduction, challenge.[11] They also deal with how powerfully language positions: how it changes the way we understand meaning, for instance, if the semantic force of a word like "queer" is so different in a first-person from what it is when used in a second- or third-person sentence.

My sense is that, in a span of thought that arches at least from Plato to Foucault, there are some distinctive linkages to be traced between linguistic performativity and histories of same-sex desire. I want to go further with an argument implicit in *Epistemology of the Closet*: that both the act of coming out, and closetedness itself, can be taken as dramatizing certain features of linguistic performativity in ways that have broadly applicable implications. Among the striking aspects of considering closetedness in this framework, for instance, is that the speech act in question is a series of silences! I'm the more eager to think about performativity, too, because it may offer some ways of describing what *critical* writing can effect (promising?

smuggling?): Anything that offers to make this genre more acute and experimental, less numb to itself, is a welcome prospect.

PROJECT 3 involves thinking and writing about something that's actually structured a lot of my daily life over the past year. Early in 1991 I was diagnosed, quite unexpectedly, with a breast cancer that had already spread to my lymph system. The experiences of diagnosis, surgery, chemotherapy, and so forth, while draining and scary, have also proven just sheerly *interesting* with respect to exactly the issues of gender, sexuality, and identity formation that were already on my docket. (Forget the literal-mindedness of mastectomy, chemically induced menopause, etc.: I would warmly encourage anyone interested in the social construction of gender to find some way of spending half a year or so as a totally bald woman.) As a general principle, I don't like the idea of "applying" theoretical models to particular situations or texts—it's always more interesting when the pressure of application goes in both directions—but all the same it's hard not to think of this continuing experience as, among other things, an adventure in applied deconstruction.[12] How could I have arrived at a more efficient demonstration of the instability of the supposed oppositions that structure an experience of the "self"?—the part and the whole (when cancer so dramatically corrodes that distinction); harm and help (when at least one of the chemicals slipped into my bloodstream was initially developed as a chemical warfare agent); fear and hope (when I feel —I've got a quarterly physical coming up—so much less prepared to deal with the news that a lump or rash *isn't* a metastasis, than it is); past and future (when a person anticipating the possibility of death, and the people who care for her, occupy temporalities that more and more radically diverge); thought and act (the words in my head are aswirl with fatalism, but at the gym I'm striding treadmills and lifting weights); or the natural and the technological (what with the exoskeleton of the bone-scan machine, the uncanny appendage of the IV drip, the bionic implant of the Port-a-cath, all in the service of imaging and recovering my "natural" healthy body in the face of its spontaneous and endogenous threat against itself). Problematics of undecidability present themselves in a new, unfacile way with a disease whose very *best* outcome—since breast cancer doesn't respect the five-year statute of limitations that constitutes cure for some other cancers—will be decades and decades of free-fall interpretive panic.

Part of what I want to see, though, is what's to be learned from turning this experience of dealing with cancer, in all its (and my) marked historical specificity, and with all the uncircumscribableness of the turbulence and threat involved, back toward a confrontation with the theoretical models that have helped me make sense of the world so far. The phenomenology of life-threatening illness; the performativity of a life threatened, relatively early on, by illness; the recent crystallization of a politics explicitly oriented around grave illness: exploring these connections *has* (at least for me it has) to mean spinning my energies out to inhabit the very farthest of the loose ends where representation, identity, gender, sexuality, and the body can't be made to line up neatly together.

OUT, OUT—. It's probably not surprising that gender is so strongly, so multiply valenced in the experience of breast cancer today. Received wisdom has it that being a breast cancer patient, even while it is supposed to pose unique challenges to one's sense of "femininity," nonetheless plunges one into an experience of almost archetypal Femaleness; from the beginning it was universally suggested to me by friends and advisors of all kinds that my proper recourse for counsel, encouragement, solidarity in dealing with breast cancer would be (i.e., I inferred, *had better* be) other women in their most essential identity as women. Judith Frank is the friend whom I like to think of as Betty Ford to my Happy Rockefeller—the friend, that is, whose decision to be public about her own breast cancer diagnosis impelled me to the doctor with my worrisome lump; she and her lover, Sasha Torres, are only two of many women who have made this experience survivable for me: compañeras, friends, advisors, visitors, students, lovers, correspondents, relatives, care givers (these being anything but discrete categories). Some of these are indeed people I have come to love in feminist- and/or lesbian-defined contexts; beyond that, a lot of the knowledge and skills that keep making these women's support so beautifully à propos derive from distinctive feminist, lesbian, and women's histories. (I'd single out, in this connection, the contributions of the women's health movement of the seventies—its trenchant analyses, its grassroots and anti-racist politics, its publications,[13] the attitudes and institutions it built and some of the careers it seems to have inspired.)

At the same time, though, another kind of identification was plaited inextricably across this one—not just for me, but for other women I have been close to, as well. Many or all of us, even in our quite various identities *as* women, have been intimately formed by, among other things, the availability for our own identifications of men and of male "perversion," courage, care, loss, struggle, and creativity. (I also know that men as well as women have been intimately formed by my and many other women's availability for identification in these ways.) Probably my own most formative influence from a quite early age has been a viscerally intense, highly speculative (not to say inventive) cross-identification with gay men and gay male cultures as I inferred, imagined, and later came to know them. It wouldn't have required quite so overdetermined a trajectory, though, for almost any forty-year-old facing a protracted, life-threatening illness in 1991 to realize that the people with whom she had perhaps most in common, and from whom she might well have most to learn, are people living with AIDS, AIDS activists, and others whose lives had been profoundly reorganized by AIDS in the course of the 1980s.

As, indeed, had been my own life and those of most of the people closest to me. "Why me?" is the *cri de coeur* that is popularly supposed to represent Everywoman's deepest response to a breast cancer diagnosis—so much so that not only does a popular book on the subject have that title, but the national breast cancer information and support hotline is called Y-ME! Yet "Why me?" was not something it could have occurred to me to ask in a world where so many companions of my own age were already dealing with fear, debilitation, and death. I wonder, too, whether it characterizes the responses of the urban women of color forced by violence, by drugs, by state indifference or hostility, by AIDS and other illnesses, into familiarity with the rhythms of early death. At the time of my diagnosis, the most immediate things that were going on in my life were: First, that I was co-teaching (with Michael Moon) a graduate course in queer theory, including such AIDS-related material as Cindy Patton's stunning *Inventing AIDS*. Second, that we and many of the students in the class, students who indeed provided the preponderance of the group's leadership and energy at that time, were intensely wrapped up in the work (demonstrating, organizing, lobbying) of a very new local chapter of the AIDS activist organization ACT UP. And third, that at the distance of far too many miles I was struggling to communicate some comfort or vitality to a beloved friend, Michael Lynch, a pioneer in gay studies and AIDS activism, who seemed to be within days of death from an AIDS-related infection in Toronto.

The framework in which I largely experienced my diagnosis, then—and the framework in which my friends, students, house sharers, life companion, and others made available to me almost overwhelming supplies of emotional, logistical, and cognitive sustenance[14]—was very much shaped by AIDS and the critical politics surrounding it, including the politics of homophobia and of queer assertiveness. The AIDS activist movement, in turn, owes much to the women's health movement of the seventies; and in another turn, an activist politics of breast cancer, spearheaded by lesbians, seems in the last year or two to have been emerging based on the model of AIDS activism.[15] Paragraphs from an obituary I wrote for Michael Lynch (while he was still alive, so he could read it; he died on July 9, 1991) suggest only a few of the complicated ways in which "his" illness and "mine" intersected:

> Last weekend visiting Toronto I had a few minutes to look through the log book kept by Michael's care team. I leafed back to February, to the time of my diagnosis and mastectomy, and was amazed to find that one caregiver's shift after another had been marked by the restlessness, exhaustion, and pain of Michael's anxiety about what was going on with me in Durham. Of course it didn't surprise me that he was worried about me or compassionated with me, during such a difficult passage. But what I had felt I was experiencing from him at the time—remember that these were the same weeks when Michael was supposed to die, but instead got stronger and stronger—was the tremendous plenitude of the energies he somehow had available to inject into me. The friend who had been, only weeks before, so flickering and disconnected that I worried that it was torturing him to make him talk on the phone, now was at my ear daily with hours of the lore, the solicitude, the ground-level truthtelling and demand for truthtelling that I simply had to have. I also felt miraculously revitalized by the joy of having a real Michael, not the dry-mouthed struggling shade of him, there again to communicate with. I didn't know where these energies came from in Michael—I thought they were produced as if magically by my need of them; to some extent I still think they were—but I see now that they were also carved directly out of Michael's substance, his rest and his peace of mind.
>
> But also a lot of what I needed so unexpectedly to learn from Michael I had already had opportunities to learn. So much about how to be sick—how to occupy most truthfully and powerfully, and at the same time constantly to question and deconstruct, the sick role, the identity of the "person living with life-threatening disease"—had long been embodied in him, and per-

formed by him, in ways which many of us, sick and
well, have had reason to appreciate keenly. These are
skills that could not have evolved outside of the context
of liberatory identity politics and AIDS activism, but
their flavor is also all Michael's own.[16] I have sometimes
condensed them to myself in the unbearably double-
edged performative injunction, "Out, out—." As if the
horrifying fragility of a life's brief flame could somehow
be braced and welded, in the forge of the signifier, as if
orthopedically to the galvanizing coming-out imperative
of visibility, defiance, solidarity, and self-assertion. From
Michael I also seem always to hear the injunction—not
the opposite of "Out, out" but somehow a part of it—
"Include, include": to entrust as many people as one
possibly can with one's actual body and its needs, one's
stories about its fate, one's dreams and one's sources of
information or hypothesis about disease, cure, consolation, denial, and the state or institutional violence that
are also invested in one's illness. It's as though there were
transformative political work to be done just by being
available to be identified with in the very grain of one's
illness (which is to say, the grain of one's own intellectual, emotional, bodily self as refracted through illness
and as resistant to it)—being available for identification
to friends, but as well to people who don't love one;
even to people who may not like one at all nor even wish
one well.

MY WAR AGAINST WESTERN CIVILIZATION. That there were such
people—that, indeed, the public discourse of my country was
increasingly dominated by them—got harder and harder to ignore during the months of my diagnosis and initial treatment.
For the first time, it was becoming routine to find my actual
name, and not just the labels of my kind, on those journalistic
lists of who was to be considered more dangerous than Saddam
Hussein. In some ways, the timing of the diagnosis couldn't
have been better: If I'd needed a reminder, I had one that, sure

enough, life *is* too short, at least mine is, for going head-to-head with people whose highest approbation, even, would offer no intellectual or moral support in which I could find value. Physically, I was feeling out of it enough that the decision to let this journalism wash over me was hardly a real choice—however I might find myself misspelled, misquoted, misparaphrased, or (in one hallucinatory account) married to Stanley Fish. It was the easier to deal psychically with having all these journalists scandalize my name because it was clear most of them wouldn't have been caught dead reading my work: The essay of mine that got the most free publicity, "Jane Austen and the Masturbating Girl," did so without having been read by a single one of the people who invoked it; it reached its peak of currency in hack circles months before it was published, and Roger Kimball's *Tenured Radicals*, which first singled it out for ridicule, seems to have gone to press before the essay was so much as *written*.

Not that I imagine a few cozy hours reading *Epistemology of the Closet* would have won me rafts of fans amongst the punditterati. The attacks on me personally were based on such scummy evidential procedures that the most thin-skinned of scholars—so long as her livelihood was secure—could hardly have taken them to heart; the worst of their effects on me at the time was to give an improbable cosmic ratification (yes, actually, everything *is* about me!) to the self-absorption that forms, at best, an unavoidable feature of serious illness. If the journalistic hologram bearing my name seemed a relatively easy thing to disidentify from, though, I couldn't help registering with much greater intimacy a much more lethal damage. I don't know a gentler way to say it than that at a time when I've needed to make especially deep draughts on the reservoir of a desire to live and thrive, that resource has shown the cumulative effects of my culture's wasting depletion of it. It *is* different to experience from the vantage point of one's own bodily illness and need all the brutality of a society's big and tiny decisions, explicit and encoded ones, about which lives have or have not value. Those decisions carry not only institutional and economic but psychic and, I don't doubt, somatic consequences. A thousand things make it impossible to mistake the verdict on queer lives and on women's lives, as on the lives of those who are poor or are not white. The hecatombs of queer youth; a decade squandered in a killing inaction on AIDS; the rapacious seizure from women of our defense against forced childbirth; tens of millions of adults and children excluded from the health care economy; treatment of homeless people as unsanitary refuse to be dealt with by periodic "sweeps"; refusal of condoms in prisons, persecution of needle-exchange programs; denial and trivialization of histories of racism; merely the pivot of a disavowing pronoun in a newspaper editorial: Such things as these are facts, but at the same time they are piercing or murmuring voices in the heads of those of us struggling to marshal "our" resources against illness, dread, and devaluation. They speak to us. They have an amazing clarity.

A CRAZY LITTLE THING CALLED RESSENTIMENT. There was something especially devastating about the wave of anti-"PC" journalism in the absolutely open contempt it displayed, and propagated, for *every* tool that has been so painstakingly assembled in the resistance against these devaluations. Through raucously orchestrated, electronically amplified campaigns of mock-incredulous scorn, intellectual and artistic as well as political possibilities, skills, ambitions, and knowledges have been laid waste with a relishing wantonness. No great difficulty in recognizing those aspects of the anti-"PC" craze that are functioning as covers for a rightist ideological putsch; but it's surprised me that so few people seem to view the recent developments as, among other things, part of an overarching history of anti-intellectualism: anti-intellectualism left as well as right. No twentieth-century political movement, after all, can afford not to play the card of populism, whether or not the popular welfare is what it has mainly at heart (indeed, perhaps especially where it is least so). And anti-intellectual pogroms, like anti-Semitic or queer-bashing ones, are quick, efficient, distracting, and almost universally understood signifiers for a populist solidarity that may boil down to nothing by the time it reaches the soup-pot. It takes care and intellectual scrupulosity to forge an egalitarian politics not founded on such telegraphic slanders. Rightists today like to invoke the threatening specter of a propaganda-ridden socialist realism, but both they and the anti-intellectuals of the left might meditate on why Hitler's campaign against "degenerate art" (Jewish, gay, modernist) was couched, as their own are, in terms of assuring the instant, unmediated, and universal accessibility of all the sign-systems of art (Goebbels even banning all art criticism in 1936, on the grounds that art is self-explanatory). It's hard to tell which assumption is more insultingly wrong: that the People (always considered, of course, as a monolithic unit) have no need and no faculty for engaging with work that is untransparent; or that the work most genuinely expressive of the People would be so univocal and so limpidly vacant as quite to obviate the labors and pleasures of interpretation. Anti-intellectuals today, at any rate, are happy to dispense with the interpretive process and depend instead on appeals to the supposedly self-evident: legislating against *"patently* offensive" art (no second looks allowed); citing titles as if they were texts; appealing to potted summaries and garbled trots as if they were variorum editions in the original Aramaic. The most self-evident things, as always, are taken—as if unanswerably—to be the shaming risibility of any form of oblique or obscure expression; and the flat inadmissability of openly queer articulation.

THOUGHT AS PRIVILEGE. These histories of anti-intellectualism cut across the "political correctness" debate in complicated ways. The term "politically correct" originated, after all, in the mockery by which experimentally and theoretically minded feminists, queers, and leftists (of every color, class, and sexuality) fought back against the stultifications of feminist and left anti-intellectualism. The hectoring, would-be-populist derision that difficult, ambitious, or sexually charged writing today encounters from the right is not always very different from the reception it has already met with from the left. It seems as if many academic feminists and leftists must be grinding their teeth at the way the right has willy-nilly conjoined their discursive fate with that of theorists and "deconstructionists"— just as, to be fair, many theorists who have betrayed no previous interest in the politics of class, race, gender, or sexuality may be more than bemused at turning up under the headings of "Marxism" or "multiculturalism." The right's success in grouping so many, so contestative movements under the rubric "politically correct" is a *coup* of cynical slovenliness unmatched since the artistic and academic purges of Germany and Russia in the thirties.

What the American intellectual right has added to this hackneyed populist semiotic of *ressentiment* is an iridescent oil slick of elitist self-regard. Trying to revoke every available cognitive and institutional affordance for reflection, speculation, experimentation, contradiction, embroidery, daring, textual aggression, textual delight, *double entendre*, close reading, free association, wit—the family of creative activities that might, for purposes of brevity, more simply be called *thought*—they yet stake their claim as the only inheritors, defenders, and dispensers of a luscious heritage of thought that most of them would allow to be read only in the dead light of its pieties and its exclusiveness. Through a deafening populist rhetoric, they advertise the mean pleasures of ranking and gate-keeping as available to all. But the gates that we are invited to invigorate ourselves by cudgelling barbarians at open onto nothing but a *Goodbye, Mr. Chips* theme park.

What is the scarcity that fuels all this *ressentiment?* The leveraged burnout of the eighties certainly took its toll, economically, on universities as well as on other professions and industries. In secretaries' offices, in hospitals and HMOs, in network news bureaus, in Silicon Valley laboratories and beyond, the bottom line has moved much closer to a lot of people's work lives—impinging not just on whether they *have* work, but on what they do when they're there. But academic faculty, in our decentralized institutions, with our relatively diffuse status economy and our somewhat archaic tangle of traditions and prerogatives, have had, it seems, more inertial resistance to offer against the wholesale reorientation of our work practices around the abstractions of profit and the market. For some faculty at some colleges and universities, it is still strikingly true that our labor is divided up by task orientation (we may work on the book till it's done, explain to the student till she understands) rather than by a draconian time discipline; that what we produce is described and judged in qualitative as much as quantitative terms; that there is a valued place for affective expressiveness, and an intellectually productive permeability in the boundaries between public and private; that there are opportunities for collaborative work; and most importantly, that we can expend some substantial part of our paid labor on projects we ourselves have conceived, relating to questions whose urgency and interest make a claim on our own minds, imaginations, and consciences.

Millions of people today struggle to carve out—barely, at great cost to themselves—the time, permission, and resources, "after work" or instead of decently paying work, for creativity and thought that will not be in the service of corporate profit, nor structured by its rhythms. Many, many more are scarred by the prohibitive difficulty of doing so. No two people, no two groups would make the same use of these resources, furthermore, so that no one can really pretend to be utilizing them "for" another. I see that some must find enraging the spectacle of people for whom such possibilities are, to a degree, built into the structure of our regular paid labor. Another way to understand that spectacle, though, would be as one remaining form of insistence that it is not inevitable—it is not a simple fact of nature—for the facilities of creativity and thought to represent rare or exorbitant *privilege*. Their economy should not and need not be one of scarcity.

The flamboyance with which some critical writers—I'm one of them—like to laminate our most ambitious work derives something, I think, from this situation. Many people doing all kinds of work are able to take pleasure in aspects of their work; but something different happens when the pleasure is not only taken but openly displayed. I like to make that different thing happen. Some readers identify strongly with the possibility of a pleasure so displayed; others disidentify from it with violent repudiations; still others find themselves occupying less stable positions in the circuit of contagion, fun, voyeurism, envy, participation, and stimulation. When the pleasure is attached to meditative or artistic productions that deal, not always in an effortlessly accessible way, with difficult and painful realities among others, then readers' responses become even more complex and dramatic, more productive for the author and for themselves. Little wonder then that sexuality, the locus of so many showy pleasures and untidy identities and of so much bedrock confrontation, opacity, and loss, should bear so much representational weight in arguments about the structure of intellectual work and life. Sexuality in this sense, perhaps, can *only* mean queer sexuality: So many of us have the need for spaces of thought and work where everything doesn't mean the same thing!

So many people of varying sexual practices, too, enjoy incorrigibly absorbing imaginative, artistic, intellectual, and affective lives that have been richly nourished by queer energies —and that are savagely diminished when the queerness of those energies is trashed or disavowed. In the very first of the big "political correctness" scare pieces in the mainstream press, *Newsweek* pontificated that under the reign of multiculturalism in colleges, "it would not be enough for a student to refrain from insulting homosexuals. . . . He or she would be expected to . . . study their literature and culture alongside that of Plato, Shakespeare, and Locke."[17] *Alongside?* Read any Sonnets lately? You dip into the Phaedrus often?

To invoke the utopian bedroom scene of Chuck Berry's immortal *aubade*: Roll over, Beethoven, and tell Tchaikovsky the news.

NOTES

Thanks for encouragement and ideas to Ken Wissoker, Mark Seltzer, and Michael Moon. My work on this essay was supported by a grant from the National Humanities Center.

1. Paul Gibson, "Gay Male and Lesbian Youth Suicide," U.S. Dept. of Health & Human Services *Report of the Secretary's Task Force on Youth Suicide*, vol. 3, pp. 110–142.
2. Thomas H. Johnson, ed., *The Complete Poems of Emily Dickinson* (Boston and Toronto: Little, Brown and Company, 1960), poem no. 325, p. 154.
3. T.A. Kellogg et al., "Prevalence of HIV-1 Among Homosexual and Bisexual Men in the San Francisco Bay Area: Evidence of Infection Among Young Gay Men," *Seventh International AIDS Conference Abstract Book*, vol. 2, 1991 (W.C. 3010), p. 298.
4. G. Remafedi, "Male Homosexuality: The Adolescent's Perspective," Adolescent Health Program, University of Minnesota (unpublished), 1985. Cited in Gibson.
5. Gibson, pp. 113–115.
6. On October 13, 1989, Dr. Louis W. Sullivan, Secretary of the Department of Health and Human Services, repudiated the section of the report concerning gay and lesbian youth suicide—impugning not its accuracy, but, it seems, its very existence. In a written statement Sullivan said, "The views expressed in the paper entitled 'Gay Male and Lesbian Youth suicide' do not in any way represent my personal beliefs or the policy of this Department. I am strongly committed to advancing traditional family values. . . . In my opinion, the views expressed in the paper run contrary to that aim." (*New York Native*: 13 November 1989, p 14; 27 November 1989, p. 7.)
7. The binary calculus I'm describing here depends on the notion that the male and female sexes are each other's "opposites," but I do want to register a specific demurral against that bit of easy common sense. Under no matter what cultural construction, women and men are more like each other than chalk is like cheese, than ratiocination is like raisins, than dark is like light, or than 1 is like 0. The biological, psychological, and cognitive attributes of men overlap with those of women by vastly more than they differ from them.
8. Michel Foucault, *The History of Sexuality*, vol. 1: *An Introduction*, tr. Robert Hurley (New York: Pantheon, 1978), pp. 38–40.
9. Foucault, p. 61.
10. For a discussion of the history of the concept of heterosexuality, see Jonathan Ned Katz, *Gay/Lesbian Almanac: A New Documentary* (New York: Harper & Row, 1983), pp. 147–50.
11. One of the most provocative discussions of performativity in relation to literary criticism is Shoshana Felman's *The Literary Speech Act: Don Juan with J. L. Austin, or Seduction in Two Languages*, tr. Catherine Porter (Ithaca: Cornell University Press, 1983); most of the current work being done on performativity in relation to sexuality and gender is much indebted to Judith Butler's *Gender Trouble: Feminism and the Subversion of Identity* (New York: Routledge, 1989).

12. That deconstruction can offer crucial thought-resources for survival under duress will sound astonishing, I know, to anyone who knows it mostly from the journalism on the subject—journalism that always depicts "deconstructionism," not as a group of usable intellectual tools, but as a set of beliefs involving a patently absurd dogma ("nothing really exists"), loopy as Christian Science but as exotically aggressive as (American journalism would also have us find) Islam. I came to my encounter with breast cancer not as a member of a credal sect of "deconstructionists" but as someone who needed all the cognitive skills she could get. I found, as often before, that I had some good and relevant ones from my deconstructive training.

13. The work of this movement is most available today through books like the Boston Women's Health Book Collective's *The New Our Bodies, Ourselves* (New York: Simon & Schuster, Inc., 1984). An immensely important account of dealing with breast cancer in the context of feminist, anti-racist, and lesbian activism is Audre Lorde, *The Cancer Journals*, second ed. (San Francisco: Spinsters, Ink, 1988), and *A Burst of Light* (Ithaca: Firebrand Books, 1988).

14. And physical: I can't resist mentioning the infallibly appetite-provoking meals that Jonathan Goldberg, on sabbatical in Durham, planned and cooked every night during many queasy months of my chemotherapy.

15. On this see Alisa Solomon, "The Politics of Breast Cancer," *The Village Voice* 36.20 (May 14, 1991), pp. 22–27; Judy Brady, ed., *1 in 3: Women with Cancer Confront an Epidemic* (Pittsburgh and San Francisco: Cleis Press, 1991); Midge Stocker, ed., *Cancer as a Women's Issue: Scratching the Surface* (Chicago: Third Side Press, 1991); and Sandra Butler and Barbara Rosenblum, *Cancer in Two Voices* (San Francisco: Spinsters Book Company, 1991).

16. The best sample of this in writing is Michael Lynch's "Last Onsets: Teaching with AIDS," in *Profession 90*.

17. Jerry Adler et al., "Taking Offense: Is this the new enlightenment on campus or the new McCarthyism?," *Newsweek*, 24 December, 1990, pp. 48–55, quoted from p. 48.

HANDLING "CRISIS"

GREAT BOOKS, RAP MUSIC, AND THE END OF WESTERN HOMOGENEITY

Houston A. Baker, Jr.

The 1992 president of the Modern Language Association, Houston A. Baker, Jr., is one of America's most prominent critics of African-American literature. Educated at Howard University and UCLA, Baker began his career as a scholar of the Victorian period. His interests have since enlarged to cover African-American culture, with a particular emphasis on the writings of women, and on rap and popular culture. He has taught at Yale and now teaches at the University of Pennsylvania, where he directs the Center for the Study of Black Literature and Culture. His books include Workings of the Spirit: The Poetics of Afro-American Women's Writing *and* Long Black Song: Essays in Black American Literature and Culture. Black Studies, Rap, and the Academy *is forthcoming from the University of Chicago Press. His piece is excerpted from an essay that first appeared in* Callaloo, *a journal edited by Charles Rowell and published at the University of Virginia.*

In his play *The Slave* (1964), LeRoi Jones (Amiri Baraka) presents an exchange between Professor Bradford Easley and one of his former students, Walker Vessels. Easley is white; Vessels is black and has led a revolutionary army to the professor's home. Easley asks Vessels what he hopes to accomplish through revolution. Are blacks better than whites? Will they—as rulers and bosses—introduce more love, beauty, or truth into the world? Walker responds: "Probably. Probably there will be more . . . if more people have a chance to understand what it is."

But the former slave to Western culture—particularly in its self-congratulatory academic guise—goes on to say that the introduction of love, truth, and beauty into the world has never been the preoccupation of white leaders and bosses of the West. Their goals have been power, money, and lordship over subject peoples. In a wry, postcolonial dismissal, Walker says: "The point is that you have had your chance, darling, now these other folks have theirs." "God," responds Easley, "what an ugly idea."

Actually, Walker's idea seems more deconstructively luminescent than "ugly," more demographically informed than aesthetically inept. And while LeRoi Jones emphasizes the apocalyptic and ritually dramatic aspects of the Easley/Vessels con-

frontation, there is a way in which we might read the scene as
prophetic for what currently in the United States is called a
"crisis in the humanities."

In *The Slave*, the house of Easley must be thunderingly
shattered; only the ambivalent, slightly drunk, and shaken Vessels escapes. In our era—confronted as we are by the demo-
graphics and challenges of global reorganization and capital
redistribution—we needn't resort to a liberal apologetics (*pace*
Easley) that attempts to aestheticize old power relations by
shaming newly emergent peoples and their voices into a colo-
nizing sense of their "ugliness." (By "newly emergent peoples"
I mean African-Americans, gay and lesbian spokespersons, Chicano and Chicana critics and artists, Asian-American theorists
and activists, Latin American commentators, recent scholars of
postcolonial discourse and postmodernism, and all others who
are seriously interrogating formerly unquestioned Western hegemonic arrangements of knowledge and power.) Nor—under
conditions of a profounder and more self-confident analysis than
Vessels's—do newly emergent peoples have to wound themselves attempting to prove the hierarchical superiority of their
beauty or waste time demolishing a master structure whose
manifold code violations have already condemned it to a
ghostly, anachronistic account in the histories of a transnational
future.

What seems certain is that an unchallenged sense of global,
Western, whitemale superiority, or beauty, or authority, has
"had its chance," and we are now engaged with the dynamics
of the articulate ascendence of OTHERS. These dynamics are,
it seems to me, what many commentators mean when they
speak of a "crisis." Finally, the "crisis" is one of the OTHER's
sound. For the moment, however, we should note that one
man's "crisis" can always be an-OTHER's field of dreams,
ladder of ascent, or moment of ethical recognition and ethnic
identification. Which of us has not heard the amusing account
of the moment when Native Americans ride over the hill, caus-
ing the masked man to shout: "We're in deep trouble now,
Tonto!" A crisis, indeed, seems at hand for the masked man.

But the appearance of the riders produces for Tonto an awakening to pronoun-chartings of colonialism: "What do you mean 'WE'?" asks the formerly faithful companion.

This familiar anecdote might prompt the question: "Whose 'crisis' is it, anyway?"

Where the humanities in our present era are concerned, the answer would be too glib and narrow if we designated a single agent, saying the "crisis" is a white, Western American male exclusive—a gender-coded, midlife malaise that produces strange fits of passion such as the verbal tantrum about Shakespeare and Zulus. Such single attribution may be solacing, even ethnically gratifying; but it ignores the fact that we OTHERS are not on another planet. Invoking Baraka again, we recall his quip that when those in power talk of blowing up the world they mean with us in it.

Which is to say, if there is a whitemale "crisis"—one that leads to Star Wars paranoia, arms proliferation, atmospheric pollution, CORE reading lists in tandem with nuclear reactor CORES—then we might have a *mind* to designate the "crisis" as "their" problem, but our *bodies* are clearly on the line as well. There is, then, a "crisis" that implicates us all.

To the extent that multinational capitalism, shifts in world trade balances, and the decentering of post–World War Two geopolitical arrangements of peoples and nations have left whitemale overseers of the United States in the blue-funk of debtors without a cause, one understands why the American condition is projected in dire syllables. For if our economy and Yankee ingenuity are under siege, how can we conceive of our humanity or of our humanities as healthy—even if their current variability, indeterminacy, and hybridity reflect global realignments of value and evaluation? Surely the gloomy sobriety of "crisis thinking" can be read as a symptomatic, if limited, response to real problems faced by the United States.

No one who has surveyed the condition of public education, spent time in secondary and university classrooms, or assessed the status of conventional knowledge and its transmission, reception, and application in the United States can doubt that an old order of literacy has passed. The pastoral, idyllic lyrics of "Schooldays, schooldays, dear old golden rule days," have given way to the postmodern indirection that Spike Lee calls "School Daze." A traditional order of "reading and writing and arithmetic" has yielded—in some cases, to alternative pedagogies and subjects, but more often to deliberate or slovenly indifference. All of these matters seem indisputably true. But the question of their interpretation and address remains very much an open-ended one. There may well exist a dire problem of literacy in our society, but we need seriously to ask in what terms we are to confront this problem. We seem, for example, to have given up on one traditional approach.

"Why Johnny can't read" is not, for example, a serious query today. For if it were a serious query, then the decidedly economic overdetermination of Johnny's plight would not be so consistently ignored, erased, or denied.

We are told, instead, that Johnny is a sufferer in the wake of wild-eyed radicals ("thugs" is sometimes the word used) of the sixties who brought the United States to desperate straits by abandoning Western ideals, misreading Nietzsche, and kicking prayer and the hickory stick out of the American classroom.

We are urged to return to old, common ideas that "every American" needs to know, to put a legacy of acknowledged "Great Books" back into place, and to let the philosophers have their head in the maintenance of State affairs.

One virtually hears Barbra Streisand in the background crooning "The Way We Were" as Allan Bloom exhorts a tearful congregation of ex-Cornell professors, and William Bennett passes the collection plate for suggested "required readings" to reclaim a legacy. Meanwhile, Deacon Hirsch counts entries.

Who is there to challenge this new Zion of whitemale literary evangelism? This chosen interpretation of a "crisis" and its solution?

Johnny himself, of course—perhaps not in the voice and guise of Homer and the Classics, but surely in the voice and person of a new hybridity of interests and values. And Johnny, like his sister Johnetta, has a huge stake in such a challenge, because it is, finally, not book-learning, but the bodies of OTH-ERS that are most decisively in "crisis." That is to say, while whites may have the privilege of endlessly rehearsing a bookish dilemma, what I have described as newly emergent people and voices have no such luxury. For behind the facade of a "battle of the books," as I have already suggested, lies a terrain of global realignment and multinational economic competition where what the French social scientist Pierre Bourdieu calls "cultural capital" has created radically new balances of exchange.

What is expendable in the United States, Johnny and his fellows realize, is *any body* that attempts to ally itself with this current multicultural and shifting flow of world "cultural capital." While Spartan Greek youth wear walkmans from Japan and dance to the hip-hop rhythms of Run DMC, Salt-n-Peppa, N.W.A., and Public Enemy, whitemale cultural literacists nostalgically croon for a return of Homeric highlights and virtually sanction the disappearance of the very bodies that make the United States' popular, public culture a valued currency of global exchange—and an informed source of critique for a postmodern world.

In a too shorthanded manner, then, one might say that Johnny and Johnetta can't read "the classics" because neither the classics nor their advocates have realigned themselves and their project to read Johnny or Johnetta—or to listen to them, or to comprehend their postmodern connectedness to a reformed future. You simply cannot teach a class of people whose life, language, and mores you don't in the least comprehend or respect. Indoctrinate, yes; teach, no. Rather than acknowledge and learn traditions and rhythms that would produce a relational pedagogy—one combining what some hold to be a precious and privileged "legacy" with the long-ignored voices and inheritances that are emerging and being transmitted across cultural frontiers and international, telecommunal viewing spaces today—the American literacists who preach of "crisis" have adopted a strategy of willful ignorance and, ultimately, sanctioned aggression.

Conserving the definite article *the* for humanities conceived only in selective, Western terms is the first move in the dance. Backward glances to a glorious past—one free of colonial expansion, racism, sexism, and self-interested imperialism—a past that never was—is the second move. The third and decisive move is—in a telecommunal age—to couch *the* crisis of *the* humanities in bookish terms, as though reading and writing were not mere technologies that favored an order of privileged ascendency and selective power and ideological control known even to Thoth and his King long ago.

The fourth move in the current "crisis" project is to rid the kingdom of the very bodies of those who represent a "cultural" threat to what the literacists define as "our" national interest. Multiple incidents of campus and university violence against Black and Women, Chicano and Chicana, Asian, Native American, gay and lesbian students by Anglomale perpetrators— incidents that have frequently gone unpunished by Anglomale administrators and ignored by white academics bent on keeping their heads in cultural sands—testify to the expansiveness of this fourth initiative in the current dance of cultural "crisis." There were more than 250 incidents of bias-related aggression on American campuses between 1987–1989. Of course, the inner-city public schools of America and the deteriorating, crime-filled neighborhoods in which they fight to serve an educational mission in the absence of adequate funding or enlightened concern from the federal government offer further testimony to a killing indifference of our "crisis" thinkers.

The OTHERS' defense of self is, thus, an inferable necessity of the current "crisis" in the humanities.

Such a defense begins with dramatically reconceptualized self-definitions by people who are products of a history that has yet to be written. (A ritual and transformative drama teaching us our own beauty plays itself out at every turn.) With bodies on the line and life itself at stake, it hardly seems strange that Johnny might regard our current "crisis" advocates of "cultural literacy" as avatars of those white missionaries who paved the way for slavetraders, armies, and curious colonial scholars of the past. Faced with the prospect of such an enslaving and myopic "cultural literacy," Johnny and his fellows have bolted from the schools and given birth to energetic expressive forms such as postmodern hip-hop, interventionist film culture, and radical scholarship into gender, class, and race determinants of power and knowledge in the world we inhabit.

In many ways, the powerful, syncretic, corporally minimalistic urgings of African-American rap music signal this *légitime défense* (self-defense) of a new humanity and a new humanities that will outlast the current "crisis" and create new room for the new people.

One hears Public Enemy cautioning those who might be drawn into a sham "battle of the books" with the injunction: "Don't, don't, don't believe the hype!"

Perhaps it is because rap is so effective in its expressive counters to a bookish "crisis" that those who "have had their chance" seek so forcefully to suppress it. Rap is the metonym for all of those shared sonics that emergent generations have brought to their own defense, to their own expressive soundings of the world. It summons in its urgings *corridos* of the southwest, Native American chant poems, Latin American magical realism, African and Caribbean lyrics, lesbian and gay signifiers, and so very much more that is undreamed of in the philosophies and books of the "crisis" people. The following letter may be taken as a representative response by "crisis thinkers" to a postmodern world in which rap and its correlates are emergent:

A song recorded by the rap group N.W.A. on their album "Straight Outta Compton" encourages violence against and disrespect for the law enforcement officer and has been brought to my attention. I understand your company recorded and distributed this album, and I am writing to share my thoughts and concerns with you. Advocating violence and assault is wrong, and we in the law enforcement community take exception to such action. Violent crime, a major problem in our country, reached an unprecedented high in 1988. Seventy-eight law enforcement officers were feloniously slain in the line

of duty during 1988, four more than in 1987. Law enforcement officers dedicate their lives to the protection
of our citizens, and recordings such as the one from
N.W.A. are both discouraging and degrading to these
brave, dedicated officers. Music plays a significant role
in society, and I wanted you to be aware of the FBI's
position relative to this song and its message. I believe
my views reflect the opinion of the entire law enforcement community.

The letter was written to Priority Records by Milt Ahlerich,
an FBI assistant director, who reports directly to William Ses-
sions, and who acknowledges that the letter represents not his
personal opinion, but the Bureau's official position. The letter
is, to Ahlerich's best knowledge, the first instance in which the
FBI has assumed such an official "cultural" position toward any
expressive product.

When asked for a comment on the Bureau's response to their
rap ". . . Tha Police," one member of N.W.A. said: "Oh, I
didn't know *they* were buying records, too!"

The economic savvy and levity of this response seem
appropriately deconstructive until one discovers that neither
Ahlerich nor the FBI even owns a copy of "Straight Outta
Compton," nor has anyone in the agency (including Ahlerich
prior to writing this letter) ever listened to the rap to which the
Bureau has now "officially" objected.

The "crisis" in the humanities (as I suggested earlier) may
finally be like the FBI's buffoonish objectionism—a crisis of
audition, a violent, reactionary cry by whitemen who have
never bothered to listen to the rhythms and lyrics of OTHERS.
Such willful disregard and lamentable ignorance may serve the
moment, but, finally, they offer the surest path to white cultural
illiteracy.

As the rap group Public Enemy counts the numbers: "It
takes a nation of millions to hold us back!" Nobody in America
can afford such wasted manpower when our nation is already
belated, behind the times and hard-pressed for any future what-

soever. Today's "crisis" will only begin to abate when American whitemale nostalgia for ancient exclusionism gives way to conscientious audition and constructive pedagogy and scholarship based on the sounds of a postmodern world. James Baldwin once asserted in a famous essay about alienation and blackness that it was time for all of those who are nostalgic for prelapsarian days of exclusion to realize that the world "is no longer white, and will never be again." If we add "bookish" or "Great Bookish" to Baldwin's announcement we have, I think, fundamental postulates for listening beyond the thresholds of our present "crisis" to sounds of a safer and more liberating future.

When asked what the phrase "poetry for the next society" suggested to him, one of my graduate students responded: "There ain't going to be a next society." Upon soberer reflection—although it is hard to imagine what can be soberer than apocalypse—he said "rap" and "MTV" are poetry for the next society. He went on to speak about his friend Eberle Umbach, Poet Laureate of Idaho, who is a radical feminist and who travels a Plains State circuit reading her work successfully to young and old, men and women, churchgoers and hard-pressed farmers alike.

The admixture of my student's thinking about "poetry for the next society" seems characteristic of turn-of-the-century human moments when we seek new definitions and hopeful signs to illuminate the despair of endings. In response to the *bon mot* "Fin de siecle," a character in a late-nineteenth-century British novel retorts "*Fin du Globe!*" But the exchange occurs in a comedic work designed precisely to dispel a staid sobriety and solipsism that would kill a century with censure before it can pass decently into the indeterminate spaces of the future. My student's alternative response to his almost instinctive despair was the suggestion that popular culture and a literate, radical feminism mark at least two sites of poetic energy destined to survive our own "*fin de siecle.*" Since he is twenty-six and I am forty-six, I take it that he and not I should be designated a citizen of the "next" society. And if even he will not sustain that definition, then certainly his children or the students he will teach qualify as a future constituency. Which is to say he and his cohorts seem closer by far to the "next" society than I.

Having begun, therefore, to question the citizenry of the next society, I decided to continue—in the service of a kind of ageist accuracy. Besides, I am a literary critic—a member of a species whose dim and inaccurate prophecies are betrayed by countless anthologies filled with writers whom we never read and embarrassingly short on entries for those who have become stars. No one in his or her right mind saddles up to a literary critic on days of the Triple Crown for advice.

So I asked my graduate seminar what they considered "poetry for the next society." To a man and woman, they responded "MTV" and "Rap." We didn't stop to dissect their claims, nor did we attempt a poetics of the popular. Instead, we tried to extrapolate from what seemed two significant forms of the present era a description of their being-in-the-world. Terms that emerged included "public," "performative," "audible," "theatrical," "communal," "intra-sensory," "postmodern," "oral," "memorable," and "intertextual." What this list suggests is that my students believe the function of poetry belongs in our era to a telecommunal, popular space in which a global audience interacts with performative artists. A link between music and performance—specifically popular music and performance— seems determinative in their definition of the current and future function of poetry.

They are heirs to a history in which art, audience, entertainment, and instruction have assumed profoundly new meanings. The embodied catharsis of Dick Clark's bandstand or Don Cornelius's soultrain would be virtually unrecognizable—or so one thinks—to Aristotle. Thus, Elvis, Chuck Berry, and the Shirelles foreshadow and historically overdetermine the Boss, Bobby Brown, and Kool Moe Dee as, let us say, *People's Poets*.

My students' responses, however, are not nearly as natural or original as they may seem on first view. In fact, they have

a familiar cast within a history of contestation and contradis-
tinction governing the relationship between poetry and the
State.

The exclusion of poets from the republic by Plato is the ur-
Western site of this contest. In Egypt it is Thoth and the King;
in Afro-America it is the Preacher and the Bluesman. It would
be overly sacramental to speak of this contest as one between
the letter and the spirit, and it would be too Freudian by half
to speak of it again as an *agon* between the law and taboo. The
simplest way to describe it is in terms of a tensional resonance
between homogeneity and heterogeneity.

Plato argues the necessity of a homogeneous State designed
to withstand the bluesiness of poets who are always intent on
worrying such a line by signifying and troping irreverently on
it and continually setting up conditionals. "What if, this?" and
"What if, that?" To have a homogeneous line, Plato (like Alan
Bloom) advocates that the philosophers effectively eliminate the
poets.

If the State is the site of what linguists call the *constative*,
then, poetry is an alternative space of the *conditional*. If the State
keeps itself in line, as Benedict Anderson suggests, through the
linear, empty space of homogeneity, then poetry worries this
space or line with heterogeneous performance. If the State is a
place of reading the lines correctly, then poetry is the site of
audition, of embodied sounding on State wrongs. What, for
example, happens to the State Line about the death of the Black
Family and the voiceless derogation of Black youth when Run
DMC explodes the State Line with the rap:

> Kings from Queens from Queens comes Kings
> we're raising hell like a class when the lunch bell rings
> the King will be praised and hell will be raised
> suckers try to phase him but D won't be phased

In considering the contestation between homogeneity and
heterogeneity, I am drawing on the work of the scholars Homi
Bhabha and Peter Stallybrass, who suggest that nationalist or
postrevolutionary discourse is always a discourse of the split

subject. In order to construct the Nation it is necessary to preserve a homogeneity of remembrance (such as anthems, waving flags, and unifying slogans) in conjunction with an amnesia of heterogeneity. If poetry is disruptive performance, or, in Homi Bhabha's formulation, an articulation of the melancholia of the people's wounding by and before the emergence of the State Line, then poetry can be defined as an audible space of opposition.

Rap is the form of audition in our present era that utterly refuses to sing anthems of, say, whitemale hegemony.

Created by young black people—preeminently males—in their late teens and early twenties, rap situates itself with respect to rhythm and blues, intermixing in its collaged styles the saxophone solos, bridges, and James Brown shouts and energy of that music. Adopting a driving, rhyming, rhythmic format, rappers such as Kurtis Blow, Run DMC, Doug E. Fresh, Rakim and Eric B., LL Kool J, Roxanne Shante, Salt-n-Peppa, Public Enemy, and the Jungle Brothers proceed to take apart the conventional wisdom and skewed ethics of the State Line. Summoning heroes like Malcolm X, Martin Luther King, Mohammed Ali, Marcus Garvey, and Minister Louis Farrakhan, these young black poets describe cityscapes and an Afro-American existence of the street that are entirely original.

They refigure traditional language, sample and remix conventional history in a sometimes absurdist and completely memorable—almost hypnotic—fashion. Theirs is a poetry of Afro-American pride intended for the people. In its very structure, rap interrogates the politics and technologies of record production in the United States. It is a poetry and music of the voice that originated in New York among black teenagers. Its first-order production requires—like the earliest Afro-American musical productions—only the body of the rapper and his or her "crew" or "posse." The steady back beat can be provided by voice or by bodydrumming equivalent to the hambone.

When rap moves into the studio of record production, what is fascinating about its corporal minimalism is that it signifies on, or deconstructs, the very processes of record production and the mechanics of utilization or instrumentalism in an age of mechanical reproduction. Turntables become mere mechanisms for converting already-produced and fetishized records into cacophonous "scratchings": microphones are mere voice-boosters (not Midas converters of the black voice unself-consciously into whitegold) that can be possessed only by the rapper who has proved that he is not a "sucker D.J." in need of "bum rushing."

While there is a marked component of self-aggrandizement and epic boasting in rap, there is also an insistent element of didacticism, polemical challenge, and ethical caution. Drugs and violence are roundly condemned. The State is put on notice that the black community is aware of its "hype."

Rapping as art is endorsed as a challenging form of creativity that converts oppression and lack into a commercial and communal success in which, as Doug E. Fresh states it, one gets "paid in full."

The test of this success *vis-à-vis* the individual rapper's performance is measured, at least in part, by the danceability of his or her performance. As my student Mark Hunter states in a very suggestive essay on rap: "The test of the lyrics is their link to the consciousness of the streets, usually of life in the hard center of the ghetto where greatest suffering as well as greatest strength and creativity abide . . . the test of the beat is in dancing, whether it can rock you and cause the delight which only a truly hard, tight rhythm can."

Rap is the poetry of youth; it is the continuation in our era of a black musical tradition that has always been syncretic: a collusion of voice and limited instrumentation, social commentary and fortifying entertainment. Rap is also the poetry of what Homi Bhabha calls "melancholia in revolt." Its very form is of heterogeneity—a collaging of all the sources of Afro-American malaise into an energetic sounding. Bits of history combine with boasts of new dress codes, which commingle with juxtapositions between philosophers and teachers, which, in turn, provide a segue into cautionary tales against drug dealing and gang violence, which, in their turn, become an overlay for self-reflexive histories of black music—including rap itself.

Rap is black life unwholly realized, but holy in its fragmentation. It is a spirited critique of a homogeneous State Line.

To say that it is the poetry of the next society is not, finally, to predict, but to describe. And the description provides a theoretical opening for the refiguration of time frames and expectations that the phrase "poetry for the next society" connotes to an audience of literary-critical aficionados and aspiring literary poets . . . in English. For the recognition of rap *as poetry* by my graduate students is coextensive, it seems to me, with a profound shift in conceptions of art and history that has marked the past twenty years. As Doug E. Fresh puts it:

> Brainwish education
> Of our nation,
> Publicized in its prime.
> To be behind time.
> Verbal abuse,
> Our History's a mystery,
> Or what's the use?

Rap in its general, popular appeal and heterogeneity—in its challenging recovery of both a sociohistorical past and past expressive traditions—is a metonym or an acronym for all of the neglected poetries that are surfacing and competing for audition today. And here, if there were world enough and time, I would enumerate spectacular and specular European, Indian, Latin American, Caribbean, African, and Asian "surfacings." For the attempt is to discover an acronym for a general revolt and not to hug the revolution ceremoniously and chauvinistically to one's own chest. In its unequivocal questioning of a homogeneous, whitemale harmony, it can be decoded as *R.* (to be pronounced) *A.P.: Recovered Audition of the People.*

Such audition is what Benjamin in his essay on translation calls the "incommensurable perplexity of the living present." And if the example of rap is not mistaken, our poetry for the next society will consist of a recovery and hearing of all those distinctive voices that have been suppressed by conventional, whitemale definitions of "poetry." We shall hear, for example, Andrew Levy's friend Eberle Umbrach writing of "Natural History" as follows:

> The Romans built Cities of the Dead the size of actual cities. They, too, had a passion for the past; only a handful of craftsmen, sculptors, writers were necessary to invent history—a history that never existed, that explained how inevitable, how natural, it was that Rome should conquer. Romulus and Remus were set in stone, in books; bit by bit the mosaic takes shape; one day you looked up and traced their outlines in the stars, you looked down and could trace the lines in the emperors' faces back to them; the world becomes decipherable. Certain problems arise in a world where only the male line carries meaning, but they can be solved; substitute a wolf for the mother of Romulus and Remus after she has been raped and put to death; or a row of female torsos cut open to show the fetus.

Where Afro-American expressive culture is concerned, the time of "the next" is a summons to moments of the past. As in rap, "next"—or a now and future "defness"—is radically dependent upon a sampling of the past. *Next* means an audition and refiguration for our era of what has been violently suppressed in a racist and sexist past. Hence, poetry for the next society in Afro-American terms is not only rap, but also what rap recovers for our attention—a litany of committed expressive production whose history has yet to be invented. Only "sucker D.J.s" of an illing, academic cast will fail to get busy with respect to such a litany.

If today's critic wishes to assume the futurity of the heterogeneous artist and be adequately predictive, then he or she must understand the rap artist as critic and stop chilling with respect to alterity. Such a desirous present-day critic must come to realize that writers such as Langston Hughes, Scott Momaday, Chicano singers of the *corrido*, the makers of the Native American chant poem, Rita Dove, and Toni Morrison are artists of whom one can only, like Run DMC, rap, righteously, saying:

> Just like King Midas, as I've been told,
> Everything that they touch turns to gold,
> They're the greatest of the great,
> Get it straight, they're great,
> Like the butcher, the baker, the candlestick maker.
> They're makers, breakers, and they're title takers.
> Like the Little old Lady who lived in a shoe,
> If cuts weren't theirs, they would be through.
> Ain't lying y'all, they're the best I know.
> And if I lie, my nose will grow.
> Like the little wooden boy named Pinocchio,
> And you all know how the story goes.

"You know what I'm saying, y'all?" "Get busy, y'all." WORD.

The fact that today's college and university students choose to graduate without taking courses in Western civilization, history, foreign languages, English and American literature, mathematics, or the natural and physical sciences is less a matter for theology and faith than for careful, student-focused inquiry. Is it because such courses are not required that students avoid them, or is it simply that the rapid, postmodernist expansion of specialized information leaves little time for students who wish fully to engage their majors to explore "general education"? Do students of American colleges and universities in the late twentieth century truly compose a body homogeneous enough in Western great bookishness to warrant their group training in a "common" Western discourse of "our own"? Isn't the commonality of college and university students less traditionally bookish than postmodernly telecommunal? Aren't "our" students bonded more in their postmodernity than in an ahistorical holiness of the Western past stored in Great Books?

Isn't it virtually impossible to achieve more than the forced ideological indoctrination of such students if teachers refuse to engage them in their postmodern, hybridly cosmopolitan, telecommunal, popular-cultural, everyday assumptions and bondings? Such queries are designed as counter-interrogatives for required questions. They are meant to suggest that there are questions far more pressing today than the regnant curriculum doxologists allow.

"Why today, more than two decades ago, should any college or university course be *required*?" "What agreed-upon ends are served by *requiring* any course whatsoever?" "Upon what basis should any *required* course build?" Everything today seems as open to question—from a heterodox perspective—as ever. And the current numbers, finances, offices, and intimidations from conservative benches must not compel us to gloss over or to cede to Western orthodoxy the task of aggressively addressing such questions in demandingly secular ways.

We must come realistically to know our students and to participate intellectually and affectively in the sounds of their everyday lives before we can meet them where they are. And it is only by meeting them where they most decidedly are that we can begin instructive conversations about an infinite variety of possible heritages they share in a postmodern, resoundingly hybrid, and increasingly non-white era of study.

THINKING

LIKE

OTHER

PEOPLE

J. Hillis Miller

*J. Hillis Miller is the chief American expo-
nent of deconstructionism, as well as a major
authority on nineteenth- and twentieth-
century literature, English and American. He
has written many books, including studies of
Dickens, the workings of narrative, and the
"linguistic moment" in modern poetry. His
most recent books are* Illustration, *published
by Harvard University Press, and* Ariadne's
Thread, *published by Yale. Miller holds degrees from Oberlin and Harvard and has
taught at Williams College, Johns Hopkins,
and Yale; he now teaches at the University
of California at Irvine.*

MATTHEW ARNOLD BEGINS HIS ESSAY ON SHELLEY with an anecdote. It is a story told Arnold by a lady who had advised Shelley's mother to send her son to a school "where they will teach
him to think for himself!" To this Mrs. Shelley (imagine being
Shelley's mother!) answered: "Teach him to think for himself?
Oh, my God, teach him rather to think like other people!"

Which of these women is right? Should education teach
people to think for themselves or should it teach them to think
like other people? Though Arnold's essay is famous for ending
with a characterization of Shelley as "in poetry, no less than in
life" as "a beautiful *and ineffectual* angel, beating in the void his
luminous wings in vain," the essay does not come down un-
equivocally on one side or the other. On the one hand, Arnold
is conspicuously thinking for himself throughout the essay, as
in his work generally. On the other, his famous dictim about
following "the best that has been thought and said in the world"
sounds as if it means thinking like other people.

In this essay I have been asked to account for myself. This
demand has made me feel "as if I were in the witness-box
narrating my experience on oath," to borrow the way George
Eliot in *Adam Bede* describes her truth-telling as a novelist. How,
I have been asked, can I both admire Matthew Arnold and at
the same time practice "deconstruction," whatever *that* means?

I say "whatever *that* means" to remind my readers that deconstruction, as I and others have repeatedly said, is a complex and
diverse cultural phenomenon, by no means amenable to being
reduced to a few formulas about "free play" and "différance"
taken out of context from the early work of Jacques Derrida.
"Deconstructions," as it is better to say, have many forms, not
only in literary study and philosophy but also in architecture,
art history, cultural studies, women's studies, religious studies,
legal studies, and the creative arts. Even the work by a single
writer associated with so-called "deconstruction"—for example, Derrida himself—is complex and diverse.

Arnold is often invoked these days as an antidote to all that
is bad in the humanities. The false charges are well known: We
humanists teach too much theory, especially French theory, in
a cacophony of conflicting schools. We have ceased teaching
the canon of great works in the Western tradition. We have
installed in its place a chaos of multicultural studies. We universally apply a political correctness test in deciding what should
be taught and who should teach. We have frittered away our
heritage in peripheral programs in film studies, studies in mass
media and popular culture, women's studies, African-American
studies, Chicano/Chicana studies, cultural studies, and colonial
studies. All would be well, our critics sometimes suggest, if we
would just return to the program Arnold proposed for preserving our heritage through study of "the best that is known
and thought in the world." (Arnold varies the formula, sometimes putting it in the present tense, sometimes in the past.)
Then we would all "think like other people," in a happy unanimity. I propose to investigate here what Mathew Arnold
really says and what would really happen if we followed him.

I begin with an observation: In his titles, Arnold puts *and*
where we expect *or: Culture and Anarchy;* "Hebraism and Hel-
linism"; "Literature and Science"; *Literature and Dogma; St. Paul
and Protestantism; God and the Bible.* We might have expected *or*
because all these titles seem to present a binary opposition offering a choice: culture or anarchy, literature or dogma, liter-

ature or science. Why does Arnold say *and* rather than *or*? Is this detail significant or is it a superficial anomaly?

To want to know is to evoke a way of study, teaching, and writing in the humanities. Two assumptions underlie this procedure. They come from two different, perhaps even contradictory, parts of the traditional American ethos. One is the assumption basic to science that everything can and should be accounted for. The other is the assumption basic to American Protestantism that everything needs to be tested and thought out for oneself.

The Protestant attitude assumes that nothing can be taken for granted just because it comes from authority. If you want to find out what is in the Bible, read it for yourself. Don't trust the commentators. In my case, this suspicion of authority carried over to my study of literature. This suspicion, for me, is linked to the realization that to understand a work fully it must be read in its original language.

The scientific bent has been just as important as my religious training in determining the way I approach literature. For my first two years in college I was a physics major. Then in the middle of my sophomore year I realized that what I most wanted to do was to read literary works and explain them to myself and other people. The shift from physics to literature was motivated not only by a love of reading but also by a desire to account for literature in the same way a physicist accounts for the stars or for the interior of the atom. The modern, post-Enlightenment university was founded to apply the principle of sufficient reason to all things worth studying. If physics, why not literature?

Science assumes that things are likely to be both stranger and more complicated than they appear—strange in the sense of not fitting received explanations; complicated in the sense that the fine grain of the physical or biological worlds may stretch to the limits our senses and reason. Though the goal is to find explanations as simple and inclusive as possible, the most surprising and counterintuitive facts are likely to arise, making simplification difficult. Science is progressive. What is received opinion in one generation is likely to be proved wrong by the experience of the next. These experiences will be guided, at least in part, by the assumption that anomalies, strange blips in the data, odd features that do not quite fit the standard hypotheses, may turn out to be important clues. Finding an explanation for the blips will allow a breakthrough to another level of understanding. To apply these methodological presuppositions to literature may seem peculiar, but that is what I wanted, and still want, to do.

This goal is based on a conviction that, looked at with an innocent eye, literature is extremely strange. Try reading a page of Faulkner, Shakespeare, Milton, or Toni Morrison. They take some explaining. I remember feeling that in particular about Tennyson's poetry, for example the fiftieth section of *In Memoriam*: "Be near me when my light is low,/When the blood creeps, and the nerves prick/And tingle; and the heart is sick,/And all the wheels of Being slow." Or this from the ninety-fifth section: "And all at once it seemed at last/The living soul was flashed on mine,/And mine in this was wound, and whirled/About empyreal heights of thought,/And came on that which is, and caught the deep pulsations of the world." I found these passages moving and powerful, but how could anyone use language in that way? What was its rationale? What was its purpose? No one around me talked like that. I wanted to understand why Tennyson used words the way he did, just as an astrophysicist seeks to know why radiation waves at various frequencies are received from the far reaches of space.

The scientist assumes that the prolonged detailed study of some delimited region of the world will take her or him on an unpredictable journey deeper and deeper into knowledge of reality, just as Newton, in Wordsworth's phrase, "voyaged through strange seas of thought alone." In a similar way my feeling was then, and still is, that reading a new book will take me somewhere that I have never been. No secondary reading "about" the work can give you much foretaste of what that journey will be like. Nor will the book take you there without any effort. An active, interventionist reading is necessary. Theory sometimes helps with that.

This scientific approach was reinforced by the assumption made by the "New Critics" that every detail of a literary work should be accounted for in a reading. My interest in literary theory therefore has primarily focused on its ability to facilitate reading. Theory, in my view, is of little use except as an aid to reading. It is the reading perhaps more than the theoretical reflection to which it gives rise that re-enters present-day culture and makes a difference there. Reading, teaching, and writing about literature do not simply give new knowledge. They are also inaugural, performative.

Good literary theory, contrary to what is sometimes thought, always arises from the reading of some particular work or works, just as a good scientific theory is generated to explain some particular data. It is often forgotten in the accounts of theoretical formulations—for example, those in Jacques Derrida's writings—that they are almost always a response to reading some work or other—in his case, works by Plato, Celan, Ponge, Joyce, Hegel, Kafka, Kant, Shakespeare, and a host of others. The measure of a theory is not its cogency or plausibility but whether it adequately accounts for the data in question. The data in the case of science may be the spectra of stars. The data in the case of literature are the words on the page. Good literary theory begins with those words as events that are both singular and repeatable and goes out from them to what those events may make happen. Nevertheless, no theory can fully account for what happens in reading. This generates an asymmetry between theory and reading. Reading continually checks and modifies theory, often even disqualifies it. The life of literary study is this coming and going between reading and theory. Theory is a name for that attempt to account for what happens in reading. Reading is a name for what must be accounted for. The two can never quite be brought together. Moreover, if a reading is truly inaugural, then what it does exceeds the knowledge it gives. Like reading and theory, the power and knowledge reading brings are not congruent.

Just how then is theory an aid to reading? Why can we not just read without theoretical forethought? No reading is free from theoretical presuppositions, even though these may be so much taken for granted that they do not need ever to be formulated explicitly. Unless they are made as explicit as possible, however, the reading may happen according to blind preprogrammed ideological assumptions about what the work is going to mean. Reading in this way will make certain the work is not read at all. What is needed, in literary study as in science, are new perspectives on the data that will allow them to reveal patterns that may be obscured by prejudice, the horizon of expectations about what you are going to find. The function of reading theory is to facilitate what Kenneth Burke called "perspective by incongruity." Such a new angle of approach will allow the reader to notice hitherto unnoticed features and perhaps give a clue as to how to account for them. All the "theoretical" writers I have found useful—Aristotle, Freud, William Empson, Kenneth Burke, G. Wilson Knight, Georges Poulet, Paul de Man, Jacques Derrida, and others—have attracted me not because of their theoretical formulations but for the way they relate these formulations to original and persuasive readings.

The scientist assumes that nature may be unexpectedly complicated, yet seeks the simplest possible explanation. Literature also turns out to be unexpectedly complicated. Looked at with a candid eye (let's say the eye of the one equipped only with the limited preparation offered by an American public high school), Chaucer or Shakespeare, Milton or Wordsworth, Melville or Faulkner appear dauntingly complex. I find that complexity fascinating. Even the simplest-appearing poem shows itself to be more and more complicated, harder and harder to explain, the more you question it, ask it why it is the way it is, what it really says and does, what social and linguistic conventions it presupposes.

The complexity in question is embodied in language. However important may be the biography of the author, social conditions at the time, the history of the work's reception, the

uses to which the work has been put, the primary data remain
the words on the page. Though language can apparently be
approached like any other object of scientific study, special
features make it different. For one thing, we dwell intimately
within language. In literary study you must use language to
study language—a particularly awkward situation. It is impossible to get outside language and study it as an indifferent
or neutral phenomenon. Moreover, language, particularly language as used in literature, is one of the media (along
with painting, sculpture, music, and now film) in which our
sense of ourselves over the centuries, in all the diversity of
languages and cultures, has been embodied. It is impossible
to be indifferent or impassive when one reads, for example,
this chorus in Sophocles's *Oedipus at Colonus* (I quote Robert
Fagles's translation): "Not to be born is best/when all is reck-
oned in, but once a man has seen the light/the next thing,
by far, is to go back/back where he came from, quickly as
he can." Another passage is from the words of Jesus in the
Gospel of Matthew: "For whosoever hath, to him shall be
given, and he shall have more abundance; but whosoever
hath not, from him shall be taken away even that he hath"
(Matthew 13:12). This is from William Butler Yeats's "The
Cold Heaven": "Suddenly I saw the cold and rook-delighting
heaven/That seemed as though ice burned and was but the
more ice,/ . . . /And I took the blame out of all sense and
reason,/Until I cried and trembled and rocked to and fro,/
Riddled with light." Finally, from Matthew Arnold: "My
dearest Clough these are damned times—everything is against
one—the height to which knowledge is come, the spread of
luxury, our physical enervation, the absence of great *natures*,
the unavoidable contact with millions of small ones, newspapers, cities, light profligate friends, moral desperadoes like
Carlyle, our own selves, and the sickening consciousness of our
difficulties."

No one is likely to read such passages and not be moved.
The critic's responsibility is to be moved and yet understand
and explain, as when Walter Benjamin says the "disturbing

power (*trüber Einfluss*)" of Goethe's *Elective Affinities* can be coped with only if the reader is protected by "an indefectible rationality (*unbestechliche Vernunft*)": "Under the protection of such rationality the heart may dare to abandon itself to the prodigious, magical beauty of this work." Only if you feel the disturbing power of literature, its strangeness, will you have need of an indefectible rationality to cope with that effect. The most effective form of such rationality is close attention to the language of the text.

I have therefore been chiefly attracted to the work of those critics who most adequately account for the linguistic complexity of literary works: the New Critics (among them my colleague at Johns Hopkins, Earl Wasserman) for their attention to detail and their assumption that every detail in a work counts; Burke for the way he understands and articulates the social function of literature, sees it as a "strategy for encompassing a situation"; Empson for his admirable sensitivity to multiple incongruous meanings in familiar texts (he calls it "ambiguity"); Poulet for his strategy of unfolding in a dialectical progression the complexity assembled in the interior space of a given writer's work; Derrida and de Man for their extraordinary gifts as readers and for their ability to convey to others what they see when they read. Decisive events for my intellectual life were my first reading of Poulet's *Études sur le temps humain*, my hearing in the late sixties of papers by de Man on Lukacs and on "The Rhetoric of Temporality," my attendance at a seminar by Derrida on short passages from Plato and Mallarmé, later incorporated in "La double séance" in *La dissémination*. These works, in all their diversity, are paradigmatic, even though they are impossible to imitate, of what good reading can be. They pass on a sense of the complexity and force of the original. They make something happen when they are listened to or read.

In spite of the diversity of these examples of good reading, all but Wasserman share the assumption that the complexity of a literary work may make it heterogeneous, not reducible without falsifying omission to some "organic unity." Though I recognize the heuristic value of assuming that every detail counts because all together make an organic unity, the danger of forcing everything to fit some preconceived scheme seems to me to outweigh the advantages of the assumption of unity. Moreover, my experience of reading has been that most works—I should even dare to say all works—are in fact not organic unities. Each work is divided against itself, inhabited by its own other. One name for that heterogeneity or self-division is "irony," though other names exist, such as Derrida's "différance."

I value all those critics I have mentioned because they account for the rhetoric of literature, in the broad sense of that term. "Deconstruction," at least in one meaning for that multivalenced word, is a contemporary version of rhetoric. Rhetoric is one of the three parts of the basic medieval educational scheme, the "trivia," meaning the place where three roads cross—or perhaps where they do not cross, where they pursue their separate ways. The other two roads are grammar and logic. Rhetoric is both the art of persuasion and the knowledge of tropes. What various experimental protocols are to science, rhetoric is to the study of literature. The distinctions among various tropes—not only metaphor, simile, and metonymy, but prosopopoeia, catachresis, irony, allegory, parable, and the rest—are a precious resource, developed over the centuries, for the exploration of language. Nothing could be more hallowed by tradition in the West than rhetoric. Rhetorical reading should be the center of literary study. This does not mean I think studies in biography, literary history, social contexts, culture, colonialism, postcolonialism, even literary or critical theory as separate topics, are not important. They are. But they all presuppose, and are in aid of, good reading.

Matthew Arnold is not usually thought of as a rhetorician. Reading him, however, has strengthened my commitment to rhetorical reading. I read Arnold first because he was there to be read, just as mountaineers climb a mountain because it is there to be climbed. I read Arnold because it was my institutional responsibility to do so. Hired to teach Victorian literature, I would have had some difficulty not teaching Matthew Arnold, though I suppose it might have been possible to avoid it. But

I was less free to do that than I was to exercise that most precious of academic freedoms for the teacher in America: to teach Arnold or anyone else more or less in any way I liked. I was free, that is, to report in teaching and writing on what I actually found when I read Arnold. Arnold was there, as a conspicuous object on the landscape of Victorian literature as traditionally conceived. So I read him for myself, to find out what he really says.[1]

If that explains how I first came to read Arnold, my continuing admiration for Arnold arises from the fact that I have learned much in trying to understand him. This, in turn, has helped me in formulating those procedures in literary study I have described. Arnold too borrows attitudes and assumptions from Protestantism and even from science.

Though Arnold has many sharp things to say about the narrow side of Protestantism—what he calls Puritanism or "dissent"—he is nevertheless deeply Protestant in the sense I have defined it. In spite of the many ways Arnold shares a specifically Victorian ideology, he also presupposes that received opinion may be wrong. He takes it for granted that he must think things out for himself, read things for himself. He praises Goethe for this: "Goethe's profound, imperturbable naturalism is absolutely fatal to all routine thinking; he puts the standard, once for all, inside every man instead of outside him; when he is told, such a thing must be so, there is immense authority and custom in favour of its being so, it has been held to be so for a thousand years, he answers with Olympian politeness, 'But *is* it so? Is it so to *me*?' "

Arnold thinks for himself in his books on religion: *St. Paul and Protestantism* (1870), *Literature and Dogma* (1873), and *God and the Bible* (1875). Those books are an extraordinary attempt to save Christianity from the social and intellectual changes that were making it less and less relevant. In order to do this he returns to the Bible, reads it for himself, and presents his way of reading it as one that should be universally accepted. In *Literature and Dogma* he asserts that the Old Testament prophecies of the Messiah are *not* fulfilled by Jesus, since the prophets imagined the Messiah coming in "glory and power." "It is impossible to resist acknowledging this," says Arnold, "if we read the Bible to find from it what really those who wrote it intended to think and say, and not to put into it what we wish them to have thought and said." In spite of the intentionalist formulation, that is an admirable recipe for good reading, though of course knowing the slogan will by no means ensure that you will be a good reader.

As for scientific method, though Arnold's "Literature and Science" is a strongly argued defense of the humanities (including the study of Greek) against Huxley's claim that in the modern world science should form the basis of a liberal education, Arnold too had appropriated science's need to account for things. He too appeals to experimental proof and, somewhat surprisingly, uses the word *science* in a positive sense. In *Literature and Dogma* he notes the opposition between "the idea that *righteousness tendeth to life*," as held by ancient Israel, and "Messianic ideas." The latter are "Aberglaube, Extra-belief," meaning "belief beyond what is certain and verifiable." The idea that righteousness tendeth to life, on the other hand, "has a firm, experimental ground, which the Messianic ideas have not."

So I have found confirmation and reinforcement of my own assumptions and procedures as a critic in Arnold's writings. But there are other even deeper reasons for Arnold's abiding interest for me. I have found him a fascinatingly complex and equivocally attractive figure, by no means easy to understand and account for. He is among other things one of the great ironists in English literature. His use of irony in scornful polemic against those he attacks is famous, but a flavor of irony pervades his work generally and often makes it difficult to know just how to take what he says. I was introduced to his work as a model of good prose and as a repository of noble ideas. Would that it were possible to learn to write with Arnold's suavity, grace, and ironic power! Arnold's writings on politics and society, *Culture and Anarchy* (1869) and the essay on "Equality," show how irony can be used as a powerful polemic weapon.

Arnold is attractive in part because the real Arnold is so different from the pictures of him frequently given.[2] There he is in the old photographs, with his muttonchop whiskers, his slightly wavy dark hair parted in the middle, a largish nose, a wide, somewhat sensual mouth, and an odd expression mixing faint ironic amusement with stern self-repression and a slight admixture of condescending censoriousness. He does not look like a wholly happy man. He looks as if he had spent most of his time surrounded by people he considered fools. In his writings may be found something of the same mixture. Arnold is like a man holding his head high and aloof as a flooding stream rises rapidly around him.

Arnold's poetry and those admirable letters to his university friend Arthur Hugh Clough confirm this image. The prose cannot be rightly understood except in the light of the poems and letters. These form a kind of self-revelation that not so many years ago would have been called "existential," with reference to Kierkegaard, Sartre, and Camus, meaning the self-conscious suffering of alienation from one's time, one's fellows, the prevailing opinions of others, even alienation from oneself in a painful self-division. Arnold feared anarchy because he had experienced it in himself, not only in the "confused multitudinousness" of Victorian public and intellectual life but in the pains of what, in a strikingly modern phrase in the Preface to the *Poems* of 1853, he called "the dialogue of the mind with itself." His essay on Heine describes the modern situation as he saw it in 1863. It is also appropriate as a description of our situation today, a situation the college teacher must address.

Modern times find themselves with an immense system of institutions, established facts, accredited dogmas, customs, rules, which have come to them from times not modern. In this system their life has to be carried forward; yet they have a sense that this system is not of their own creation, that it by no means corresponds exactly with the wants of their actual life, that, for them,

it is customary, not rational. The awakening of this sense
is the awakening of the modern spirit. . . . It is no longer
dangerous to affirm that this want of correspondence
exists; people are even beginning to be shy of denying
it. To remove this want of correspondence is beginning
to be the settled endeavour of most persons of good
sense. Dissolvents of the old European system of dominant ideas and facts we must all be, all of us who have
any power of working; what we have to study is that
we may not be acrid dissolvents of it.

This passage and others like it, in the diagnosis of modern
times that makes up such a large part of Arnold's work, hardly
confirms those who try to cite him in support of a reactionary
move to teaching the Western canon as it used to be taught.
His goal rather was to transform teaching of the humanities to
make them effective now, in the light of a clear-sighted vision
of what our present situation really is. For all his admiration
for the great classics—Homer, Dante, Chaucer, Shakespeare,
Milton, and, as he says, "parts of Wordsworth"—Arnold saw
clearly the extreme difficulty of preserving traditional moral and
aesthetic values without the solid transcendent ground that
would validate them. He saw clearly that this search for grounds
was being made in a time when social changes had rendered
the old forms and values, even the old expressions of them in
great works of literature, no longer wholly appropriate or applicable.[3] Nowadays the "sea of faith," as he puts it in "Dover
Beech," is "retreating" with a "melancholy, long, withdrawing
roar." Arnold had the courage, most of the time, to report
clearly his inability to find the needed transcendent ground and
build on it. The traditional name for this combined belief in the
necessity of a transcendent ground of values and an inability to
find one is "nihilism." By this definition Arnold is frequently
a nihilist. In "Stagirius" he imagines himself not going down
deeper to find a solid ground on which to stand, but, in another
characteristic figure, climbing higher and higher to reach God
but failing to do so: "When the soul, growing clearer,/Sees God

no nearer;/When the soul, mounting higher,/To God comes no nigher . . ."

In the letters to Clough, Arnold speaks movingly of himself: "I am past thirty, and three parts iced over—and my pen, it seems to me is even stiffer and more cramped than my feeling. . . . I am nothing and very probably never shall be anything— but there are characters which are truest to themselves by never being anything, when circumstances do not suit." Arnold found his situation intolerably painful and did everything he could to pretend he was not in it, to hide it, or to figure some way to get out of it. An example is his repudiation of "Empedocles on Etna." This poem expresses Arnold's sense of his own situation. In the Preface to the *Poems* of 1853 he speaks of his poem as one "in which the suffering finds no vent in action; in which a continuous state of mental distress is prolonged, unrelieved by incident, hope, or resistance; in which there is everything to be endured, nothing to be done. In such situations there is inevitably something morbid, in the description of them something monotonous." Arnold's whole career as a writer both in poetry and in prose is an unremitting attempt to deal with the situation in which he found himself, either by finding a solid ground for values or by figuring out a way to preserve values without such a ground—by lifting himself by his own bootstraps, so to speak, or, as Nietzsche puts it in *Also Sprach Zarathustra*, by climbing upward on his own head, a neat trick if you can do it.

A famous instance of this climbing on your own head is the alogic of "Dover Beech." In that poem the speaker, presumably Arnold himself, implores his beloved: "Ah, love, let us be true/ To one another!" and then goes on to give as the reason for doing so the fact that "the world . . . /Hath really neither joy, nor love, nor light,/Nor certitude, nor peace, nor help for pain." Love, let us be true to each other because there is no love! It does not make sense. A woman would be foolish to accept such a proposal. Arnold's formulations in the letters to Clough of this characteristic alogic balance precariously between presuming that the ground is there already and admitting that it has to be chosen arbitrarily, so is not there at all. Therefore, it must be confirmed by an unaided human choice. In these letters Arnold analyzes himself in the guise of analyzing Clough. Your problem, he tells Clough, is "that you would never take your assiette[4] as something determined final and unchangeable for you and proceed to work away on the basis of that: but were always poking and patching and cobbling at the assiette itself —[you] could never finally, as it seemed—'resolve to be thyself.'" Here is another version of the bootstrap image or the image of climbing on one's own head. Arnold sets Clough (and implicitly himself) an impossible task. The ground on which the whole edifice of selfhood is to be built must both be constructed by that self, since it is a matter of "resolve," and at the same time be assumed to be already there, so that to poke and patch at it is like sawing off the branch on which you sit. But the branch-sitter has himself constructed the branch on which he perches.

Arnold's ironic condemnations cut both ways. Arnold always gives the reader the tools to dismantle his affirmations, assuming we apply to them the same analysis he applies to the positions he is attacking. His late book on religion, *Literature and Dogma*, ironically mocks "dogma." Arnold means by dogma the whole edifice of theology: seeing God as like a man with a long gray beard, along with all those ideas about "substance, identity, causation, design" in which theology puts so much stock. In place of this Arnold posits a claim, supported by a great many citations from the Bible, that religion is morality touched by emotion, that God is only a falsely anthropomorphizing name for "the Eternal not ourselves that makes for righteousness," and that the language of the Bible is poetic, not scientific. It rather is "language *thrown out* at an object of consciousness not fully grasped, which inspired emotion." Not many pages later he is defining the "idea that *righteousness tendeth to life*" as something with "a firm, experimental ground," while what he wants to put in question as "Aberglaube, Extrabelief" is called poetry. I have referred to this passage already, but now we are in a better position to understand it: "*Extrabelief*, that which we hope, augur, imagine, is the poetry of life, and has the rights of poetry. But it is not science; and yet it tends always to imagine itself science, to substitute itself for science, to make itself the ground of the very science out of which it has grown." What Arnold at first called poetry—the throwing out of language toward an eternal "something" that always exceeds it—he now calls science. He now uses the word *poetry* to name the parts of Christianity he wants to question, because it is belief beyond what is certain and verifiable—for example, belief that Jesus fulfills the Messianic ideas in the Old Testament. Arnold himself gives us the formula to define what he has been doing.[5] He has been making poetry the substitute for science, making it the ground of the very science out of which it has grown. That which is to be proven is taken for granted in the terms in which the proof is worked out. It is another case of climbing on your own head.

This constant self-deconstruction, if I may dare to use that word, characterizes Arnold's work throughout, from the poems and early letters to the late books on religion. Such self-undermining, followed by a moving on to a new position that is undermined in its turn in the forms of language that affirm it, is the life of Arnold's writing. Arnold is important not as a model to be blindly followed in America now, but as a complex exemplary case of a certain stage in the intellectual or ideological history of England, the stage of a desperate attempt to preserve some form of old dogmas in a modern world they clearly did not fit. Arnold's situation has many analogies to our own. By reading him carefully, by trying to find out what he really thought and said, rather than putting into his work what we wish him to have thought and said, we may come to understand our own situation better.

The peculiar combination of affirmation and self-undermining in Arnold explains that apparently anomalous *and* in Arnold's titles. To say "literature *and* dogma" rather than "literature *or* dogma" is appropriate because literature and dogma turn out not to be opposites but differential versions of the same thing, as do other apparent opposites in Arnold's titles. Another meaning may also be given to that *and*. We need Matthew Arnold *and* a reading of him that does not take as necessarily true what received opinion says about him. We need Matthew Arnold *and* a whole panoply of other writers both in the Western canon and outside it. The heterogeneity and complexity of Arnold's work reveal themselves when we make a serious effort to read it. Such reading is a good preparation for dealing with the complexity and heterogeneity of literature generally, then making use of it in our own lives. Each work and each tradition is self-divided, inhabited by its own other, just as Arnold's work constantly puts in question its own affirmations. Each tradition can best be understood if its hegemonic authority is at least provisionally suspended and if it is seen in the context of the other traditions that seem its antagonists. Like Goethe we must learn to ask, "But *is* it so? Is it so to *me?*" This is another form of the *and,* that indispensable "perspective by incongruity" Kenneth Burke recommends.

I promised when I began this essay to tell the truth as though I were in the witness-box narrating my experience on oath. I promised also to explain how I reconcile the kind of criticism I do with an admiration for Matthew Arnold. I have done my best to fulfill both promises.

NOTES

1. For my previous writing on Arnold, see "Matthew Arnold," *The Disappearance of God* (Cambridge: Harvard University Press, 1963), pp. 212–269; *The Linguistic Moment* (Princeton: Princeton University Press, 1985), pp. 15–43; "The Search for Grounds in Literary Study," *Theory Now and Then* (London: Harvester Wheatsheaf, 1990; Durham: Duke University Press, 1991), pp. 265–268.

2. That does not mean I have not learned from what other readers of Arnold have said. Lionel Trilling's *Matthew Arnold* (1939) is still essential reading, as is A. Dwight Culler's *Imaginative Reason: The Poetry of Matthew Arnold* (1966). But in order to find out the degree to which these critics are right, one has to read Arnold for oneself.

3. It is necessary to add, however, that ideas about racial or national essence that are so dangerous in Paul de Man's wartime writings, though vigorously contested in his later work, and that are present in some currents of American polemics today, both on the left and on the right, pervade Matthew Arnold's work. Such ideas are found, for example, in *On the Study of Celtic Literature,* in the distinction between Hebraism and Hellenism in *Culture and Anarchy,*

and in dozens of other places where the essential specificity of the French, German, American, or English national spirit is taken for granted. Nor are these nationalist and Eurocentric ideas adventitious to Arnold's thinking. They are "essential" to it. Through his influence on American education, Arnold bears some responsibility for the problematic organization of literary studies into separate departments for each of the national literatures. Nor is the discipline of comparative literature as it has descended from nineteenth-century beginnings free of these Arnoldian assumptions. These issues are beginning to be thought through in present-day "cultural studies," for example by Gerald Graff in *Professing Literature* and by Edward Said in his forthcoming book on imperialism. About those wartime writings of Paul de Man I have written elsewhere. See "Paul de Man's Wartime Writings" and "An Open Letter to Jon Wiener," *Theory Now and Then* (London: Harvester Wheatsheaf, 1990; Durham: Duke University Press, 1991), pp. 359–384.

4. "Assiette" means plate, support, or ground. Arnold uses the latter word when in a poem he says he wants a "joy whose grounds are true."

5. Another example of that in *Literature and Dogma* is the ironic phrase Arnold uses to describe the way the New Testament conflates and modifies incompatible formulations in Old Testament prophecy to make them confirm Jesus as the Messiah: "Certainly it was a somewhat violent exegetical proceeding." That is a splendid formulation for Arnold's own exegetical proceeding when through etymological legerdemain he redefines the personal God of the Bible as "the Eternal not ourselves that makes for righteousness," or as "the stream of tendency by which all things seek to fulfil the law of their being." In Arnold's hands Deuteronomy 6:4 ("Hear, O Israel! The Lord our God is one Lord") is transformed: "Israel said, not indeed what our Bibles make him say, but this: 'Hear, O Israel! *The Eternal is our God, The Eternal alone.*' "

PRAGMATISM AND THE SENTENCE OF DEATH

Richard Poirier

Richard Poirier is the foremost practitioner of literary critical pragmatism in America. His work both describes and renews a tradition that moves through Emerson, William James, Gertrude Stein, Robert Frost, and Wallace Stevens. He has written a number of influential books on American literature, including A World Elsewhere, Robert Frost: The Work of Knowing, *and, most recently,* Poetry and Pragmatism. *He is chairman of the board of the Library of America and editor of* Raritan; *he teaches English at Rutgers. He was educated at Amherst College, Cambridge University, Yale, and Harvard.*

"Why don't you write the way you talk?"
"Why don't you read the way I write?"
—Gertrude Stein,
replying to an American reporter
in New York, 1934

A COMPELLING INTEREST IN HOW A PIECE OF WRITING is getting itself written and how it asks to be read; a preoccupation with the toil of language in a passage or a phrase, rather than with its ideas or themes or references to life; a conviction that the most important question is not "what does this writing mean" but "what is it like to read this?" confusing? reassuring? intimidating? cozy? all of these at once?—; and a conviction, too, that no matter when a work was composed, it is, while being read, effectively being written, moment by moment finding its way; that it is to be taken as a performance, an exploration into the words at its disposal, a struggle with words and not a putting forth of something predigested in the mind; that writing and reading are actions nearly indistinguishable one from the other; that writing emerges from the reading by the writer of what has just previously found its way onto the page, often as an echo of something put on another page centuries before; that the most worthy acts of writing and reading are signs of vibrant, creative life perhaps especially when the sentiments being expressed are of total deprivation or loss—these are the assumptions that have guided everything I've tried to do for several decades as a critic and as a teacher. It is what literature asks us to do with it, no matter what anyone else wants to do with it besides.

I have to wonder, though, why I've become ever more convinced of this, why it seems to me a matter of cultural life or death. I wonder especially because in these convictions there lurks another, apparently contrary conviction, that it is possible to lead a good and creative life without caring about literature at all and without even knowing how to read or write. This belief is implicit in my asking that the emphasis in reading should be relocated, as it so often is in the greatest writing, from communicated values of a philosophical nature, roughly speaking, to the values of performance, from the idea of the work as a cultural monument in which truths await our apprehension, to the idea of the work as an exemplification of actions carried out with that most plastic and most tricky of all cultural inheritances, which is words. It is in this light that I applaud Gertrude Stein's reiteration, most notably in *The Geographical History of America*, that it does not matter if a masterpiece is lost, because the actions that produced it are forever discoverable in the human mind. She could have picked this up from Emerson's "Art" or "Intellect," and it finds a somberly beautiful expression in Stevens's "The Planet on the Table," where, speaking of his poems, he says that "It was not important that they survive./What mattered was that they should bear/Some lineament or character,/ . . . /Some affluence, if only half-perceived,/In the poverty of their words,/Of the planet of which they were a part." "Criticism," Emerson remarks in his *Journals* (May 18, 1840), "must be transcendental, that is, must consider literature ephemeral & easily entertain the supposition of its entire disappearance."

My own criticism is more pragmatist than transcendental, because even though I can "entertain the supposition of [literature's] entire disappearance," I cannot "easily" do so. My persistent emphasis on the necessity and benefit of close reading obviously shows a reverence for the materiality of literature in the language of texts, no matter how much of that reverence is displaced onto the actions that are transforming that language. But when I veer at some points toward the transcendental, dispensing with the text in order to admire the work, I probably part company with at least some of the friends and associates who taught a course with me instituted at Harvard in the 1950s by Reuben Brower, on an earlier Amherst model, and called Hum 6. In their careers since, these colleagues have ranged in their activities from the now president of Harvard, Neil Rudenstine, to the most prominent advocate of deconstruction in America, the late Paul de Man. I discuss the course and its uniqueness, including its distinctions from the new criticism of Brooks and Warren, in the final chapter of *Poetry and Pragmatism*. It should be obvious in any case that the sort of reading I try to practice and inculcate is intended, in the spirit of Hum 6, to produce results wholly different from those called for by new critical pedagogy, with its emphases on the difficult achievement of order and unity in works of art, a new criticism, furthermore, that could never accommodate the far more disruptive and open-ended practices of the greatest readers of the first half of this century, who are haphazardly called New Critics, Empson, Blackmur, and Kenneth Burke.

Out of the huge accumulation of writing done over many centuries, I would identify only some very small part of it as literature, not by virtue, obviously, of its having the formal characteristics of poetry or fiction or drama, but because it shows evidences of this active, struggling, exploratory, and exultant performing presence. Its energies are ignited by the impositional threat of the words it also finds itself using, with their already complacent, already accrued meanings, and by the desire to make these words serve some different, individually determined purposes. When in "What Pragmatism Means" William James describes a similar activity with words, he uses the phrase "practical cash-value." Literary interpreters of a New Historicist disposition are delighted to find in such a phrase the confirmations they have learned to expect—of how even those American writers who could aspire to political correctness turn out, inevitably, to be submissive to "bad" capitalistic assumptions. But as with Emerson's equivalent (and equivalently derided) phrasing in "Experience," when he refers to the loss of his son as the loss of an estate, James's financial metaphor is

actually put to use in the process of showing, as Emerson succeeds in doing over the whole length of his essay, the limitations
of such terminology and of how it provokes the desire and the
will to move around or away from it. James, who, in "Some
Metaphysical Problems Pragmatically Considered," will remark that "Pragmatism, so far as keeping her eye bent on the
immediate practical foreground, as she is accused of doing,
dwells as much upon the world's remotest possibilities," really
means by the phrase "practical cash-value" something like
"trade-in value."

How much, he wants to find out, can a word get to mean,
not when you come to rest with it, but when when you trope
or reinvest it, when you mess around with it. In the immediately
preceding sentence he had been complaining about the human
habit of trying to solve the riddle of the universe by seeking
answers "in the shape of some illuminating or power-bringing
word or name." He opposes the notion that our "quest" should
ever find completion in some stated principle or idea, in some
handed-down word or prevailing discourse. Instead, he urges
us to get to "work," a repeated injunction of his. "Work" for
him, as earlier for Emerson and Thoreau, and thereafter in the
work poems of Frost like "After Apple-Picking," is a metaphor
for an energetic involvement with words. Work is troping.
They want to suggest that work of almost any kind can be a
metaphor for their own work with words, and they like to hold
out this possibility, I suspect, so as not to appear unduly aes-
thetical and literary, and in order to intimate that the effort
involved is muscular, that it is taking place on this earth and
not merely on a page, by way of reading and writing. "But if
you follow the pragmatic method," he writes, "you cannot look
on any such [power-bringing or illuminating] word as closing
your quest. You must bring out of each word its practical cash-
value, set it at work within the stream of your experience. It
appears less as a solution, then, than as a program for more
work, and more particularly as an indication of the ways in
which existing realities may be *changed*."

James's pragmatism is far more substantially indebted to

Emerson than he cared to know. This account of the pragmatic method with respect to language is responsive, for example, both to "Nature" and to "The Poet" in *Essays: Second Series*. In "Nature" we are told that "Our music, our poetry, our language itself are not satisfactions, but suggestions," and in "The Poet" that "Every thought is also a prison; every heaven is also a prison. Therefore we love the poet, the inventor, who in any form, whether in an ode, or in an action, or in looks and behavior, has yielded us a new thought. He unlocks our chains and admits us to a new scene." When in the same essay he claims that language is "good" not when it is like a "homestead" but when it is "vehicular," like a ferry or a horse, he obviously means that it must be made "good" by the poet, who can be any one of us; language can be made "good," in James's way of putting it, if we treat words not as a solution but as a "program for more work."

What seems to be being called for at such moments are wholly conscious acts of will in the uses of language, with the further inference that these acts are to be carried out by individuals who are already firmly implanted within language. This may seem disturbingly at odds with cautionary notes in Emerson to the effect that the authenticity of the self is actually diminished by too willful a use of language, as when it is said in "Self-Reliance" that "he who has once acted or spoken with eclat" becomes "a committed person." It may seem at variance, too, with James's important claim in "The Stream of Thought" that in his own work he is bent upon "the re-instatement of the vague to its proper place in our mental life." He warns that our analyses of transitive words can so retard their mobility as they move through speech, thought, writing, or reading that we end up only with some buoyed sense of substantives and concepts: "the full presence comes"—where before there had been only vague intimations, mere hints of tendency—and "the feeling of direction is lost." He wishes instead to insist that even "namelessness is compatible with existence"; just because we have no word to apply to something does not mean that it ceases to be real.

James's determination to find a privileged place in our thinking for "the vague"; his solicitude for the ignored, easily dismissed "fringes" of experience, including the unarticulated
affinities among words and sensations; his rhetorical outrage at
the syntactical advantage enjoyed in our sentences by substantives, to the neglect of transitives—an issue raised with considerably more humor in Stein's lecture "Poetry and Grammar"
—and which have meant, he alleges, that "all *dumb* or anonymous psychic states" have gotten "cooly suppressed"; his
attention to the nonverbal language of the body, the "faint
brain-process upon our thought, as it makes it become aware
of relations and objects but dimly perceived"—these concerns,
exposed with such bravado and subtlety in James's greatest
single work, *The Principles of Psychology*, tend to be overlooked
by interpreters who crowd round his louder commitments to
acts of will, his fear of introspection, and his reiterated exaltation
of effortfulness, personal heroism, and purposeful movement.

A good illustration of how James, like Emerson, can be
understood too easily even by very astute interpreters can be
found in a commentary on Gertrude Stein's story "Melanctha"
in Lisa Ruddick's admirable *Reading Gertrude Stein*. The story,
as Ruddick elucidates it, becomes an allegory of Stein's effort
both to identify herself with James, her cherished teacher when
she was at Radcliffe, and to define herself against him. On the
one hand, she is understandably attracted early in her career—
the story was written in 1905—to James's love of success and
his endorsement of the work ethic. These can be said to be
represented in the story by Jeff Campbell, Melanctha's lover.
On the other hand, however, the style of the story might indicate that the author is temperamentally and artistically
attracted to the reverse, to what Stein calls Melanctha's "wandering after wisdom," her relaxed perambulations, her "always
wanting new things just to get excited."

Even though this reading one-dimensionalizes James, it does
show how his "pragmatic method" conditioned the structural
principles as well as the style of a woman of genius, one who
on several occasions made grateful references to James and to

Emerson. Along with Frost, she was, on that score at least, among the more generous-spirited of a group of American writers, all of whom were undergraduates at Harvard while James, who retired in 1907, was one of the most renowned members of its faculty: Stein from 1893 to 1897, Frost from 1897 to 1899, Wallace Stevens from 1897 to 1900, and Eliot from 1906 to 1910. (W. E. B. DuBois, an admirer and friend of James, was in residence there from 1888 to 1892.)

As will already be apparent, James seems to me, as he does to Ross Posnock in his stunningly argued *The Trial of Curiosity*, to have already included within himself, and in creative tension with the Jeff Campbell side of his disposition, another side closer to Melanctha and inferrable from the style of the story. That is, he exhibits both a need for purposeful action *and* a predisposition to vagrancy, to wandering desire. Stein does turn away from James in her story, but as I read it the turn is a sexual one. For though she makes only a hinted allowance for Melanctha's own lesbian experience, Stein manages to have written what is, so far as I know, the first great story of homosexual cruising, of endlessly peramulating and unsettled desire, of literally wandering the streets searching for an object that might excite desire, but with no intention of locating that object in familiar, approved, or communally endorsed figures, and with no aspiration to settle down with the Jeffs of this world, especially when they do become available.

James has a similar predilection for mobility prompted by desire, but it finds expression in ideas about grammar rather than about sex. In his terms Melanctha would be a transitive, Jeff a substantive. Some sentences from "The Stream of Thought" will clarify the differences and also indicate James's solicitude toward transitives, which Stein doubtless appreciated, even though he sees little hope of rescuing them from a compelled and destructive conformity to substantives:

> As we take, in fact, a general view of the wonderful stream of our consciousness, what strikes us first is this different pace of the parts. Like birds' life it seems to be

made of an alternation of flights and perchings. The rhythm of language expresses this, where every thought is expressed in a sentence, and every sentence closed by a period. The resting-places are usually occupied by sensorial imaginations of some sort, whose peculiarity is that they can be held before the mind for an indefinite time, and contemplated without changing; the places of flight are filled with thoughts of relations, static or dynamic, that for the most part obtain between the matters contemplated in the periods of comparative rest.

Let us call the resting-places the "substantive parts," and the places of flight the "transitive parts," of the stream of thought. It then appears that the main end of our thinking is at all times the attainment of some more substantive part than the one from which we have just been dislodged. And we may say that the main use of the transitive parts is to lead us from one substantive conclusion to another.

Now it is very difficult, introspectively, to see the transitive parts for what they really are. If they be but flights to a conclusion, stopping to look at them before the conclusion is reached is really annihilating them. Whilst if we wait till the conclusion *be* reached, it so exceeds them in vigor and stability that it quite eclipses and swallows them up in its glare. . . .

The results of this introspective difficulty are baleful. If to hold fast and observe the transitive parts of thought's stream be so hard, then the great blunder to which all schools are liable must be the failure to register them, and the undue emphasizing of the more substantive parts of the stream.

Intellectualists—James's name for his chosen enemies in philosophy and in life—are those who, simply because they cannot name or fix the transitive parts of the stream of thought, have decided that in fact these parts do not exist. Intellectualists live in the reduced world of names, of substantives, of concepts.

Frost, who spoke glowingly of Emerson and James, who was an enthusiastic reader of *Principles* and *The Will to Believe* and who taught *Talks to Teachers of Psychology* at Plymouth Academy, offers examples everywhere in his much neglected prose of how a pragmatist skepticism about conceptual certainties, and especially about intellectualists, can generate a style of brilliantly contrived and targeted casualness. Its aim is best described in his letter of January 1, 1917, to Louis Untermeyer. After a brief mention of Henri Bergson, the Parisian friend and ally of James who provided the occasion, in *A Pluralistic Universe*, for an essay called "Bergson and His Critique of Intellectualism," Frost writes:

> You get more credit for thinking if you restate formulae or cite cases that fall in easily under formulae, but all the fun is outside saying things that suggest formulae that won't formulate—that almost but don't quite formulate. I should like to be so subtle at this game as to seem to the casual person altogether obvious. The casual person would assume that I meant nothing or else I came near enough to meaning something he was familiar with to mean it for all practical purposes. Well well well.

In referring, twice over, to "casual persons" who necessarily miss what he is up to, Frost is suggesting that a pragmatist style like his own is itself anything but casual. Its casualness is only apparent; it is quite anxiously, meticulously, mischievously worked out so that it may sound easy and intimate—sound, that is, like the reverse of intellectualist discourse. It is this manipulative use of the idiomatic and conversational modes, however, that makes Emerson, Stein, Stevens, and Frost sometimes extraordinarily hard to get hold of, and, for the noncasual reader, hard to appreciate. As I've tried to show at length in other places, their writing—once you decide to attend to it in the way Frost hopes you will, as if, say, you were rereading a love letter—is far more challenging than is the sort of writing recommended in 1921 by Eliot in "The Metaphysical Poets" and elsewhere, a writing that "must be *difficult*," he italicizes, and for reasons unique "to our civilization, as it exists at present." None of the writers I'm favoring here thought of the twentieth century as better than any other, but none thought it was assuredly worse. They kept in mind that writers in every century have complained about the deterioration of the language under the pressure of social and historical degenerations. One of the sustaining myths of literature is that its authors are beleaguered cultural heroes, fighting to rescue language, as it needs always to be rescued, from what Wordsworth in "Preface to the Second Edition of *Lyrical Ballads*" (1800) called "a multitude of causes, unknown to former times" that "are now acting with a combined force to blunt the discriminating powers of the mind, and unfitting it for all voluntary exertion, to reduce it to a state of almost savage torpor." And so it goes. Emerson's American Scholar is "man thinking," but so, too, are good scholars anywhere. In controversies about language since Plato, the argument has always been made that it is incumbent upon us to release words from the posturing embrace of Thought so that they may enter the turbulent embrace of Thinking. "The creator's attitude toward language," according to Octavio Paz in "Return to *The Labyrinth of Solitude*," "should be the lover's attitude. An attitude of fidelity and, at the same time, of lack of respect toward the loved object. Veneration and transgression. The writer should love language, but ought to have the courage to transgress it."

The situation in which writing finds itself never changes, and for the simple reason that its medium is not this or that aspect of always variable history; its medium is language, and language has always resisted what any single individual wants to do with it; it has always been everybody's property, but also, always, the prey to special interests. Frost speaks as a pragmatist's poet when, in a letter to Louis Untermeyer in 1936, he remarks that "Marx had the strength not to be overawed by the metaphor in vogue. . . . Great is he who imposes the metaphor." Historical conditions may at one time or other favor this or that claimant, but this only localizes or serves to characterize the poet's oppositional task without essentially changing

it. One can say as much, however, while remarking that pragmatist criticism, and the writers who show in their writing how
that criticism might proceed, have benefited over the past century by a more general acknowledgment: That while problems
posed by language can be exacerbated by particular cultural and
historical developments, these problems are inherent in the very
nature of language.

It has always been suspected, by some at least, that language
finally depends only on itself for confirmation. It is impossible
to know what is on the other side of language, once God has
been removed, and it is therefore necessary to suspect that whatever *might* be there is made unrecognizable to itself once it passes
into our descriptions of it. In attempted compensation, Emerson
and James try to picture what cannot be better named: "it"
becomes a stream or a flow or a transition or a movement. This
is as good a way as any to talk about the problem, to come
decently, susceptibly, more or less cheerfully to terms with it.
That seems to me what Gertrude Stein is doing in her lecture
"Poetry and Grammar." In much the way Paz describes how
best to live with all of language, she there describes her attempts
to live with nouns:

> Poetry is concerned with using with abusing, with losing
> and wanting, with denying with avoiding with adoring
> and replacing the noun. It is doing that always doing
> that, doing that and doing nothing but that. Poetry is
> doing nothing but using losing refusing and pleasing and
> betraying and caressing nouns. That is what poetry does,
> that is what poetry has to do no matter what kind of
> poetry it is. And there are a great many kinds of poetry.

I have been proposing that a markedly wary, markedly generative, affectionate, and abusive relation to language has shaped
itself into a pragmatist tradition wherein James looks back to
Emerson and both then look ahead to some writings in this
century whose veritable subject is its own relation to language.
The relation is described succinctly in Lawrence's foreword to
Women in Love, where he refers to "the struggle for verbal

consciousness." "It should not be left out in art," he continues. "It is a very great part of life. It is not superimposition of theory. It is the passionate struggle into conscious being." The poem or essay or story asks to be appreciated as an enactment, going on even as you read, of the effort usually thought to have occurred prior to the work, the effort to make words yield at least some approximation of an always elusive promised truth. One beneficial result of proceeding on this assumption is that it reveals the extent to which literature itself has always been pragmatist. Though Lawrence ignores Emerson in his *Studies in Classic American Literature*, and nowhere mentions William James, his own amazingly fluid sensitivity to language as a living and therefore potent and perilous organism taught him all he might have learned from them. Writers who provide themselves with such stylistic incentives—or "compositional resources" in Henry James's phrase—as Cleopatra or Falstaff, Satan or Ahab, Huck Finn or Dorothea Brooke, have always subscribed to "the pragmatist method," as does Wordsworth, without of course calling it that, in his Preface to *Lyrical Ballads* (1800).

Appropriately, James's *Pragmatism* is subtitled *A New Name for Some Old Ways of Thinking*. Any critical theory, I would argue, has long since been put into practice within those literary works of the past that display an agitated, critical responsiveness to their own language. Already traceably at work in Shakespeare's *Troilus and Cressida* for example, or in the satires of Marvell and Swift or in the novels of Henry James, are what have since come to be called deconstruction and New Historicism. Literature itself invents these theories while, more often than not, allowing them to be only *procedurally* useful; they become in writers like Emerson or Emily Dickinson or Stevens incidental to the enormous, generative resources of the work's language, and they never accumulate the determining power nowadays attributed to them. Currently influential schools of academic criticism end up isolating a few ideologically weighted features of a literary work, as if any work of art can do without them, while remaining oblivious to countervailing tendencies that would exonerate the writers from ideological complicity.

As an alternative to this rampant all-knowingness, I am not proposing that we should look to the language of literature for some saving transcendence. Literature itself doesn't do that. My emphasis on the creative struggles that go on in writing and reading assumes that literature, except here and there for Dickensian purposes of self-promotion, is in fact quite free of the sentimental notion that writing can ever arrive at transcendence. To do so would be to leave language behind altogether. When, in "The Stream of Thought," James says, so calmly as to be taking it for granted, that "Here, again, language works against our perception of the truth," he does so while discussing examples of how, in descriptions of what is going on, we almost always focus on those parts of the description that can be most easily named. This means, as we've noted, that we tend to focus on substantive parts of speech, to the detriment of transitive parts, until the latter become no more than pathways drawing us toward entities, concepts, abstractions. "So inveterate has our habit become of recognizing the existence of the substantive part alone," he writes in "The Stream of Thought," which is chapter IX of *The Principles of Psychology*, "that language almost refuses to lend itself to any other use." That word *almost* loses some of its already plaintive force when, later in the paragraph, he describes the results of language's intransigence with undisguised annoyance:

> All *dumb* or anonymous psychic states have, owing to this error, been cooly suppressed; or, if recognized at all, have been named after the substantive perception they led to, as thoughts "about" this object or "about" that, the stolid word *about* engulfing all their delicate idiosyncracies in its monotonous sound. Thus the greater and greater accentuation and isolation of the substantive parts have continually gone on.

Inferable from the posture which language seems naturally to assume is Emerson's discovery in "Nature" that in "every act [there is] some falsehood of exaggeration." But "the craft with which the world was made," he goes on, "deceives us to

our benefit." The very deceptions inherent in life and art generate a desire for excess, a Jamesian will to believe, and the
supreme fictions of Stevens, which owe more to James, I think,
than to Santayana. In an anticipation of Stevens, James, in
"Pragmatism and Humanism," describes how the fictions we
engender necessarily depend on earlier ones:

> . . . you can't weed out the human contribution. Our
> nouns and adjectives are all humanized heirlooms, and
> in the theories we build them into, the inner order and
> arrangement is wholly dictated by human considera-
> tions, intellectual consistency being one of them. Math-
> ematics and logic themselves are fermenting with human
> rearrangements; physics, astronomy and biology follow
> massive cues of preference. We plunge forward into the
> field of fresh experience with the beliefs our ancestors
> and we have made already; these determine what we
> notice; what we notice determines what we do; what we
> do again determines what we experience; so from one
> thing to another, although the stubborn fact remains that
> there *is* a sensible flux, what is *true of it* seems from first
> to last to be largely a matter of our own creation.

Our relation with God, to name an especially persistent hu-
manized heirloom, is, in Frost's way of adducing it at the end
of "Education by Poetry," a purely pragmatic one. We don't
necessarily believe in God, but by entering into a relationship
with Him, or with some comparable fiction, we put ourselves
in a position "to believe the future in—to believe the here-
after in."

The greatest cultural accomplishment of pragmatism remains the least noticed, and one that it never very clearly enun-
ciates as a primary motive even to itself. It managed to transfer
from literature a kind of linguistic activity essential to literature's
continuing life but which pragmatism now wants effectively to
direct at the discourses of social, cultural, and other public formations, always with an eye to their change or renewal. Neither
Emerson nor James, however, ever directly sets forth in any

extended theoretical fashion the value of bringing into the language of everyday life those same compositional/decompositional urgencies that lead Frost, in a letter to R. T. Coffin in 1938, to say that "poetry is the renewal of words forever and ever." There is no single essay by Emerson or by James devoted to the exploration of this possibility. It is instead left to insinuate itself into a rhetoric favorable to an always vaguely defined "action," or in praise of heroic individuals, or in such metaphors for linguistic movements as can be inferred from their preoccupation with wandering off, transitions, strolling, or, to quote James in "What Makes a Life Significant," "the divinity of muscular labor."

Sexual desire and sexual love do make an appearance in pragmatist writing as metaphors for making out with language, but far less in Emerson and James than in the poets I am linking to them. Thus Whitman, while participating in "the procreant urge of the world," says early on in *Song of Myself:* "I mind how we lay in June, such a transparent summer morning;/You settled your head athwart my hips and gently turned over upon me,/And parted the shirt from my bosom-bone, and plunged your tongue to my barestript heart,/And reached till you felt my beard, and reached till you held my feet." I take his reference to "you" as a reference to the poet himself as the male lover of Whitman the man, or more accurately to the muse or genius who is "beside myself," helping to write the poems. As in many other instances, Whitman is here anticipating the Stevens, of, say, "Final Soliloquy of the Interior Paramour," or, for that matter, predicting Stein, when she, too, projects herself into her own same-sex lover, Alice B. Toklas, so as to write Toklas's—that is, Stein's—*Autobiography*. Frost, much given to sexual figurations for the writing of poetry (and so resolutely heterosexual that it is as if homosexuality had not yet been invented) develops a theory of metaphor in "Education by Poetry" that directly echoes Wordsworth's furtive sexual reference, in his Preface to *Lyrical Ballads*, to "the perception of similitude in dissimilitude," a principle, so he maintains, that "is the great spring of the activity of our minds" and the origin of "the direction of the sexual appetite, and all the passions connected with it." But while Emerson in the *Journals* for March 1841 cries, "Away with your prismatics, I want a spermatic book. Plato, Plotinus, & Plutarch are such," and while he puns in "Nature" on the word *rape*—rapt, wrap, rapturous—sexual metaphors, given the immense and free-wheeling extent of his writing, are relatively infrequent, and in James, so far as I can discern, they are barely inferable. The reticence may be decorous but more significantly involves their recognition that to equate literary figuration with sexual intercourse—in their case only women are imagined as possible partners for men—would inevitably raise the problem of giving women an equality of opportunity for "action," that is for "turning," to use a frequent action cited by James, or, for "riding," as when Emerson in "The Poet" claims that he rides on words "as the horses of thought." Hard to do sidesaddle.

However, their hesitant use of sexual activity as a metaphor for creative actions with words is best understood, I think, as a clue to a shared hope that their rhetorics of action will prove more generally appealing if left vague, if released from anything intimidatingly specific or lurid. "Words are also action, and actions are a kind of words," Emerson typically remarks in "The Poet." No one can possibly feel excluded from *that*. Action in Emerson and James is a term literally left up for grabs, suspended between wordly enterprise and poetic enterprise, between athleticism and aestheticism. It is a way of insisting, again, that we are all poets without insisting that therefore we must actually write poetry. Above all, their indefiniteness as to specific actions avoids any need to specify the results of action; there are to be "actions," that is, but not designed to give birth to encumbrances like texts or monuments or actual sons and daughters. Emerson had trouble enough exorcising the dead Waldo! No wonder Wordsworth shrewdly dropped his image of heterosexual copulation as soon as it was uttered.

It is true that these writers desperately ask for offspring, especially if, like Whitman, Stein, and Crane, their sexual preferences make it highly unlikely that they will have any. But if there are to be no surviving biological heirs, then all the more urgent may be the desire for cultural ones, future readers and writers. "I stop somewhere waiting for you," says Whitman at the end of *Song of Myself;* "when this you see/remember me," says Stein. It does not matter in pragmatist poetics who first imagined the wheels around the sun; it does matter that in "A Postcard from the Volcano" Stevens can imagine children in the future wandering near a ruined mansion that they do not recognize as the imagined ruins, I would guess, of Stevens's own literary estate. The children, wholly ignorant of Stevens and of his repeated references to the sun as a figure for poetry, are nonetheless "still weaving budded aureoles." That is, they are, again in ignorance, engaged in actions that are emulations of his poetic ones; they are creating images of the halo round the sun that poetry has already put there.

In a valuable reformulation of Emerson and James, Kenneth Burke asks, by way of one of his titles in *Language as Symbolic Action,* the pertinent question "What Are the Signs of What?" and then goes on to offer as its subtitle "A Theory of Entitlements." At issue is whether we shouldn't reverse the commonsense view that words are the signs of corresponding things so that we can entertain the possibility that things are the signs of words. As a result of previous human actions, that is, things have acquired a fund of significance on which anyone may instinctively call. Tropes have become part of the object that, to begin with, came into human consciousness by an act of naming, and this is what encourages the furtherance of such acts. Burke's proposition could be extended to explain some differences, within an underlying similarity, among Emerson's and James's poetic successors. Frost's "The Tuft of Flowers" in that way becomes a dramatization of how such entitlements are gratefully accepted; Stein's descriptions of objects in *Tender Buttons* can be read as so many entitlements wittily evaded; Stevens sometimes pretends to reject entitlements outright, as when he says of the sun that "the solar chariot is junk."

Emerson had already taken a theory of entitlements for granted, it seems to me, when he claims as in "Nature" that "we talk of deviations from natural life, as if artificial life were not also natural," while James, in "Philosophical Conceptions and Practical Results," comes close to enunciating the theory. He characteristically asks us to think that entitlements, though he does not use the word, result only from the most vigorous sorts of action: They are made, he says, by "the axe of the human intellect." Indeed, at one point his rather curious syntax allows us to think of poets and philosophers as "so many spots and blazes" themselves, and not simply as persons who make them:

> Philosophers are after all like poets. They are pathfinders. What every one can feel, what everyone can know in the marrow of him, they sometimes find words for and express. The words and thoughts of the philosophers are not exactly the words and thoughts of the poet—worse luck. But both alike have the same function. They are, if I may use a simile, so many spots or blazes—blazes made by the axe of the human intellect on the trees of the otherwise trackless forest of human experience. They give you somewhere to go from. They give you a direction and a place to reach. They do not give you the integral forest with all its sunlit glories and its moonlit witcheries and wonders. Ferny dells, and mossy waterfalls, and secret magic nooks escape you, owned by the wild things to whom the region is a home. Happy they without the need of blazes! But to us the blazes give a sort of ownership. We can now use the forest, wend across it with companions, and enjoy its quality. It is no longer a place merely to get lost in and never return. The poet's words and the philosopher's phrases thus are helps of the most genuine sort, giving to all of us hereafter the freedom of the trails they made. Though they create nothing, yet for this marking and fixing function of theirs we bless their names and keep them on our lips, even whilst the thin and spotty and half-casual character of their operations is evident to our eyes.

Close to the time in which he wrote this, James remarks in "The Stream of Thought" that "the truth is that large tracts of human speech are really but signs of direction." He has in mind such signs as transitives, conjunctions, particles, interjections, all the idioms we coast with. His phrase "the trackless forest of human experience" embraces more than these particular signs, however. It is obviously a metaphor for everything that language can include and, also, for what language suppresses, or cannot grasp, given its partiality for the substantive parts of experience. James is so fluent a writer, so willing to be casually companionable with the reader, that, as with Frost, we are almost dissuaded from attending to the gentle urgings of his disclaimers and exceptions. It may be necessary, then, to call attention to a few inflections that could easily slip by. Note that his poets and philosophers can only "sometimes" find words for what "everyone can feel"; note, too, that they cannot in their words ever represent the "integral forest." That is, not only can't they express everything going on in us, but they cannot manage, even in what they do express, adequately to protect what we have heard him call "all *dumb* or anonymous psychic states." These states correspond, in "the forest of human experience," to things like "the ferny dells," which must be left, he says, to "the wild things to whom the region is a home."

The immense charm of James's writing can be explained, in part, by his frequent willingness to let himself become so fully taken over by the "story" or the image of the metaphor he is developing that both he and the reader tend to forget the subject of the metaphor and to decide, as here, that James is not being a philosopher of language at all, but some nice sort of environmentalist. And yet close by in the passage, after his slightly self-deprecating comparison between philosophers and poets, note that he has chosen to make a gently recuperative aside—"if I may use a simile," even though I am a philosopher and not a poet—in order to alert us to a high degree of calculation in the simile he then goes on to develop. Thus, these "spots and blazes" do allow us to "use" the forest; they help us make sense *out* of our human experience. He is also careful to suggest that thanks to these markings we can do our explorations "with companions." We are provided, that is, with signs that are not simply personal but communal, with a shared language—along with the conformities that this shared usage involves. The price of this treasure of "spots and blazes"—nothing less than the essential clues to self-recognition and human community—is that we must consign "sunlit glories" and "moonlit witcheries and wonders" to the ownership of "the wild things." "The wild things" are equivalent, I would say, to that "good third of our psychic life" noticed in "The Stream of Consciousness"—"the fringe of unarticulated affinities," "the delicate idiosyncrasies," as he calls them, the flow of feeling, sensation, consciousness. Hardly any of these get into words, and just as soon as we do try to put them there they disappear. It is like putting "the wild things" in a cage.

The tough-mindedness of pragmatism is nowhere more evident than here, confronting, as it must, not only the tenuousness of the human claims upon the world but also, in consequence, the human inclination to seek a refuge, some place of rest, of surcease, leaving "the wild things" alone or to heaven or to the control of a priest or a psychoanalyst. It is just at this point that pragmatism, while allowing for the utility of a belief in God, also becomes most unrelenting in its call for human action, here and now, and most hopeful of its success. Because once it can be admitted that language is all we can muster in any effort to create our Gods or to come to terms in some other way with reality, and once it is admitted, too, that language can never adequately meet the demands made of it, then to that very extent is its hold upon us loosened, its authority transferred from the past to present usage, and those who wish to do so may try to free themselves from the definitional fates that other people's language, and our own, threaten to impose. "Nothing is secure but life, transition, the energizing spirit," says Emerson in "Circles." It is not for wisdom or for redemptive values that one turns, therefore, to James's "poets and philosophers," but for what he calls their "marking and fixing function," their indications of "somewhere to go from." On that account alone, strict constructionists of the American Constitution are already outside their country's greatest intellectual tradition. Again, Emerson comes to mind, for proposing in "Nature" that "the real value of the Iliad, or the Transfiguration, is as signs of power."

Only praise and gratitude can be intended, therefore, when James says of his poets and philosophers that the character of their operation is "thin and spotty." What else could it be, given the nature of their medium? Further on in the essay, he will remark that in fact it is poets and philosophers who know better than anyone else that "what their formulas express leaves unexpressed almost everything that they organically divine and feel." This distrust of language among people who spend their lives working with it becomes in itself the occasion in pragmatist writing for attitudes ranging from jubilation to stoical resolve. For what each of these writers "divines" are movements of life that forever elude their words and that, when approached, disappear into them, the way James's transitives dissolve and die in the gravitational pull of substantives. But this does not provoke in any of them, least of all in Stein and her Melanctha, the lugubrious conclusions, reached at the end of Eliot's "Burnt Norton," that "Desire itself is movement/Not in itself desirable" or that it is somehow too bad that "Words . . . will not stay in place,/Will not stay still." Pragmatist writers never turn away from the dilemmas posed by language so as to embrace nostalgic illusions that this was not always the case or that there is a reprieve somewhere in an Unmoved Mover. Rather, the dilemma is an opportunity, an invitation to make writing itself into a representation of those energies in life that have been released into motion by the removal of God, the Substantive of Substantives, the black hole of all transitives. To participate in an always unfinished creation, writing cannot effectively become a raid on the inarticulate without also becoming a raid, and a destructive one, on the already articulated. Before deconstruction became a movement in the academy, it was simply part of the pragmatic method designed to reverse the movement within language itself.

I want now to construct a pragmatist dialogue among these writers, an exchange, occurring over a century and more, of ideas, remarks, figures of speech, tones of voice. The sounds are those of a close-knit family whose members are very attentive to one another, though they pretend otherwise. I want to listen in on them as they echo, interpret, resist, extend, celebrate, and change one another, especially in the effort to explain their own writing, the mystery of its coming into existence at all, and the highly problematic relation of writing and reading to that larger existence—they call it "life" and there is no better word for it—in which they are uniquely endowed with a consciousness of self and the use of speech. Writing and reading are finite experiences from which truth, some sense of truth, may emerge. James says as much in "Pragmatism and Humanism," when he claims that

> For pluralist pragmatism, truth grows up inside of all finite experiences. They lean on each other, but the whole of them, if such a whole there be, leans on nothing. All "homes" are in finite experience; finite experience as such is homeless. Nothing outside the flux secures the issue of it. It can hope for salvation only from its own intrinsic promises and potencies.

James himself leans heavily and rather ungratefully, as family members will, on Emerson, and their twentieth-century offspring nearly everywhere lean on and build out from them. One instance, a letter sent by Frost in March 1935 to the *Amherst Student*, a college newspaper, illustrates just how much he assents to James's description of the human situation, and then proposes to cope with it in terms also borrowed from his mentor:

> The background is hugeness and confusion, shading away from where we stand into black and utter chaos; and against the background any small man-made figure of order and concentration. What pleasanter than that

this should be so? . . . To me any little form I assert
upon it is velvet, as the saying is, and to be considered
for how much more it is than nothing. If I were a Platonist I should have to consider it, I suppose, for how
much less it is than everything.

Less is more in this situation because, like his associates from
Emerson to Stevens, Frost finds in "any little form" all the
security he can reasonably hope for. In his case, "the little form"
is a poem. A poem is "not necessarily a great clarification," he
observes in "The Figure a Poem Makes"; it is perhaps better
for being only "a momentary stay against confusion." To repeat
James's phrase, a poem "gives you somewhere to go from,"
not something on which to repose. It is to be recalled that in
Emerson there is the threat that repose may prove dangerously
long even when it is momentary. "Power ceases in the instant
of repose," he says in "Self-Reliance"; "it resides in the moment
of transition from a past to a new state."

Stevens joins this chorus of mixed voices with the advice,
in "An Ordinary Evening in New Haven," that "The poem is
the cry of its occasion." "Its" and not *the* "occasion"; "its"
refers to the act of the poems getting written and getting read.
In what sounds like a direct echo of James—from the passage
where we have heard him protest the authoritarian ubiquity of
the word *about*, with its capacity to engulf all "delicate idiosyncrasies in its monotonous sound"—Stevens dismisses the
usual assumption that a poem is principally "about" a subject.
It is rather a sign of its maker at a moment of creative and
performative energy:

The poem is the cry of its occasion,
Part of the res itself and not about it.
The poet speaks the poem as it is,

Not as it was: part of the reverberation
Of a windy night as it is, when the marble statues
Are like newspapers blown by the wind. He speaks

By sight and insight as they are. There is no
Tomorrow for him. The wind will have passed by,
The statues will have gone back to be things about.

For good measure, there is also an echo here of Emerson, especially audible in the phrase "There is no tomorrow for him." In "Self-Reliance," he says of some roses (they are to branch off into a rose Stein will make forever famous): "These roses under my window make no reference to former roses or to better ones; they are for what they are; they exist with God today. There is no time to them. There is simply the rose. . . ."

All these writers are convinced that, if improperly conceived—conceived, that is, as monuments or as "statues [that] will have gone back to be things about"—art can actually repress the "signs of power" still coursing through its works, signs that, like the "blazes made by the axe of the human intellect" in James's imaginary forest, can induce in later generations emulative actions with words. It might be remembered that James's seemingly relaxed grammar, as it applies at this point in his passage to poets and philosophers, encourages the inference that these persons are themselves so many "spots or blazes . . . in the otherwise trackless forest of human experience" and are not to be thought of simply as agents who have left these marks behind them. In effect, the marks, when later come upon, promise to *produce* philosophers and poets. This is in accord with the suggestion, inherent in the vague pragmatist use of terms like *action* and *work*, that all of us are poets. "But do your work," says Emerson in "Self-Reliance," "and I shall know you." In other words, even if you do not write or read books—and there are many other things to read—any evidence of your creative desire will allow me to recognize in you some distinctive workings of the mind we share in common. It is not only literary persons who inherit that human mind. As Stevens puts it in "The Sail of Ulysses," " 'In the generations of thought, man's sons/And heirs are powers of the mind,/His only testament and estate.' " Had Emerson put it that way in "Experience," he might have been spared the fury of certain readers who come ready to pounce upon what he does say: "In the death of my son, now more than two years ago, I seem to have lost a beautiful estate,—no more. I cannot get it nearer to me."

Stevens's "estate" is a trope of Emerson's, a turning away from the suggestion that the loss of a child of one's flesh counts only so much as does the loss of a piece of property. Stevens is on less contested ground when he refers to "heirs" as "powers of the mind." But surely it would be no less unfeeling and obnoxious to describe Waldo, two years after his death, as a power of the mind than it is to describe him as an economic unit. It is still a question, however, why Emerson elects to use so displeasing a metaphor to describe his loss, while admitting his own displeasure in it. It is as if he were purposefully surrendering his feelings to economic discourses prevalent in the 1840s, and conceding that this is the best that a great writer could do under the circumstances: "I cannot get it nearer to me." Can this be Emerson as New Historicist of his own writing? That is, I think, just what he intends to sound like at this point. He does so, however, only within a drama of writing already being enacted on his pages, a struggle to find a truer way to talk about the larger issue, for a writer, of profit and loss. I mean the issue of the loss of his creative powers altogether.

For his true subject in the essay is how to cope with the discovery that what he is in danger of losing is the gift to him of creativity itself. It was sufficient to father a son and his earlier work, but is it sufficient to father this essay? However ineffectual he imagines himself to be in the opening paragraphs, he asks there only that he not remain ineffectual—a prey, one might say, to New Historicists. On that score, it is important that in initially reporting his depression he doesn't in fact mention Waldo, who comes on the scene only for a few sentences in the third paragraph. Waldo is a symptom and not a cause of his distress. In fact, the essay begins with a question not about Waldo's whereabouts but about Emerson's, and I take it to be addressed both to Emerson and to his equally distracted muse: "Where do we find ourselves?" The death of Waldo only illustrates a hovering sense that all of his powers are waning and, along with that, his vital sense of life. To attribute such feelings only to the loss of the son would be to localize it trivially, to deceive himself, thereby delaying the possibility that he might recover powers mysteriously withdrawn, powers transmittable not through biological lines in any case, but only through, as Stevens calls them, "the generations of thought." "Generations" here refers to powers of production, as well as to those inheritors who might one day find entitlements, in what has been produced, for productions of their own, especially when faced with that "black and utter chaos" that Frost posits as the surrounding condition of human existence. That is why I chose to read the beginning of the essay as a supplication to Emerson's muse or genius, a supplication whose quiet superciliousness is itself a hint of constricted energy: "Ah, that our Genius were a little more of a genius!"

Emerson is asking for what he calls "superfluity of spirit for new creation." Do I have enough spirit, he means, not simply to go on living but to go on writing? Why "superfluity" of spirit? In part because any new creation would be something additional to the already amazing generosity that allowed his participation in the creation of Waldo, of his essays and poems. (In his *Journals* for October 31, 1836, the day after Waldo's birth, he wrote that the arrival of the baby "makes the Universe look friendly to me," all the more because he has trouble imagining himself as more than "merely a brute occasion" for it.) Superfluous, too, because any new creation will depend on his having more fluidity and fluency than is required by most other actions; he needs the energy to effect those transitions that will release him from repose and inertia. Superfluous, finally, because the deed of life itself, his individual life, quite apart from the deed of his literary gift, is already beyond anything one could bargain for.

Stein's assurance—that "it is not any loss if we lose a masterpiece"—already descends, as we've seen, from Emerson's conviction that "we must consider literature ephemeral." It is an extension, too, of his admission in "Experience" that the loss of yet another creation, a son, has only taught him the shallowness of grief for losses of any kind. Loss, reduction, riddance, abandonment, bareness—these, for a pragmatist, are the necessary precondition for the renewal of life. As "Experience" nears its end, the sense of loss felt at the beginning has become attenuated, and so has the influence upon him of what he calls "the lords of life"—Illusion, Temperament, Succession, Surface, Surprise, Reality, Subjectiveness—which, he now admits, were found "in my way" as he tried to bring the essay to conclusion. At last, he is left with nothing but, in his compelling phrase, "these bleak rocks." Here is to be the final emptying out of all that the self has acquired, including its own subjectivity, so that it may face more directly, and at whatever risk, upon the mystery of a life to which individual human life and its works are forever incidental. "These bleak rocks" set the stage for Frost's "The Most of It," where a crying out on "life" is only ambiguously answered on some "boulder-broken beach," and the prediction no less for Stevens's "The Rock," with its speculation, just as the rock seems to flower, that it is "As if nothingness contained a métier."

Emerson's "bleak rocks" are the Plymouth Rock of American pragmatism. "We must," Emerson says of them, "hold hard to this poverty, however scandalous, and by more vigorous self-recoveries, after the sallies of action, possess our axis more firmly." "Sallies" may imply that actions taken heretofore—and these include the previous sections of the essay—have proved to be precipitous and over-committed. The opportunity now is that a newfound poverty, the disposal of accumulations, has left us unencumbered, free to revolve on, even revolt against, ourselves. Such are the implications of the word *axis;* an axis is where a body may be supposed to turn. "Turning" is also everywhere recommended in James, who in "Pragmatism and Religion" equates "turning places" with "growing places . . . the workshop of being, . . . where we catch fact in the making." Ideally, this means catching "fact" before it is made over, or "faked," as James elsewhere puts it, by being put into language. In a short paragraph in "What

Pragmatism Means" he describes a pragmatist as one who "turns his back resolutely and once for all upon a lot of inveterate habits dear to professional philosophers," "who turns away from abstraction," who "turns toward concreteness and adequacy." Except in some simplistic, hortatory sense, which is the one popularly attributed to James, he can mean only one thing by the word *turn:* It refers to movements of mind, especially, for him, movements in language, writing, and reading. We are being urged always to turn against or to turn round or to turn over any usage in which we might be tempted, by others or by ourselves, to repose. To "turn" is to create something new in the process of losing something familiar; it is to part from something you already have and which will be lost anyway since, as Emily Dickinson frequently reminds us, what already "is" is marked for death.

If the creation is to proceed, there can be no end to turning and therefore no end to the fragmentation of whatever appears to be whole or complete in itself. In that respect, it is altogether right that Emerson waits until his essay is nearly finished before he tells us that "I am a fragment, and this is a fragment of me." Emerson exists as a breaking away from something larger; his individual life is at odds with, even as it joins, the larger flow of life. His essay is thus a further breaking away from the fragment that is Emerson. Like the dead Waldo, "Experience" will be a part of him but at the same time apart from him, behind him. Both author and essay are examples of what Emerson means when, mentioning the *Iliad* and the *Transfiguration,* he speaks of "signs of power." Signs are made by a breaking away from already constituted or imagined life, an act of resistance within life, of "a strange resistance in itself," to recall a telling phrase in Frost's "West-Running Brook," by which life runs counter to its own movement toward death. This same imperative—to make the human presence known in life against the pressure of anonymous participation—compels those "blazes made by the axe of the human intellect" that in the James passage are left "on the trees of the otherwise trackless forest of human experience," a place that in the absence of "blazes" would be left entirely to "the wild things," and unavailable to our knowing of it in words. To say with Stevens that a poem is "part of the res and not about it" is, then, to place it within antagonistic forces. On the one hand, it is an act or performance that partakes of the energies at work in the larger creation of life, life as described with surpassing and awesome serenity of purpose in Stevens's "The River of Rivers in Connecticut"; on the other hand, by locating that energy in language, a poem calls attention to itself as only a sign, a thing that, in a double sense, stays the course of nature.

In sum, writing and reading partake of life, of the creative powers moving through it, but they are self-conscious forms of that power, making use of language that is already a mediation, a distancing between us and it. Language gives us a wholly unique apartness within the wholeness of which we are still a part, a wholeness Emerson characterizes with ghoulish reserve in "The Method of Nature," when he says of it that "its smoothness is the smoothness of the pitch of the cataract." The human consciousness of time compels us to measure the flow of this cataract—or of "West-Running Brook" or of Stevens's river or of Melanctha's "wandering very widely . . . always in search of new things and excitements." We measure the movement because however much it constantly renews itself it moves each of us meantime inexorably toward death. Its destination cannot be changed by poets or philosophers or by their writing, which may be one reason why many of those whose profession includes the reading of literature want to evade literature's intimacy, its cryptic alliance with death, contenting themselves instead with its fancied betrayals of reader and writer to so-called discursive formations. They are hunting for small and easy game. Literature, as any pragmatist knows, can indeed be misused so as to solidify, stabilize, and give authority to value systems abstracted from it, but its true function is best described by Gertrude Stein in a few lines from a longer gathering of hers called "Patriarchal Poetry," where she is obviously counseling herself:

Reject rejoice rejuvenate rejuvenate rejoice
reject rejoice rejuvenate reject rejuvenate
reject rejoice

By such actions and counteractions, literature leaves its mark on us, as well as on things, entitling us to suppose, however credulously, that, for the sake of those we love, the world may be re-created in the face of death. Literature can turn language, for a moment at least, against the sentence of death.

BIBLIOGRAPHY OF
RELATED WRITING

Atlas, James. "The Battle of the Books." *The New York Times Magazine*, 5 June 1988.

Aufderheide, Patricia, ed. *Beyond P. C.: Toward a Politics of Understanding*. Saint Paul, Minnesota: Graywolf, 1992.

Berman, Paul, ed. *Debating P. C.* New York: Laurel, 1992.

Bérubé, Michael. "Public Image Limited—Political Correctness and the Media's Big Lie." *The Village Voice*, 18 June 1991.

Bloom, Alan. *The Closing of the American Mind: How Higher Education Has Failed Democracy and Impoverished the Souls of Today's Students*. New York: Simon and Schuster, 1987.

Bromwich, David. *Politics by Other Means: Higher Education and Group Thinking*. New Haven: Yale University Press, 1992.

D'Souza, Dinesh. *Illiberal Education: The Politics of Race and Sex on Campus*. New York: Free Press, 1991.

Ehrenreich, Rosa. "What Campus Radicals?" *Harper's Magazine*, December 1991.

Gates, Henry Louis. *Loose Canons: Notes on the Culture Wars*. New York: Oxford, 1992.

Genovese, Eugene D. "Heresy, Yes—Sensitivity, No." *The New Republic*, 15 April 1991.

Gless, Darryl J., and Barbara Herrnstein Smith, eds. *The Politics of Liberal Education*. Durham: Duke University Press, 1992.

Howe, Irving. "The Value of the Canon." *The New Republic,* 18 February 1991.

Kimball, Roger. *Tenured Radicals: How Politics Has Corrupted Our Higher Education.* New York: Harper and Row, 1990.

Lehman, David. *Signs of the Times: Deconstruction and the Fall of Paul de Man.* New York: Poseidon, 1991.

Menand, Louis. "Illiberalism" (Review of D'Souza's *Illiberal Education*). *The New Yorker,* 20 May 1991.

———. "Lost Faculties" (Review of Kimball's *Tenured Radicals*). *The New Republic,* 9 & 16 July 1990.

———. "What Are Universities For?" *Harper's Magazine,* December 1991.

Pollitt, Katha. "Why Do We Read?" *The Nation,* 23 September 1991.

Said, Edward. "The Politics of Knowledge." *Raritan,* Summer 1991.

Searle, John. "The Storm over the University" (Review of Kimball's *Tenured Radicals;* Gless and Herrnstein Smith's *Politics of Liberal Education;* and *Michael Oakeshott on Education*). *The New York Review of Books,* 6 December 1990.

Stimpson, Catharine R. "On Differences: Modern Language Association Presidential Address 1990." *PMLA* 106 (1991).

West, Cornell. "Diverse New World." *Democratic Left,* July/August 1991.

Wiener, Jon. "What Happened at Harvard." *The Nation,* 30 September 1991.

Woodward, C. Vann. "Freedom and the Universities" (Review of D'Souza's *Illiberal Education*). *The New York Review of Books,* 18 July 1991.

FOR THE BEST IN PAPERBACKS, LOOK FOR THE

In every corner of the world, on every subject under the sun, Penguin represents quality and variety—the very best in publishing today.

For complete information about books available from Penguin—including Pelicans, Puffins, Peregrines, and Penguin Classics—and how to order them, write to us at the appropriate address below. Please note that for copyright reasons the selection of books varies from country to country.

In the United Kingdom: For a complete list of books available from Penguin in the U.K., please write to *Dept E.P., Penguin Books Ltd, Harmondsworth, Middlesex, UB7 0DA.*

In the United States: For a complete list of books available from Penguin in the U.S., please write to *Dept BA, Penguin,* Box 120, Bergenfield, New Jersey 07621-0120.

In Canada: For a complete list of books available from Penguin in Canada, please write to *Penguin Books Canada Ltd, 10 Alcorn Avenue, Suite 300, Toronto, Ontario, Canada M4V 3B2.*

In Australia: For a complete list of books available from Penguin in Australia, please write to the *Marketing Department, Penguin Books Ltd, P.O. Box 257, Ringwood, Victoria 3134.*

In New Zealand: For a complete list of books available from Penguin in New Zealand, please write to the *Marketing Department, Penguin Books (NZ) Ltd, Private Bag, Takapuna, Auckland 9.*

In India: For a complete list of books available from Penguin, please write to *Penguin Overseas Ltd, 706 Eros Apartments, 56 Nehru Place, New Delhi, 110019.*

In Holland: For a complete list of books available from Penguin in Holland, please write to *Penguin Books Nederland B.V., Postbus 195, NL-1380AD Weesp, Netherlands.*

In Germany: For a complete list of books available from Penguin, please write to *Penguin Books Ltd, Friedrichstrasse 10-12, D-6000 Frankfurt Main 1, Federal Republic of Germany.*

In Spain: For a complete list of books available from Penguin in Spain, please write to *Longman, Penguin España, Calle San Nicolas 15, E-28013 Madrid, Spain.*

In Japan: For a complete list of books available from Penguin in Japan, please write to *Longman Penguin Japan Co Ltd, Yamaguchi Building, 2-12-9 Kanda Jimbocho, Chiyoda-Ku, Tokyo 101, Japan.*